REA

FRIENDS
OF ACPL

P9-EMH-268

12-12-67-

THE HELLENISTIC
AND ROMAN AGE

THE HELLENISTIC AND ROMAN AGE

BY ÉMILE BRÉHIER

TRANSLATED BY WADE BASKIN

Phoenix Books

THE UNIVERSITY OF CHICAGO PRESS
CHICAGO AND LONDON

v. 2

This book is also available in a clothbound edition from
THE UNIVERSITY OF CHICAGO PRESS

DEC 1 2 '67

Originally published in 1931 as Histoire de la philosophie:
L'Antiquité et le Moyen Age. II: Période Hellénistique
et Romaine. © *1931, Presses Universitaires de France*

*The present bibliography has been enlarged
to include recent publications. These
have been supplied by the translator
and William Bondeson*

*The University of Chicago Press, Chicago & London
The University of Toronto Press, Toronto 5, Canada*

© *1965 by The University of Chicago
All rights reserved. Published 1965
Second Impression 1965
First Phoenix Edition 1965*

Printed in the United States of America

1459140

CONTENTS

THE SOCRATICS

To THE same man who engendered the intellectual movement of the philosophy of the concept is linked historically a number of contemporaneous schools known as the Socratics, all decidedly hostile to the movement even though they disagreed among themselves. Linked to Socrates are the Megarian school, founded by Eucleides of Megara; the Cynic school, led by Antisthenes; and the Cyrenaic school, associated with Aristippus of Cyrene.

For several reasons it is difficult for us to determine the importance of the Socratic schools. To begin with, their prestige is lessened by the influence of Plato and Aristotle. Furthermore, the writings of the best thinkers are known mainly through collections of titles which are themselves in many instances suspect, their doctrines through doxographical summaries, often written in the language of later schools, and their lives through collections of anecdotes or *chreiai* intended for the edification of the reader and indebted more to hagiography than to history. Finally, they are overshadowed by the great dogmatic schools, Epicureanism and Stoicism, which were founded after the death of Alexander the Great.

It is nonetheless true that these latter schools could not have existed in the absence of the "minor" Socratics. The Platonic spirit, surreptitiously weakened, never recovered from their attacks. They set the stage for the schools that were to dominate the intellectual life of the Roman period. In addition, some of the Socratic schools continued to exist for some time alongside the doctrines of Epicurus and Zeno. The Cyrenaic school, for example, retained its characteristic originality in the face of Epicurean Hedonism, and after an eclipse (or at least what seems to have been an eclipse), the Cynic school reappeared near the beginning of the first century of the Christian Era and continued until the sixth century, the last survival of pagan philosophy.

The Socratic schools differ with the schools of Plato and Aristotle on an issue that goes deeper than a doctrinal conflict: the place and the role of philosophy. Outwardly most Socratics still preserved one trait that caused Plato to inveigh against the Sophists: they charged for their instruction. The Socratic schools in which students assembled to hear a teacher whom they paid contrast sharply with the Academy and the Lyceum, which were legally recognized as religious associations capable of owning property and of surviving those who founded them. The same contrast applies to the content and aim of instruction. Whereas Plato stipulated a rigorous and scientific preparation for philosophers, Antisthenes and Aristippus turned their students away from astronomy and music, two sciences which they considered absolutely useless. Why study mathematics, asked Aristippus, since it teaches nothing concerning good or evil? [1] And along with mathematics the Socratics rejected dialectic in its entirety, that is, the use of discussion in establishing the truth.

Teaching, discussion, and demonstration therefore gave way to suggestion, persuasion through rhetoric, and reliance on direct, personal impression. Nothing could stand in sharper contrast to the method of Plato.

It follows that there was a tendency to see convention and artifice in everything created by thought, in everything elaborated through reflection: in laws, especially, and in cities which are built on laws. The result was complete indifference to politics, an attitude diametrically opposed to the attitude of Plato.

[1]Alexander of Aphrodisias *In Metaphysicam commentaria*, ed. Hayduck (1891), 182. 32.

1 *The Megarian School*

Eucleides, the leader of the Megarian school, was nevertheless on good terms with Plato, for he received him and the other disciples of Socrates at Megara following their departure from Athens upon the death of their teacher; and Plato, by presenting his *Theaetetus* as a Socratic dialogue which was read to Eucleides, doubtless wished to offer proof of ties of friendship which endured long after the tragic event.[2] Even so, his doctrine, as well as can be determined from a few statements made by Diogenes Laertius, is antipodal to Plato's. It should be recalled that for Plato no thought or intellectual life was possible apart from a system of unified but distinct Ideas. Eucleides holds that "the Good is one, though it is called by different names: wisdom, God, intelligence or others still." Since he also denies the existence of the contraries to the Good, it seems that his intention is to resist any attempt to unite concepts other than by declaring them identical or to differentiate them other than by making them mutually exclusive. Wisdom ($\varphi\rho\acute{o}\nu\eta\sigma\iota\varsigma$), God, intelligence are the very terms which Plato tries to differentiate from each other and from the supreme Good, in the *Timaeus* for instance, even as he draws them together and builds them into a hierarchy. Eucleides, by identifying them and denying their contraries, rules out any dialectical speculation such as that found in the *Timaeus* and in the *Philebus;* diversity is only in names, not in things. Plato of course made reasoning through comparison an indispensable tool; Eucleides denies the possibility of such reasoning and refuses to recognize a similarity which is neither identical nor different. Either the terms of the comparison are similar to things, in which case things are to be preferred, or they are different and the conclusion is invalid.[3]

The famous sophisms which Diogenes Laertius attributes to

[2] Diogenes Laertius *Lives of the Philosophers* ii. 106; Plato *Theaetetus* 142a–143c.
[3] Diogenes Laertius ii. 106 and 107.

Eucleides' successor, Eubulides of Miletus,[4] seem to be aimed more specifically at Aristotelian logic and also, in the form in which Cicero presents them in the *Academica,* against Stoic logic. The principle of contradiction states that one cannot answer both yes and no to the same question at the same time. Sophisms point up cases where, by virtue of this principle, we are forced to answer both yes and no at the same time, with the result that the thought is negated. Take the sophism of the liar: "If you say that you are lying and tell the truth, you are lying." Here the speaker concedes both that he is lying and that he is not lying. In the name of logic the Megarian forces his adversary to admit that he has horns since one possesses what one has not lost and since he has not lost any horns; to acknowledge that he does not know his own father by showing him his father in disguise; that Electra knows and does not know the same things since when she meets him as a stranger she knows that Orestes is her brother but not that her brother is Orestes. He drives his adversary to despair by asking him how many grains of wheat make up a heap (soritical sophism) or how many hairs he would have to lose to be bald.[5]

All their clever arguments point up the impossibility of choosing between yes and no and therefore of discussion based on definite concepts. They must have met with great success, for it is said that Stilpo of Megara, a contemporary of Theophrastus, attracted to his courses the disciples of both the Peripatetics and the Cyrenaics. We are fairly well acquainted with two parts of his teaching, both of which penetrate to the heart of the philosophy of the concept. The first is the criticism of Ideas.[6] The method of his criticism, according to Diogenes Laertius, is that employed by Eucleides in his refutations. Eucleides attacked demonstrations not by criticizing their premises but by revealing the absurdity of the conclusion. In the same way Stilpo posits certain ideas and deduces their absurd consequences: the ideal man is so and so — for instance, speaking or not

[4] *Ibid.* 108; cf. 111.
[5] Cicero *Academica Priora* ii. 96; Diogenes Laertius vii. 187; Lucian *Sale of Lives* 22; *Academica Priora* ii. 92.
[6] Diogenes Laertius ii. 113, 114, 119.

speaking; it follows that we have no right to say that a man who is speaking is a man since he does not measure up to the concept. The ideal vegetable is eternal; therefore what you show me is not a vegetable, for it did not exist a thousand years ago. Or again, if you mean that a certain man measures up to the concept of man, and if this man happens to be in Megara, then you will have to say that there are no men in Athens since the property of the concept is its uniqueness.[7] Aristotle's attempts to answer other critics who follow the same line of attack show clearly that Philo's criticism is aimed at the Aristotelian concept as well as the Platonic Idea.

We are also acquainted with Stilpo's position on a related issue, the problem of predication. Plato had dealt at length with the problem in the *Sophist,* and his adversaries had concentrated on it the full measure of their efforts. Stilpo's approach to the problem is but another side of the method of criticism that we have just examined. If like Aristotle and Plato we try to think by means of definite, stable concepts each of which has its own essence, we are unable to set forth any proposition since by doing so we would be affirming the identity of two distinct essences. To state that horses run or that men are good is to state that horses or men are something other than themselves; or again, if we say that good is in effect the same thing as men, then we deny ourselves the right to state that healing or food is good. It is of course wrong to say, along with Colotes the Epicurean, who gives an account of Stilpo's doctrine in his treatise *Against the Philosophers,* that this thesis "puts an end to life," but it does put an end to interpreting judgments as relations of concepts, that is, to any sort of Athenian idealism.[8]

It will be remembered that Aristotle himself managed to resolve such difficulties only by introducing alongside fixed, determinate essences notions of indeterminate realities, such as potency, and that Plato jokingly accused himself of parricide when he contradicted his "father" Parmenides by stating that the life of thought re-

[7] *Ibid*. vii. 186.
[8] Plutarch *Against Colotes* chaps. xxii and xxiii.

quired the granting of existence to non-being. It is not surprising then that the Megarians are associated with Parmenides and are considered renovators of his thought. Still, it may be that they care little for his thought but are instead intent on showing that a philosophy of the concept, since it admits only fixed essences, has no right to introduce the indeterminate realities proposed by Aristotle. This seems to be the sense of the argument attributed to Diodorus Cronus, a disciple of Eubulides and a contemporary of Ptolemy Soter (323–285). His famous argument (the so-called κυριεύων λόγος) strikes at the very roots of Aristotle's philosophy by showing that the notion of the possible, and consequently of indeterminate potentiality, can have no place in his system.

Aristotle gives a simplified account of the argument (but without attributing it to Diodorus or even to the Megarians).[9] As soon as you admit in a general sense that any proposition is true or false, the principle applies as well to future events as to the present or the past; any assertion about the future will be true or false; it follows that there is no indetermination (or possibility of being or not being) with respect to the future event. The affirmation of the possible is incompatible with the principle of contradiction. Did the author of this argument wish (as Aristotle pretends to believe in refuting it on the basis of its practical consequences) to demonstrate necessity? Is it not more in line with what we know of the Megarians to believe that he wanted to show the absurdity of the consequences of a logic based on the principle of contradiction, which made it impossible for will or deliberation to have any bearing on the future? Epictetus gives a more detailed account of the argument, but his version is unfortunately very obscure.[10] The line of argument assumes on the one hand that no true assertion concerning the past can ever become false and on the other that the impossible can never be an attribute of the possible. Then he doubtless shows (in a development analogous to the one transmitted by Aristotle) that according to his adversary the principle

[9] *On Interpretation* chap. ix.
[10] *Discourses* ii. 19. 1–5.

of contradiction must be universal in scope, that is, it must apply also to assertions relative to the future; from this he deduces that in the case of an alternative (such an event will occur or will not occur), the assertion which expresses the event that will not happen refers to nothing possible since the possible is that which can be and not be, while the event in question not only is not but will never be. To say that it is possible would be then to say that the impossible is possible. The philosophy of the concept could therefore accommodate only a reality that can be strictly and completely determined.

The Megarians are always attacking the doctrines of others, but never do they offer a positive doctrine of their own. These "eristics" wish to point up the incoherence of the philosophy of the concept but seem never to have intended, as has sometimes been charged, to substitute an idealism of their own for that of Plato and Aristotle. Did a course of argument ever enable the Greek thinkers, including Plato, to establish a truth? Is it not always dialectical, that is, aimed at deducing the consequences of an assertion made by an adversary? Through an inspired transposition Plato had made dialectic a vital element of the intellectual life; with the Megarians it falls back heavily to the earth and again becomes an eristic tool.

But did this tool not prepare the ground for a new intellectual life, one that followed a course different from that indicated by Plato? Dialectic was not the only means of education. The rhetor could speak of useful things, and he could speak persuasively. It was this method of rhetorical education that was extolled by Alexinus of Elis, a Megarian who belonged to the generation of the Stoic Zeno and who, like his teacher Eubulides, is also known as the author of a slanderous book filled with personal polemics against Aristotle.[11] In a passage in his treatise *On Education*,[12] cited by the Epicurean Hermarchus, Alexinus proposes an ideal

---

[11] According to Eusebius *Evangelical Preparation* xi. 2. 4–5.
[12] Preserved by Philodemus of Gadara in book B of his *Rhetoric* col. 40. 2–18. In *Volumina rhetorica: Supplementum*, ed. Sudhaus (Leipzig, 1895).

which marks a radical departure from philosophy. In the debate that has always existed in Greece and even in the Greek soul between rhetoric and philosophy, between formal education that teaches subject matter and scientific education that penetrates to things, he unhesitatingly sides with the first; but if he criticizes the professors of literature for being too punctilious in the matter of textual criticism in their investigations, he praises them for taking up useful things in their discourses on philosophical subjects and for using common sense in deciding issues. Here we have the right side of rhetoric, in contrast to the wrong side, which is polemics. We shall find an analogous rhythm in the other Socratic schools.

II *The Cynics*

A common trait in fourth-century thought, a trait that goes back to the Sophists, is almost unlimited confidence in education (παιδεία) as a means of shaping and transforming man according to rational methods.

The trait appears for example in the writings of Xenophon. One of his main works, *Cyropaedia,* aims to show through the example of Cyrus that there is an art of governing men and that knowledge of this art should bring to an end the era of revolutions and eliminate the political crises that plague Greece. Xenophon in the *Memorabilia,* like Isocrates in the *Discourse to Nicocles,* emphasizes the qualities and virtues that a king must have in order to govern: "It is more important for a king to train his soul than for an athlete to train his body." [13] It is assumed that the training of the monarch will benefit everyone: "To train individuals is to serve only them, but to make the powerful virtuous is to serve both those who possess power and their subjects." The same tendency is reflected in Plato's conception of the philosopher king.

Nowhere is the trait more in evidence than among the Cynics, who represented themselves above all else as leaders of men. In

[13] Cf. G. Mathieu, *Les Idées politiques d'Isocrate* (Paris, 1925), pp. 95 ff.: "A la recherche d'un chef."

The Sale of Diogenes the third-century Cynic Menippus relates that
when Diogenes was offered for sale at the slave market and buyers
asked him what he could do, he replied: "Govern men."[14]

Never did the Cynics limit themselves to self-reformation. They
reformed themselves in order to direct others and in order to serve
as models. They were there to observe and oversee not themselves
but others and, if necessary, even to censure kings for their insatiable desires.

"Virtue can be taught" is the first article in Antisthenes' doxography.[15] But his system of education was not purely intellectual.
Along with the Megarians, Antisthenes was a resolute opponent of
education through dialectic and the sciences. That is why Plato and
Aristotle never spoke of him without calling up a host of scornful
epithets. "Dull-witted old man," said Plato, his junior by some
twenty-five years. "Stupid lout," added Aristotle. Against them he
used arguments similar to the arguments of the Megarians: Plato
wants to discuss, to refute errors, and to define; but neither discussion nor refutation nor definition is possible, and for the same reason that statements and thoughts are limited by things. Discussion
is impossible since the people involved will either think the same
thing and be in agreement or think different things, with the result that their discussion will be pointless. Error is impossible since
one can think only that which is, and error would consist in thinking that which is not. Finally, definition is impossible since essence
is either compound, in which case one can enumerate its primary
elements but cannot go beyond these undefinable terms, or simple,
in which case one can only tell what it resembles.[16]

Antisthenes had no less contempt for mathematics and astronomy,
and it is his contempt that is voiced by Socrates in Xenophon's
Memorabilia.

Does it follow that the first of the Cynics rejected all intellectual

[14] Diogenes Laertius vi. 9.
[15] *Ibid*. 13.
[16] Aristotle *Metaphysics* iv. 29. 1024b 32 and *Topics* i. 9. 104b 21; cf. Plato
Euthydemus 283d, 285d and *Cratylus* 429a ff.; Aristotle *Metaphysics* vii. 3. 1043b
24 and Plato *Theaetetus* 201d–202c.

training? And are we to take seriously the quip, "To avoid being corrupted by others a wise man should not learn to read"? [17] In point of fact, Antisthenes' teaching at the Cynosarges was not too different from the teaching of the Sophists. Isocrates, who often attacks him without naming him, as in the first part of his encomium *Helen* and at the beginning of his speech *Against the Sophists,* describes his teaching in detail: he was paid four or five minas by the student; he taught an eristic art involving many useless discussions and promised to acquaint the student with the road to happiness. At the end of his *Panegyricus,* Isocrates again takes him to task on account of the contrast between his capacious promises and his captious discussions. The fact is that he saw in him a rival. Several of the titles of Antisthenes' books show that the disciple of Gorgias taught judicial rhetoric, or the art of pleading causes, and that he engaged in polemics with Isocrates, whose attitude toward him is revealed in the passages just cited.

One of the subjects which must have had an important place in his school was the allegorical explication of Homer, to which is devoted almost every work in two of the ten volumes in which the writings are classified.[18] The adventures of Ulysses in particular are the subject of several books. We know that in later allegorical writings the wanderings of Ulysses represent the victories of the sage's soul over the attacks of the sensible world, and it is possible that the origin of this interpretation is to be sought in Antisthenes. In any event he is among the first, if not the first, to have seen in Homer a means of edification. Anaxagoras had already stated that Homer's poems were linked to virtue and justice, and a passage in Xenophon's *Banquet* (3. 6) shows clearly how the allegorists, whose ranks included Antisthenes, opposed the rhapsodists who merely recited Homer and wanted to utilize for moral education poems traditionally learned by heart. We know the objections raised by Plato. In the *Republic* he finds that such instruction is dangerous because a young man is incapable of distinguishing what is alle-

[17] Diogenes Laertius vi. 103.
[18] *Ibid*. 15–18.

gorical in a poem from what is not, and in the *Ion* he shows how arbitrary and superficial are the exegetes of Homer.

The moral allegories which seem so childish to us are nevertheless in keeping with the most important trait of Cynicism. "Virtue consists in acts," according to Antisthenes, "and it has no need of numerous speeches or sciences." But in a strict sense an act is not independently learned. Through exercise and training one manages to act. Does this mean that there is no place for mental training? Certainly not. For the Cynic the highest virtue, prudence ($\varphi\rho\delta\nu\eta\sigma\iota\varsigma$), is intellectual: "it is the strongest bulwark, and it must be built on impregnable reasoning." [19] Still, the words reasoning and reason, which Antisthenes uses so often, seem to designate no succession of methodical and proven thoughts, as in the case of Plato or Aristotle. Only his aphorisms have survived, and these, which are more suggestive than instructive, invite meditation rather than assent: "The sage will love, for only the sage knows that one must love." Xenophon in his *Banquet* (4. 34–35) probably characterizes Antisthenes through the words attributed to him in the speech on true wealth. Here we find two contrasting pictures: on the one hand apparent wealth in the form of money, with all the ills that it entails, and on the other true wealth in the form of wisdom, with all its advantages.

Mental training then is total, immediate response to an aphorism, or meditation on a theme rather than a reasoned construction, where meditation leading to action contrasts so strongly with mere contemplation of truth. The most important themes for meditation are provided by the examples of heroes in the domain of wisdom. Here was a popular, direct method of instruction, one designed to impress minds nurtured on the exploits of Hercules and Theseus. As a matter of fact its use was general. In *To Demonicus*, the mediocre letter of advice to a young man attributed to Isocrates, the author, who purports to be a teacher of philosophy, uses it constantly. For instance, after briefly enumerating the advantages of virtue, he says: "It is easy to grasp all this from the works of Hercules or the ex-

[19] *Ibid.* 10–73.

ploits of Theseus." And in another place: "Remember your father's deeds and you will have a good example of what I am saying." We can understand the importance of Homer's allegory and the tenor of Antisthenes' works (known to us by their titles) on Helen and Penelope, the Cyclops and Ulysses, Circe, Ulysses and Penelope and the Dog. In all of his works he showed the heroes victorious in their struggles against temptations.[20]

But for the Cynic the exemplary hero was Hercules, to whom Antisthenes devoted three books. The Cynic's life was a veritable imitation of Hercules, the beloved son whom Zeus made immortal because of his virtues, just as it was later to be an imitation of Diogenes. The Cynic wished always to play a role, to pose as a model, or to acquaint others with models. The famous image of the world considered as a theater in which each man is an actor in a divine play — an image which will have such an important place in popular moralistic literature — may have its beginning in Antisthenes' *Archelaus*.[21] Hercules was the paragon of incorruptible will and complete freedom.

In his seventh oration the emperor Julian wondered whether Cynicism was a philosophical doctrine or a way of life. The truth is that since the time of Antisthenes the Cynic had had the ordinary dress and outward appearance of the common man: a cloak (which he wrapped around himself in the winter), a beard and long hair, a staff in his hand and a double sack on his back. He retained his dress and his outward appearance, however, after the fashion had changed under the Macedonian influence, in much the same way that our religious communities have retained the habit ordinarily worn at the time of their foundation. Henceforth no one could fail to notice the eccentric vagrant with his striking attire, particularly when he made a show of his endurance by going about naked in the rain, by walking barefoot in the snow in winter, and by braving the heat of the sun in summer.[22] This sage, whose unrestrained

[20] *Ibid.* 18.
[21] F. Dümmler, *Akademika*, pp. 1–18.
[22] Diogenes Laertius vi. 13, 23, 41.

tongue spared neither the rich nor the powerful and whom Aristotle would doubtless have thought impudent and vulgar,[23] had no common tie with any segment of society. More abused than professional beggars, "without a city, without a house, without a country, a wandering beggar seeking his daily bread" (as Diogenes, citing a tragic poet, described himself), he lived in public places, took shelter in the temples and made himself the guest of everyone. Only in this way could he carry out his mission, which was that of being Zeus' messenger and observing the vices and errors of men. It is to this mission that the title of Antisthenes' book *On the Observer* must refer; it is this mission that Diogenes was carrying out when he told Philippus that he was the observer of his insatiable desires; finally, it is this mission that the Cynic Menedemus, a contemporary of Philadelphus (285–247) flaunted before everyone by disguising himself as one of the Erinyes and pretending to be an observer who had come from Hades to report the sins of men to the daimons.[24]

It is with the celebrated Diogenes of Sinope (413–327) that all the traits of the life of the Cynic are traditionally associated. From the mass of well-known *chreiai*, witticisms and apothegms collected by Diogenes Laertius and Dio of Prusa, is it possible to construct an authentic portrait of Diogenes?[25] It has been noted, and rightly so, that all these documents are contradictory and that their inextricably mingled details yield two portraits of Diogenes. There is the licentious, uninhibited, profligate Diogenes who ridicules Plato's asceticism, who so closely resembles the loose Hedonists that the witticisms of Aristippus are attributed to him, and who is so irreligious that he is credited with the clever remarks of Theodorus the Atheist.[26] There is also the austere, strong-willed Diogenes, the ascetic who as an old man says to those who advise rest: "And if I were running

[23] *Nicomachean Ethics* vi. 6.

[24] Diogenes Laertius vi. 38, 17, 43, 102; Epictetus *Discourses* iii. 22. 38; cf. Norden's article in *Neue Jahrbücher*, 1893.

[25] Cf. L. François, *Essai sur Dion Chrysostome* (1922), pp. 119–40; *Deux Diogéniques* (Paris, 1922).

[26] Diogenes Laertius iv. 25–42.

a long race, would I stop to rest near the end of the contest or would I make an even greater effort instead?" Like a singing teacher he stresses the hard notes, and he exemplifies work and effort (πόνος). It seems that the second of the two portraits is that of the real Diogenes.[27] The earliest Cynics, whose leader Antisthenes stated that "he would rather be a madman than experience pleasure," cannot be compared in this respect with Aristippus. We shall see in the next chapter that the Cynics of the third century tended on the contrary to drift toward Hedonism, giving birth to hedonistic Cynicism, the type of brutal off-handedness generally implied today by the word cynical. This new spirit is probably responsible for the introduction of a new stock of anecdotes into the life of Diogenes.

The Cynicism of Diogenes seems then to have been a practice rather than a doctrine; moreover, the further he withdrew from the sciences, the closer he pretended to bring his philosophy to the imitative and manual arts. Proof that virtue is neither an innate gift nor something acquired through knowledge but rather the result of training (ἄσκησις), is that "in imitative arts and in other arts, we see the artisan acquire extraordinary skill through training." [28] Athletes and flute-players are good examples. "Nothing in life is accomplished without training; with training, we can surmount anything." Nor is physical training which gives us strength less important than meditation; one form of training complements the other. Diogenes' Cynicism is grounded on almost complete confidence in effort, and his confidence based on experience; effort, however, is to be interpreted not as just any effort but as a reasoned effort. It is not the effort in itself that is good, for there are "useless strivings." The task of philosophy "consists in achieving happiness by choosing efforts that conform to nature; it follows that lack of judgment leads to unhappiness." This explains the prime role assigned to reason; much intellectualism remains in Cynicism since intelligence alone gives the sense of the work to be done.

[27] *Ibid*. vi. 34–35.
[28] *Ibid*. 70.

If they had not attached great importance to reason it would be impossible to explain why the Cynics devoted so much attention to prejudices and false opinions. As Menander (342–290), the poet of the New Comedy, says through the Cynic Monimos, "All opinions are like smoke." [29] One of the fruits of Diogenes' teaching is the denunciation of convention wherever it exists and the contrasting of convention with nature. According to a tradition that goes back to Diocles, Diogenes was the son of a banker of Sinope who had been exiled from his country for counterfeiting coins; Diogenes boasted of having been his accomplice as if his father's crime had prefigured his own mission; and by playing on the words, he made the act of counterfeiting coins (νόμισμα) the act of rejecting all conventional values (νόμος).[30] But the aim of the Cynics in abolishing social prejudices was not to reform society. For instance, their reason for accepting the community of women was not, as in the case of Plato, to tighten the social bond but rather to loosen it and to allow more freedom to the sage. Their aim was so far from social reform that they shamelessly took advantage of everything that the rich cities built on pride had to offer them; Diogenes said in jest that the Porch of Zeus was built in order that he might live there. The underlying reason for emancipation from prejudices was therefore an inner, individual reform.

The city envisioned by the Cynics did not exclude but rather presupposed a real city. That is what Crates (*ca.* 328), the disciple of Diogenes and teacher of the Stoic Zeno, says in a poem that has been preserved: "Charity, the Cynics' city, is built inside the red smoke of pride; there no parasite prowls, there nothing is produced except thyme, figs and bread, and men do not take up arms against each other to possess these." [31]

In direct contrast to the spirit of Plato and even to the spirit of Aristotle, the Cynic separated the moral life from the social problem and at the same time subordinated the exact sciences to the intellec-

---

[29] *Ibid.* 83.
[30] *Ibid.* 20.
[31] *Ibid.* 85.

tual meditation of the sage. Since there is no man more devoid of scientific spirit, there is none more devoid of civic spirit.

Men like Plato and Isocrates were proud of being Hellenes and descendants of the Athenians who repelled the invading Persians, but the Cynics did not share their pride. In all probability Antisthenes went so far as to say that the victory of the Greeks over the Persians was merely a matter of chance. Still, if the Cynic proclaims himself a citizen of the world, if "his politics follows the laws of virtue rather than the laws of the state," he nevertheless expresses a preference for the political forms that are incompatible with the Greek city, such as the Persian empire or the empire of Alexander. Three of Antisthenes' works are entitled *Cyrus* and may have inspired the magnification of Cyrus as the model king in Xenophon's *Cyropaedia*. The tradition was continued by the Cynics, for one of Diogenes' disciples, Onesicritus, wrote an *Alexander* which is said to be patterned after the *Cyropaedia*.

III *Aristippus and the Cyrenaics*

We find the same disparagement of the exact sciences and the same indifference toward organized society in Aristippus of Cyrene and his disciples. In this respect they followed the same course (divergent from Plato) as the Megarians and the Cynics. Why bother with the mathematical sciences? Are they not inferior to the lowest arts since they are concerned with neither good nor evil? [32] As for the social role that the philosopher reserves for himself, it is in a sense diametrically opposed to that of the Cynics, even though in practice it leads to the same indifference. As a matter of fact (if the words that Xenophon attributes to him do not distort his thought),[33] Aristippus holds the opposite view to the Cynics and says that "he does not join the ranks of those who wish to command." Only a madman would take upon himself all the penalties and expenses which must be assumed by the magistrates "whom

[32] Aristotle *Metaphysics* B. 2. 996a 32; M. 2. 1078a 33.
[33] *Memorabilia* ii. 1. 8.

the cities use as a private individual uses his slaves." His only wish
is to lead a pleasant life of ease.

Aristippus was a contemporary of Plato. Drawn to Athens by the
desire to study with Socrates, like Plato, he was later the guest of
Dionysius, the tyrant of Syracuse. According to hostile legends cir-
culated about him Dionysius subjected Aristippus to the worst insults, and because of his desire for a life of luxury and elegance,
Aristippus accepted them without recrimination. His doctrine is very
hard to reconstruct. As documents we have in Diogenes Laertius
(ii. 84–85) a list of titles of his works, many of which have been
contested since antiquity; a doxography which is attributed to the
Cyrenaics in general and which seems to stress especially the points
where Cyrenaic Hedonism differs from Epicurean Hedonism; and
finally an exposition of the theory of knowledge of the "Cyrenaics"
written by the Skeptic Sextus Empiricus,[34] who uses many technical
terms characteristic of Stoicism.

There have been attempts to enrich these sources through supposed allusions to Aristippus in the writings of Plato and Aristotle.
Such writings fall into two classes: passages in the *Philebus,* in the
Nicomachean Ethics and in the *Republic* which explain or criticize
the doctrine of Hedonism; and passages in the *Theaetetus* in which
Plato, in words attributed to Protagoras, presumably explains Aristippus' doctrine of knowledge. The writings on Hedonism comprised by the first class raise a difficult question. They speak of
Hedonists, but are they speaking of Aristippus? One of them certainly is not. In chapter two of the tenth book of the *Nicomachean
Ethics,* Aristotle names the Hedonist of whom he is speaking:
Eudoxus of Cnidos (d. 355), the famous astronomer who had at-
tended Plato's school.[35] Was Eudoxus a true Hedonist? Aristotle
tells us that he is known for his austerity and reserve, and that, not
on account of his taste for pleasure but rather in order to bear witness to truth, he states that every being seeks pleasure and avoids
pain, that pleasure is desired for itself, and finally that pleasure

[34] *Against the Mathematicians* vii. 190–200.
[35] Cf. Diogenes Laertius viii. 36.

when added to something that is already good increases its value. But these are the characteristics which everyone attributed to the Good and to the Sovereign Good. It is interesting to note that, after citing Eudoxus' arguments in favor of the thesis that pleasure is the sovereign good, Aristotle studies and criticizes the line of argument in the *Philebus* which corresponds almost point by point with that of Eudoxus. This shows clearly that the Hedonist discussed by Plato in the *Philebus* could well be Eudoxus and not Aristippus.

Still, it is worth noting that one of the theses pronounced by the pleasure-seekers in the *Philebus,* namely the thesis that pleasure consists in motion, is not found in the exposition of Eudoxus' arguments, and that it is attributed to Aristippus in Diogenes Laertius' enumeration of his opinions. But gaining acceptance in recent years, and rightly so, is the view that it is a mistake to think that Plato attributes to the Hedonists the thesis that pleasure consists in motion; he actually says nothing of the kind and uses the thesis only to show that pleasure, if it does consist in motion, cannot be the principal good. And Aristotle in the *Ethics* takes up the same thesis and considers it solely as an argument against the Hedonists and not as one of their affirmations. The truth is that as it is presented in this chapter of the *Ethics,* the polemic between proponents and opponents of the doctrine of pleasure, the same polemic that had given Plato the opportunity to write the *Philebus,* takes on the appearance of a scholarly debate within the Academy between Speusippus, who held that pleasure is always evil, and Eudoxus, who thought that it is always good. The somewhat artificial character of each of the two theses (with Speusippus defending his thesis not so much because he believes it to be true as because he wishes to thwart the pleasure-seekers) shows that the discussion is between members of the Academy.

Consequently these texts, like the passage in the *Republic* (505 *b*) which attributes Hedonism to the common people, do not seem to refer to Aristippus or to add to our knowledge of him. On the contrary, they show us that in the fourth century the value of pleasure was the subject of lively discussion everywhere.

Furthermore, Eudoxus' line of argument (everyone seeks pleasure, avoids pain, and chooses pleasure as a goal) is less original than the argument which Aristippus used to prove that pleasure was the highest good.[36] Nothing else is to be expected since in defining the goal he limits himself to stating the obvious.

The originality of the Cyrenaic school seems to reside in the effort not to go beyond the primary facts by ruling out the superimposition of any rational view, and a number of the opinions that make up the doxography of the school answer the objections of people accustomed to construct their ideal of life rationally rather than to trust their immediate impressions or valuations. We know, for example, that the fleeting, mobile character of pleasure contrasts sharply with the stable, flawless happiness envisioned by the sage; that is why, as we shall see later on, Epicurus will prefer to transform and adulterate the notion of pleasure in order to keep pleasure as the goal rather than to renounce the stability of wisdom; he will seek a calm, stable pleasure predicated on the absence of pain and not the Cyrenaics' pleasure, which is associated with gentle motion. Aristippus (or rather his successors) had a ready answer: what is here assumed to be pleasure is no different from the state of sleep; besides, the sage is not concerned with this stable, continuous pleasure since his goal is the pleasure of the moment; happiness is merely the sum total of all pleasures, not a goal. Their objection is also essentially the same as the one that consists in saying that the pleasures caused by reprehensible acts are themselves reprehensible. It introduces into the appreciation of pleasure an intellectual representation which does not belong there. For Aristippus pleasure itself, even in this instance, is a good.

We shall see a little later on how Epicurus believed that by preserving pleasure as the goal, he could make man the master of his happiness. It was enough that the only pleasure that existed was bodily pleasure, intellectual pleasure being but recall or anticipation of such pleasures. Since man has the power to direct his memory and his thought, he can accumulate pleasures. The Cyrenaics took

[36] *Ibid.* ii. 86.

the opposite view: first, the mind has its own pleasures and pains, and these have nothing to do with the body (for instance, the pleasure of saving the fatherland); next, time quickly effaces the memory of a corporeal pleasure; finally, it is a fact that the pleasures of the body always surpass the pleasures of the mind, just as physical suffering is much more painful than moral suffering.

Under these conditions the Cyrenaics could not set as their goal the virtuous, impassive, painless life which the Cynics offered the sage, for the sage is exposed to pain while the fool sometimes experiences pleasures. Nor is the sage free from passions; to be sure he has none of the passions that have their source in an intellectual construct or a "vain opinion," but he inevitably feels any immediate, positive impression, with the result that he is subject to pain and also to dread, which is the apprehension of imminent pain.

Never had anyone gone farther toward ruling out every possible criterion of good and evil other than pleasure or pain experienced immediately as "gentle motion" or as "violent motion." If some degree of reason still remains, it is because "although any pleasure is desirable in itself, its production may entail arduous effort; for instance, it is very difficult to assemble the pleasures which constitute happiness." Thus the Cyrenaic, in one way or another, eventually confronts the problem of the combination of pleasures, but from this moment on the doctrine risks being dealt a fatal blow. This we shall see when we come in a later chapter to Aristippus' third-century successors.

Sextus Empiricus notes that there is a perfect correspondence between Aristippus' moral doctrine and his theory of knowledge. Like conduct, knowledge finds certitude and support only in the immediate impression to which it must cling in order to remain certain: "We can state without lying and with truth and certitude that we feel the impression of something white or sweet, but we cannot state that the cause of the impression is white or sweet." The impression must not be the point of departure for any conclusion or the basis for any intellectual superstructure. Knowledge does not lead us to any reality beyond impression; furthermore, it does not even allow agreement among men since it is strictly personal and I do not have the right to draw from my own impression any conclusion with respect to impression. Speech is the only thing we have in common, but the same word designates different impressions.

Megarianism, Cynicism, and Cyrenaism are the counterpart to Platonism and Aristotelianism. They repudiate intellectual training and even civilization, holding that neither benefits man. Instead they try to find within him, and only within him, a moral support for man.

BIBLIOGRAPHY

I

C. M. Gillespie. "On the Megarians," *Archiv für die Geschichte der Philosophie*, XXIV (1911), 218.

E. Zeller. "Über den Kurieuon des Megarikers Diodorus," *Sitzungsberichte der Akademie der Wissenschaften zu Berlin* (1882), pp. 151–159.

A. Koyré. *Epiménide le menteur (ensembles et catégories)*. Paris, 1947.

I. M. Bochenski. *Ancient Formal Logic*. Amsterdam, 1951.

C. Field. *Plato and His Contemporaries*. 2nd edition, London, 1953.

P. M. Schuhl. *Le dominateur et les possibles*. Paris, 1960.

J. Rolland de Renéville. *Essai sur le problème de l'Un-multiple et de l'attribution chez Platon et les Sophistes*. Paris, 1961.

II

F. Dümmler. *Antisthenica*. Berlin, 1882.

J. Geffcken. *Kynika und Verwandtes*. Heidelberg, 1909.

G. Rodier. "Conjecture sur le sens de la morale d'Antisthène," *Etudes de philosophie grecque*. Paris, 1926. Pp. 25–26. "Note sur la politique d'Antisthène," p. 303.

D. R. Dudley. *A History of Cynicism from Diogenes to the 6th Century A.D*. London, 1937.

III

A. Mauesberger. "Plato und Aristippus," *Hermes,* LXI (1926), 208–30; 363.

Lorenzo Colosio. *Aristippo di Cirene*. Turin, 1925.

G. Giannantoni. *I. Cirenaici*. Florence, 1958.

{ II }

THE OLD STOA

Hellenistic Age is the name given to the period during which the Greek culture became the common property of all the Mediterranean countries. From the death of Alexander to the Roman conquest it spread gradually, from Egypt and Syria to Rome and Spain, through enlightened Jewish circles as well as through the Roman nobility.[1] The Greek language, in the form of the κοινή or common dialect, was the organ of the culture.

In some respects this period is the most important in the history of Western civilization. Greek influence extended to the Far East and, reciprocally, the Greek West was open to the influence of the East and Far East. Here we trace through its maturity and into its glittering decline a philosophy which, remote from political preoccupations, aspired to discover universal rules for human conduct and to guide the conscience of man. And during its decline we witness the gradual ascendance of the Oriental religions and Christianity. Then with the Barbarian invasions comes the disintegration of the Roman Empire and the long period of quiet contemplation that laid the foundation for modern civilization.

[1] But see M. J. Rostovstzeff, "L'hellénisme en Mésopotamie," *Scientia*, XXVII (February 1, 1933). In this region Rostovstzeff detects, especially with reference to religion, not a firm imprint but only a vague trace of the Greek influence.

23

1 *The Stoics and Hellenism*

A magnificent surge of idealism which infused the spirit of philosophy into civilization but which soon stopped and became crystallized as dogmas, and introversion and renunciation of culture as man sought support only from within himself through the exertion of his will or through the immediate enjoyment of his impressions — such is the composite portrait of the fourth century B.C., the great philosophical century of Athens. From this moment on the sciences, cut off from philosophy, followed an independent course: the third century was the century of Euclid (330–270), Archimedes (287–212), and Apollonius (260–240); it was the great century for mathematics and astronomy; and at the Museum of Alexandria, where the librarian was the geographer Eratosthenes (275–194), the observational sciences and philological criticism reached the same high stage of development.

As for philosophy, it assumed a completely new form and cannot be said, strictly speaking, to have continued in any of the directions previously described. The great doctrines that emerged during the fourth century, Stoicism and Epicureanism, do not bear the slightest resemblance to anything that preceded them; no matter how numerous their points of contact, the spirit in which they are formulated is wholly different. Two traits identify the new spirit: the first is the belief that it is impossible for man to find rules of conduct or to attain happiness without relying on a conception of the universe determined by reason. Investigations concerning the nature of things do not have their goal in themselves, in the satisfaction of intellectual curiosity; they require application. The second trait, which appears with some degree of regularity, is a tendency to subscribe to the doctrine of a school. The young philosopher does not have to verify what has been learned before him; reason and argument only serve to consolidate the dogmas of his school and to make them absolutely impregnable. But the schools put no less stress on the free, disinterested, and unrestricted pursuit of truth than on the assimilation of truths that have already been discovered.

The first of these traits separated the new doctrines from the Socratic doctrines, which minimized culture, and reintroduced into philosophy concern over reasoned knowledge. The second separated them from Platonism, for the Stoics and Epicureans were neither apostles of free inquiry like the Socratic Plato nor authoritarians and inquisitors like the author of the tenth book of the *Laws*. Theirs was rationalism, perhaps, but a doctrinal rationalism that brooks no questions and not, as in the case of Plato, a rationalism of method that poses questions.

The two radically new traits were not accepted without resistance, however, and, as we shall see, underneath the two great dogmas the Socratic tradition continued during the third century.

To understand the significance and value of the two traits, we need to examine the lives of the men who introduced them and the reactions of these men to the new historical circumstances created by the Macedonian hegemony.

Athens remained the center of philosophy even though not one of the new philosophers was an Athenian, or even a continental Greek. All the third-century Stoics known to us were aliens, born in countries on the periphery of Hellenism. Living outside the great civic and pan-Hellenic tradition, they were subject to many influences other than the Greek, particularly the influence of the neighboring Semitic peoples. A city in Cyprus, Citium, gave birth to Zeno, the founder of Stoicism, and to his disciple Persion; the second founder of the school, Chrysippus, was born in Cilicia, in either Tarsus or Soli, and three of his disciples, Zeno, Antipater, and Archedemus, were also from Tarsus; and from the Semitic countries proper came Herillus of Carthage, a disciple of Zeno, and Boethius of Sidon, a disciple of Chrysippus. Those born in lands closest to Greece are Cleanthes of Assos (on the Aeolian coast) and two other disciples of Zeno, Sphaerus of the Bosphorus and Dionysius of Heracleia (Pontus Euxinus in Bithynia); in the generation that followed Chrysippus, Diogenes of Babylon and Apollodorus of Seleucia came from distant Chaldea.

Most of these towns, unlike the cities of continental Greece, had behind them no long traditions of national independence, and their inhabitants were prepared for commercial reasons to travel to distant lands. It is said that the father of Zeno of Citium was a Cyprian merchant whose interests took him to Athens, that on his return he brought with him books by the Socratics, and that the reading of these books fired his son with the desire to go and hear the masters.[2] But the semi-civilized nations remained indifferent to the local politics of the Greek cities. This is proven clearly by the political attitude of the protagonists of the school during the century that elapsed between the death of Alexander (323) and the intervention of the Romans in Greek affairs around 205.

Here are the main outlines of the political history of Greece during this period. Greece was an enclosed arena in which Alexander's successors, particularly the Macedonian kings and the Ptolemys, joined battle. The cities or leagues of cities could only draw support from one of the two factions to avoid being dominated by the other. The constitutions of cities were changed at the whim of those who wielded the power and drew their support alternately from the oligarchic party and the democratic party. Athens in particular submitted passively to the results of a conflagration that extended throughout the East. After a vain attempt to recover her independence, Athens surrendered, through the peace arranged by Demades (322), to the Macedonian Antipater, who established an aristocratic government and became master of all of Greece. For a brief period the regent of Macedonia who succeeded him, Polysperchon, re-established democracy to strengthen his alliance (319), but Antipater's son Cassander drove out Polysperchon, reinstated the aristocratic government at Athens under the hegemony of Demetrius of Phaleron, and managed to retain control in Greece in spite of the efforts of other diadochi, Antigonus of Asia and Ptolemy, who rallied to their support the league of Aetolian towns. Still another change

[2] Diogenes Laertius *Lives of the Philosophers* vii. 31.

occurred in 307. Demetrius of Phaleron was driven from Athens by the son of Antigonus of Asia, Demetrius Poliorcetes, who gave Athens her freedom, wrested all of Greece from the control of the Macedonian, and proclaimed himself the liberator of the country. The Athenians abandoned by him were strong enough, with the support of the Aetolian League, to stop Cassander of Macedonia when he broke through Thermopylae in 300 and engaged them in battle at Elatea. A few years after the death of Cassander, Demetrius Poliorcetes gained the Macedonian throne, which remained in the possession of his descendants. After 295 B.C. Macedonian influence in Athens was hardly contested except in 263 when, under the reign of Demetrius' son Antigonus Gonatas, Ptolemy Euergetes declared himself the protector of Athens and the Peloponnesus, and Athens, supported by him and by Lacedaemon, made a last but futile effort to recover her independence (Chremonidean War). And after 295 B.C. Athens remained indifferent to events, even though resistance to the Macedonians was still active in the Peloponnesus, where Macedonia was striving to exert an influence on the petty tyrants who controlled the towns. Around 251 Aratus of Sicyon established democracy in his country and then, assuming the leadership of the Achaean League, drove the Macedonians from most of the Peloponnesus and recaptured Corinth. In spite of his efforts, however, and although he even tried to bribe the Macedonian governor of Attica, he could not enlist the Athenians in the alliance, and he turned to Ptolemy for support. The last attempt of Greece to achieve independence ended sadly; Aratus was confronted by a Greek enemy, Cleomenes, the king of Sparta, who revived the old Spartan constitution and tried to regain control of the Peloponnesus; for help in battling his enemy, Aratus turned to the Macedonian kings who, since the death of Poliorcetes, had been the traditional enemies of Greek freedom; Antigonus Doson and his successor Philip V helped him to defeat Cleomenes (221), but they regained possession of Greece as far as Corinth. Aratus was the victim of his protector, who had him poisoned, along with two Athenian orators who were too popular among the people. The Romans delivered

Athens from the Macedonian yoke (200), but not in order to make the city independent.

Such is the framework within which was unfolded the history of the Old Stoa and its three great scholarchs, Zeno of Citium (322–264), Cleanthes (264–232), and Chrysippus (232–204). This brief review was necessary for an understanding of their political attitude. Their attitude is clear: between the Greek towns that were making a last effort to preserve their liberties and the diadochi who were founding great states, they did not hesitate but gave their full sympathy to the diadochi, particularly the Macedonian kings. They were continuing in the tradition of the Cynics, who admired Alexander and Cyrus. Zeno and Cleanthes never requested Athenian citizenship, and Zeno is said to have insisted on being called a citizen of Citium.[3] The kings lavished on them privileges and flattery, convinced, apparently, that there was in the Stoic schools a moral force that could not be neglected. Antigonus Gonatas, for instance, was a great admirer of Zeno; when he went to Athens he listened to Zeno, as well as to Cleanthes later on, and he sent subsidies to both of them. At the death of Zeno he took the initiative and asked the city of Athens to erect a monument in his honor in the Ceramicus. So important a person was he that Ptolemy's ambassadors to Athens never failed to call on him.[4] Antigonus liked to be surrounded by philosophers. He had at his court Aratus of Soli, who explained Eudoxus' astronomy in his poem *Phenomena,* and he wanted Zeno himself to come there as his counselor and instructor in ethics. The latter refused because of his age but sent him two of his disciples, Philonides of Thebes and Perseus, a young man from Citium who had been his servant and whom he had trained in philosophy. Perseus became a courtier and wielded enough influence to be flattered by the Stoic Aristo, if Timon's satirical poem is accepted at face value. Many years later, in 243, he

---

[3] Plutarch *On the Contradictions of the Stoics* chap. iv, in H. von Arnim (ed.), *Stoicorum veterum fragmenta,* 4 vols. (Leipzig, 1903–24), I, No. 26.

[4] Diogenes Laertius vii. 169.

had charge of the Macedonian garrison at the Acrocorinthus; Aratus of Sicyon had laid siege to the citadel, and it seems that Perseus died during the siege, a defender of the Macedonian cause against the freedoms for which Greece fought. He intervened in the negotiations which another philosopher, the Megarian Menedemus of Eretria, who had an important political role in his native town, was conducting with Antigonus to free Eretria from the tyrants and establish democracy. It seems, then, that Perseus was only serving Macedonian politics, supported everywhere by the tyrants, when he tried to prevent Antigonus from satisfying the demands of Menedemus.[5]

As Zeno sent Perseus to Antigonus, Cleanthes sent Sphaerus to Ptolemy Euergetes. Sphaerus was the Stoic teacher who had taught philosophy at Sparta and had numbered among his pupils Cleomenes.[6] In his political reforms Cleomenes, who re-established in Sparta the constitution of Lycurgus, may have been inspired by Stoicism, but the truth is that neither he nor the Spartans had the Hellenic spirit that inspired his enemy, the leader of the Achaean League, Aratus of Sicyon.

The political universe of the Stoics then is quite different from that of a Plato. They have an important place in the city of Athens, but not as political counselors. Diogenes Laertius (vii. 10) gives a mixed account of the two decrees by which the Athenians granted Zeno a gold crown and a monument in Ceramicus. He says: "Zeno of Citium, son of Mnaseas, taught philosophy for many years in our city; he was a good man; he invited the young men who came to him to practice virtue and temperance, directed them along the path to goodness, and he offered to all the example of his own life, which conformed to the theories that he expounded." His moral qualities obviously commanded high admiration, but nowhere do we find a hint of his role in politics.

[5] *Index stoïcorum herculanensis* col. xiii (Arnim, I, No. 441); Athenaeus *Deipnosophistae* vi. 251b (Arnim, I, No. 342); Pausanias *Description of Greece* ii. 8. 4; Diogenes Laertius vii. 143.

[6] Plutarch *Life of Cleomenes* chap. i.

II *How We Know the Old Stoa*

We have only indirect knowledge of the teachings of Zeno and Chrysippus. Many treatises by Zeno and seven hundred and five by Chrysippus are known only through tiny fragments and through a few titles preserved by Diogenes Laertius. The only Stoic works that we possess, those by Seneca, Epictetus, and Marcus Aurelius, date from the time of the Empire, four centuries after the foundation of Stoicism. It is by studying the traces left by the Old Stoa in their own works or in the works of other writers that we can reconstruct their teachings; and our task is difficult, for our main sources date from a much later period; they are either eclectics like Cicero, whose philosophical writings date from the middle of the first century B.C., and Philo of Alexandria (beginning of the first century A.D.); or they are adversaries like Plutarch who wrote his works *Against the Stoics* and *On the Contradictions of the Stoics* toward the end of the first century B.C., the Skeptic Sextus Empiricus, from the end of the second century A.D., the physician Galen, who wrote against Chrysippus during the same period, and finally the Church Fathers, particularly Origen, in the third century. These treatises, which are either mutilated or malicious, are all that we have except for one valuable source, the summary of Stoic logic which Diogenes Laertius (vii. 49-83) copied from the *Compendium of the Philosophers* by Diocles of Magnesia, a Cynic friend of Meleager of Gadara, who lived at the beginning of the first century B.C. With this one exception, all the literature issued from conflicts that had existed from the second century between Stoic dogmatism and the Academy or the Skeptics. Thus, to take but one example, our main source for the Stoic doctrine of knowledge is in Cicero's *Academica,* written expressly to combat the doctrine. The polemical spirit is inimical to exact reporting, and Plutarch in particular repeatedly falsified the thought of the Stoics in order to make them contradict each other. Furthermore, these writings are from a late date and, unless the authors of the doctrines are designated by name, it is often difficult to separate the opinions of the Old Stoa (third century B.C.) from those of the Middle Stoa (second and first centuries); besides, even in the mainstream of the Old Stoa there are many divergencies of detail, in spite of general agreement. The rather artificial character of a comprehensive exposition of Stoicism, based on such paltry data, must not be hidden. Starting from Zeno's doctrine, we shall indicate whenever necessary what has been modified or abandoned by his successors, Cleanthes and Chrysippus.

III *The Origins of Stoicism*

Zeno of Citium was the pupil of Crates the Cynic, Stilpo the Megarian, Xenocrates and Polemon, the scholarchs at the Academy. He was closely associated with Diodorus Cronus and his pupil Philo the dialectician. As if these influences were not sufficiently varied, Zeno boasted of "reading the ancients," and his doctrine is considered in some respects to be a renewal of the doctrine of Heraclitus. But the influences singled out by the old historians (in particular Apollonius of Tyre, in his book *On Zeno*) still leave the beginnings of Stoicism wrapped in an enigma.[7] From the Megarians he probably acquired the taste for the dry, abstract dialectic that characterizes the teaching of the Old Stoa. Stilpo, with whom he was most closely associated, is supposed to have had the same contempt for prejudices as the Cynics and to have identified the sovereign good with the impassive soul.[8] The Academician Xenocrates, in contrast, so exaggerated the role of virtue that it seemed to him to be the condition of happiness.[9] Polemon, like the Cynics, stressed the superiority of ἄσκησις over purely dialectical training, and he defined the perfect life as one consistent with nature. Finally, Speusippus had condemned pleasure almost as vehemently as had Antisthenes. Thus the austere, naturalistic trend manifested in most schools during the time of Alexander helped to confirm and to rein-

---

[7] Known through Diogenes Laertius vii. 2; cf. vii. 16.
[8] Stobaeus *Florilegium* 108. 33.
[9] Cicero *Tusculan Disputations* v. 18. 51.

force the influence of the Cynic Crates, even though it was mitigated by the milder doctrines of the Academy.

But there was a huge gap between these general influences and the Stoic doctrine, which was not simply a moral code but a broad vision of the universe that dominated philosophical and religious thought throughout antiquity and a part of the modern age. It was in this respect a new departure and not the continuation of the moribund Socratic schools.

Is its origin to be sought on Greek soil? Partly at least, or so it would seem. Fourth-century thought was not actually exhausted by either the conceptualism of Aristotle and Plato or the teaching of the Socratics; it had much more to offer. The medical schools were prosperous, and their adherents applied themselves diligently to general questions concerning the nature of the soul and the structure of the universe. We need only recall Plato's unexpected references to medicine in the *Phaedrus* and especially in the *Timaeus*.

The physician Galen, who is one of our best sources for the history of Stoicism, explains in his book *Against Julian* that Zeno, Chrysippus, and the other Stoics wrote at great length about diseases, that in addition one school of medicine, the "methodical" school, traced its origin to Zeno, and finally that the medical theories of the Stoics were the same as those of Aristotle and Plato. He summarizes them in this way: a living body has four qualities that form two contrasting pairs, hot and cold, dry and wet; these qualities are supported by four humors, yellow and black bile, acid phlegm and salt phlegm; health is due to a felicitous mixture of the four qualities and disease (at least chronic disease) to the excess or lack of one of the qualities or to a break in the continuity of the parts of the body. We also find certain opinions of the Stoics on physics (on the seat of the soul in the heart, on digestion, on the duration of pregnancies) formally cited by Philo of Alexandria as opinions borrowed by physicists from physicians.[10]

[10] *Allegories of Laws* ii. sec. 6; *Special Laws* iii. chap. ii; *Questions on Genesis* ii. chap. xiv.

The significance of their borrowings can be determined from extant fragments of the works of Diocles of Carystos, a fourth-century physician cited by Aristotle. Diocles maintains, in keeping with the physiological doctrine ascribed to the Stoics, as we have seen, that all phenomena in the life of animals are governed by hot and cold, dry and wet, and that there is in each living body an innate heat which by altering ingested foods produces the four humors — blood, bile, and the two phlegms — whose proportions explain health and disease. But he also assumes that the outer air, drawn toward the heart through the larynx, esophagus, and pores, becomes the psychical breath in which resides the mind once it enters the heart; and that the intellect or mind permeates, distends, and supports the body and is the source of voluntary motion. "Living bodies," says Diocles, "are composed of two things: that which bears and that which is borne; that which bears is potency, and that which is borne is body." He holds that many diseases are due to the obstruction of this potency, which is identical to breath and prevented from circulating through the vessels by the accumulation of humors.

His theories are the same as those of the Stoics concerning the living being, but their explanation is generalized. In their thinking any body, whether animate or inanimate, is alive and contains a breath (pneuma) which through tension holds together its parts. Diverse degrees of tension explain the hardness of iron and the solidity of stone. The whole universe (as in the *Timaeus,* which is filled with medical notions) is thus a living entity whose soul, a fiery breath that permeates all things, holds together its parts.

Medical notions, drawn from pre-Socratic physics and systematized anew into a doctrine of physics and a cosmology, seem then to be the basis for the Stoic image of the universe. Nor were the Stoics the first during their time to have started from medical theories and evolved a vitalistic cosmology. Some Pythagoreans still survived during the second half of the fourth century B.C. Aristoxenus of Tarentum, who became Aristotle's disciple and who is known for having upheld the theory that the soul is the harmony of the body, was associated closely with them and has left us the names of four of them.[11] In addition, Alexander Polyhistor, a prolific writer of the first century B.C., has provided a summary of Pythagorean cosmology, based on *Pythagorean Notes*. Their cosmology is quite similar in its details to the opinions of the Ionian physicists of the last period (Alcmaeon, Diogenes) and to those of the fourth-century physicians: the theory of two pairs of forces — hot and cold, dry and wet — which when disproportionately distributed produce differences in seasons in the world and diseases in the body; the divine character of heat, the cause of life, whose rays emanate from the sun and produce life in things; the soul, a particle of hot ether mixed with cold, immortal like the being from which it emanates and nourished by effluvia in the blood; reason, from which emanate the sensations; many traits that need not be explained, as had been the case up to this point, by the belated influence of the Stoics on the Neo-Pythagoreans of the second and first centuries since they all reappear prior to the development of Stoicism. Furthermore, some of these traits, such as the tripartite division of the soul into reason ($\varphi\rho\acute{\epsilon}\nu\epsilon\varsigma$), intelligence ($\nu o\tilde{\nu}\nu$), and heart ($\theta\upsilon\mu\acute{o}\nu$), are tinged with an archaic flavor. Old Pythagoreanism, for example, was impregnated with physical and medical ideas. It is also worth noting that Aristoxenus' theory of the soul as the harmony of the body is closely tied to medical ideas; the musical character of the metaphor almost disappears when this harmony is compared to the health of the body and is said to consist in the equal role that the four elements have in the life of the body.[12] This is simply a paraphrase of Alexander Polyhistor's account of the medical theory of life and the cosmology of the Pythagoreans.

Thus in the reconstruction of medical vitalism, the tendency toward mechanical mathematics initiated by Plato was reversed, and the animate world of the Stoics followed in the Ionian tradition (visible even in Plato's mathematical world, considered in the *Timaeus* as a living being). But even when these influences are

[11] Diogenes Laertius viii. 46.
[12] Lucretius *On the Nature of Things* ii. 102–3; 124–5.

recognized, the main point still remains unexplained. In the place which the Stoics assigned to God, in the manner in which they conceived the relation of God to man and the universe, there were new traits that had never before appeared among the Greeks. The Hellenic God or the God of popular myth, as well as Plato's Good and Aristotle's Mind, was in a sense a being with a life of his own and one who in his perfect existence ignored both the ills of mankind and the vicissitudes of the world; the ideal of man and of the universe, he acted upon them only through the attraction of his beauty; his will had no part in it, and Plato censured those who believed that he could be moved by prayers. To be sure, Plato had also condemned the old beliefs in a god jealous of his prerogatives, but the goodness that he contrasted with such jealousy was an intellectual perfection reflected in the order of the world and had nothing to do with moral goodness. Doubtless also, beside the Olympians, the Greeks recognized in Dionysus a god whose periodic death and rebirth imbued the lives of his faithful with a certain rhythm. The faithful participated in the divine drama; by experiencing and acting out the passion of god in a mystical orgy, he united with him and became one with him. Nor did the Bacchic god descend to man; instead, he allowed man to rise to him.

But the God of the Stoics is neither an Olympian nor a Dionysus. He is a god who lives among men and reasonable beings and who arranged everything in the universe for their benefit. His power penetrates everything, and his providence overlooks not even the slightest detail. His relation to man and to the universe appears in a new light; he is no longer a solitary stranger in the world which he attracts through his beauty but the operator of the world for which he has conceived a plan. The virtue of the sage is neither the assimilation to God that Plato envisioned nor the simple civic and political virtue depicted by Aristotle; it is rather his acceptance of the divine work and collaboration in this work through his knowledge of it. 1459140

Here we have the Semitic idea of the omnipotent God who governs the destiny of men and things, and it is quite different from the Hellenic conception. Zeno the Phoenician gave the new key to Hellenism. We can be sure that his contribution to Greek thought is not without precedent; the God of Plato in the *Timaeus* is a demiurge, the one in the *Laws* is concerned with man and oversees every detail of the operation of the universe, and the God of Socrates according to Xenophon, having given men their senses, their inclinations and their intelligence still guides them through oracles and divination. We see that the demiurgic, providential theme was already common property, but that with Zeno it became the cornerstone of philosophy. We shall see in the sequel to this story how these two conceptions, the Semitic and the Hellenic, sometimes tend to fuse and sometimes stand in sharp contrast by virtue of their acknowledged divergence. And it is possible that we shall find, underneath the diverse forms assumed by the conflict that continued down to the contemporary period, one of the deepest cleavages in human nature.

IV *Stoic Rationalism*

To the fundamental theme of rationalism is subordinated the rest of the Stoic doctrine. Zeno is before all else the prophet of the Logos, and philosophy is but the awareness that nothing resists the Logos, or rather that nothing exists apart from the Logos. It is "the science of divine and human things," that is, of all rational beings and all things since nature itself is divine. Its task is therefore prefigured and, whether it involves logic, the theory of knowledge, ethics, physics, or psychology, it consists in each instance in eliminating the irrational and in seeing in nature as in conduct the influence of nothing other than pure reason. But there must be nothing illusory about the rationalism of the Logos. It is by no stretch of the imagination the successor to the conceptualism or intellectualism of Socrates, Plato, and Aristotle, for their system was predicated on nothing more than a dialectical method which permitted them to go beyond sensible data and reach intellectual forms or essences. There is no such methodical procedure in the dogmatic system of the Stoics; the object is no longer to eliminate the immediate, sensible datum but on the contrary to see Reason take shape; nor is there any progression from the sensible to the rational since there is no difference between one and the other; there where Plato accumulated differences to have us emerge from the cave, the Stoic sees only identities. Since in the Greek myths the legends of the gods remain outside the history of men while in the Bible human history is a divine drama, it follows that in Platonism the intelligible is beyond the sensible while for the Stoics it is in sensible things that Reason acquires the plenitude of its reality.

This accounts for the necessary solidarity of the three parts of philosophy according to which, following the example of the Platonists, they segregated philosophical problems: logic, physics, and ethics. For no matter to what degree each of the three parts retains a certain independence by virtue of the diversity of its object (with the result that in Aristotle, for instance, ethics can degenerate into something resembling a description of character, independent of the rest of philosophy), they are for the Stoics inseparably linked since one and the same reason connects consequent propositions to antecedent propositions in the dialectic, links together all causes in nature, and establishes perfect agreement between acts in the realm of conduct. It is impossible for the physicist and dialectician not to be a good man. It is impossible for him to achieve rationality separately in the three domains, for instance, and to apprehend reason in the march of events in the universe and not at the same time have reason dominate his conduct. Such a comprehensive philosophy, which imposes on the virtuous man a certain conception of nature and of knowledge without the possibility of progress or betterment, was something completely new in Greece and recalls the all-encompassing beliefs of the Oriental religions.

This also accounts for the difficulty of beginning and for indecision with respect to the ordering of parts which do not automatically fit into a hierarchy since they are reached simultaneously. If we agree to begin with logic, for example, physics may take second place since it contains the conception of nature from which ethics is derived, or it may take third place since it has as its crown theology which, according to an explicit statement by Chrysippus, is the mystery that philosophy is designed to reveal to us.[13] It is obvious, then, that Stoicism leans now in the direction of ethical conduct, now in the direction of the knowledge of God. Later we shall examine further the meaning and scope of such hesitation.

v *Logic of the Old Stoa*

The Stoic theory of knowledge consists precisely in making sensation the key to certainty and wisdom. Unlike Plato, who had cautiously steered philosophy away from such a course, the Stoics hold that truth and certainty are in the most common perceptions, and that these require no quality that surpasses the qualities common to all men, even the most ignorant. Wisdom, it is true, belongs exclusively to the sage but is nonetheless in the domain of sensation and retains its link to the common perceptions of which it is but the systematization.

Knowledge has its point of departure in the representation or image ($\varphi\alpha\nu\tau\alpha\sigma\iota\alpha$), which is the impression made on the soul by a real object and which is analogous according to Zeno to the impression of a seal on wax, or according to Chrysippus, to the modification produced in the air by a color or a sound. This representation is also, it would seem, like an initial judgment of things (this is white or black) which is offered to the soul and which the soul may voluntarily accept or reject. If it mistakenly gives its assent ($\sigma\upsilon\gamma\kappa\alpha\tau\alpha\theta\epsilon\sigma\iota\varsigma$), it errs and the opinion is false; if it rightly gives its assent, it then has the apprehension or perception ($\kappa\alpha\tau\alpha\lambda\eta\psi\iota\varsigma$) of the object that corresponds to the representation. And it must be noted that in the latter case the soul is not content simply to infer the object from the image but apprehends it immediately and with perfect certainty. It apprehends not images but things. In a strict sense, then, sensation is a mental act that is distinct from the image itself.

[13] Plutarch *On the Contradictions of the Stoics* chap. ix (Arnim, II, No. 42).

Still, in order that assent not be misdirected but lead instead to perception, the image itself must be faithful. This faithful image, which thereafter constitutes the criterion or one of the criteria of truth, is the famous apprehensive representation (φαντασία καταληπτική). Here apprehensive means not capable of apprehending or perceiving (which would make no sense inasmuch as the representation is pure passivity and not any form of activity) but capable of producing true assent and perception. The word apprehensive then refers to the function and not to the nature of the image, and when Zeno defines it as "a representation impressed on the soul, originating in a real object, conforming to this object and such that it would not exist if it did not come from a real object," he is merely identifying its role without stating what it is. The apprehensive representation is the image which allows true perception and which even produces it of necessity just as a weight of necessity tips a scale. But what distinguishes it from a nonapprehensive image? The question, according to the Academicians, was never answered by the Stoics. As a matter of fact, it is hard to find an answer to the question. Since it allows us not to confuse one object with another, it should doubtless be said that the apprehensive representation is the image which according to the Stoics contains the unique "personal" quality that always distinguishes one object from any other object, the image which according to Sextus possesses a distinctive trait (ἰδίωμα) that sets it apart from everything else, or the image which according to Cicero manifests in a particular manner the things that it represents.

The apprehensive representation, common to the sage and to the ignorant man, is therefore the first degree of certainty. Wisdom, which is peculiar to the sage, is but a higher degree of certainty attained through accretion and reinforcement. Wisdom is the "stable, reinforced perception which cannot be shaken by reason." [14] Indeed, it seems that the solidity of wisdom is due to the fact that in the sage perceptions corroborate and reinforce each other in such a manner that he can see their rational agreement. Art, which

[14] Philo of Alexandria, in Arnim, II, No. 95.

is midway between ordinary perception and wisdom, is for the
Stoics a "system of perceptions drawn together by experience and
directed toward a particular end useful in life." Thus reason groups
together the isolated, temporary certainties of perception and uses
them to reinforce each other. Wisdom is sure perception because it
is total, which is another way of saying that it is systematic and
rational.

Zeno summed up the whole theory of certainty in a picturesque
manner. "He would raise his hand, spread out his fingers, and say:
'This is representation.' Then he would bend his fingers slightly
and say: 'This is assent.' Then he would clinch his fist and say:
'This is perception.' Finally he would clasp his right fist in his left
hand and say: 'This is wisdom which belongs only to the sage.' " [15]
Careful attention to Cicero's words shows that representation,
whether apprehensive or not, grasps nothing, that assent sets the
stage for perception, and finally that perception alone grasps the
object while wisdom goes further still.

It is obvious that only in a very restricted sense can the Stoics be
called sensualists. There is knowledge other than that of sensible
realities, of course, but such knowledge is permeated by reason and
subject from the outset to its systematizing influence. In spite of appearances, general or innate notions such as those of goodness, justice and the gods, the notions which have been formed in all men
by the age of fourteen, do not derive from a source of knowledge
distinct from the senses; instead, they all derive from spontaneous
reasoning, starting from the perception of things. The notion of
goodness, for instance, derives from a comparison through reason
of things perceived immediately as good,[16] and the notion of the
gods is a conclusion based on the spectacle of the beauty of things.
Such reasoning is spontaneous and common to all men.

The result is that without contradicting each other individual
Stoics could choose very different criteria of truth: apprehensive
representation, sensation, and prenotion or general notion (Chrysip-

[15] Cicero *Academica Priora* ii. sec. 144 (Arnim, I, No. 66).
[16] Cicero *On the Ends* iii. chap. x.

pus); or intelligence, sensation, and wisdom (Boethus). All these criteria are interrelated, interdependent, and interchangeable since what is involved is either the image which leads of necessity to perception, or perception and its link with others. Intellectual activity can consist only in the act of grasping the sensible object; one can only abstract, add, compose, transpose, without ever getting away from sensible data.[17]

Associated with sensible things is what can be said about them or what can be expressed through speech — in a word, meanings (λεκτόν). The representation of a thing is produced in the soul by the thing itself, but what can be expressed is what the soul represents to itself with respect to the thing and not what the thing produces in the soul.[18] The distinction made here is of capital importance in understanding the significance of dialectic in Stoicism. For dialectic deals not with things but with true or false statements relating to things. The simplest of these true or false statements or judgments (ἀξιώματα) are composed of a subject expressed by a substantive or a pronoun and an attribute expressed by a verb. The attribute (κατηγόρημα) is by itself an incomplete expression, e.g., *walks,* which requires a subject. The subject and the attribute together form a complete expression (αὐτοτελές) or simple judgment: *Socrates walks.*[19]

The propositions used by the Stoics differ radically from those used in Platonico-Aristotelian logic. They do not express a relation between concepts, and the subject is always singular even though it may be either definite ("this one"), indefinite ("someone"), or intermediate ("Socrates"). The attribute is always a verb, that is, something that happens to someone. Thus Stoic logic eludes all the difficulties that the Sophists and Socratics raised concerning the possibility of stating one thing about another; and by disregarding the convertibility of propositions as well as the apprehension and ex-

[17] Diocles, in Diogenes Laertius vii. 54 (Arnim, II, No. 105); Epictetus *Discourses* i. 6. 10.

[18] Sextus Empiricus *Against the Mathematicians* viii. 409 (Arnim, II, No. 85).

[19] See Arnim, II, Nos. 181–269, for an exposition of logic, particularly that of Galen and Diocles.

tension of concepts, it relinquishes the complicated mechanism of the Aristotelian syllogism. The dialectic is based on statements of fact about singular subjects.

As a matter of fact the Stoics do retain the syllogism, but the reason for the conclusion is no longer an inclusive relation between concepts expressed by a categorical judgment; instead, it is a relation between facts stated individually through a simple proposition ("It is light. It is day"), and the relation is expressed by a compound judgment ("If it is light, it is day"). They recognize five types of compound judgments (οὐχ ἁπλᾶ ἀξιώματα): the conditional *hypothetical* (συνημμένον) which expresses a relation between an antecedent and a consequent, such as the one just cited; the *conjunctive* which links together the facts ("It is day and it is light"); the *disjunctive* which separates them in such a way that one or the other is true ("It is either day or it is night"); the *causal* which links facts through the conjunction *because* ("Because it is day, it is light"); and the *judgment* stating that one is more or less than the other ("It is more light than dark," or "It is less light than dark").

The major premise in a syllogism is always a proposition ("If it is day it is light"); the minor premise states the truth of the consequent ("It is day"); and the conclusion deduces the truth from the antecedent ("Then it is light"). Such, at any rate, is the first of the five modes or figures of irreducible or undemonstrable syllogisms recognized by Chrysippus, according to Diocles.[20] The second has as its major premise a condition ("If it is day, it is light"), as its minor premise the opposite of the consequent ("It is night"), and as its conclusion the negation of the antecedent ("Then it is not day"). The third has the negation of a conjunctive judgment as its major premise ("It is not true that Plato is dead and that he is alive"), the truth concerning the facts as its minor premise ("Plato is dead"), and the negation of the other part ("Then Plato is not alive"). The fourth has a disjunctive as its major premise ("It is either day or it is night"), the affirmation of one of the parts as its

[20] Diogenes Laertius vii. 79.

minor premise ("It is day"), and the opposite of the other as its conclusion ("Then it is not night"). Conversely, the fifth, which also starts from a disjunctive, denies one of the parts in the minor premise ("It is not night") and has the other as its conclusion ("Then it is day"). To these undemonstrable modes are added the compound modes or themes (θέματα) derived from them, such as the compound argument "If A is B is, if B is C is, etc.; C is, therefore A is."

Both of these classes of judgments and syllogisms are based on language and are patently arbitrary. It is not surprising that Crinis, one of Chrysippus' pupils, acknowledges six kinds of compound judgments instead of five, and that while Diocles tells us that Chrysippus himself acknowledged five undemonstrable syllogisms, Galen attributes only three to him.

The truth is that interest in the Stoic dialectic is not in the mechanism but in the nature of the major premise, which always expresses a relation between facts, such as the relation between an antecedent and a consequent. But under what conditions is a conditional judgment valid or sound (ὑγιές)? We should note that such a judgment is never the conclusion of a demonstration (the conclusion being always a simple judgment), that is, it can never be demonstrated. Also worth noting is the outward resemblance between such propositions ("If something is, something else is") and the propositions which physicians or astrologers, prime observers of symptoms and signs, formulated on the basis of their experience to diagnose diseases and predict the future. Theirs is the language of inductive logicians, which takes us back to the view of a world constituted by a concatenation of facts, quite different from the world of Aristotle. The Stoics themselves saw in demonstration nothing more than some sort of sign.

Still, we must distinguish between the outward form of the proposition and the way in which its value is established. Nowhere in this logic do we find anything even remotely resembling a proof through induction. As a matter of fact, if we consider the content of the judgments that they give as examples, we shall see that none is needed since the consequent is always linked logically to the antecedent. The only justification which they offer for a conditional judgment ("If it is day, it is light") contradicts the antecedent. And in the sign itself, that is, in a judgment such as "If he has a scar, it is because he has been wounded," the Stoics pretend to see a link of the same sort since the sign links not a present reality and a past reality but two statements of fact, both of which are present, and present only in the mind (νοητά), and which in the last analysis are logically identical.[21]

In short, if the logical relation is always expressed in a relation between facts observed through the senses and stated through language, the relation between the facts is valid only by virtue of the logical reason that unites them, and the validity of the conditional judgment is enhanced as it approximates a statement of identities: "*Si lucet, lucet.*" [22] The Stoic dialectic thus has the same ideal as the theory of knowledge: complete penetration of facts through reason. We shall soon see how the conditional proposition, which is their main tool, is particularly appropriate for expressing their vision of things, just as logic is not a simple tool for them, as in the case of Aristotle, but a division of philosophy or a type of philosophy.

vi Physics of the Old Stoa

The Stoic physics is directed toward the representation through the imagination of a world wholly dominated by reason. In this world there is no irrational residue, no room for chance or disorder as in the world of Aristotle and Plato. Everything fits into the universal order. Movement, change, and time are not the mark of imperfection or incomplete being, as in the case of the geometrician Plato or the biologist Aristotle. At each instant the world which is forever changing and forever in motion has the plenitude of its perfection, for motion is "at each of its instants an act and not a passing to the act," [23] and time, like place, is an incorporeal without

---

[21] Sextus Empiricus *Against the Mathematicians* viii. 177.

[22] Cicero *Academica Priora* ii. sec. 98.

[23] Simplicius *Commentary on the Categories* 78b (Arnim, II, No. 499).

substance or reality since it is only because it acts or is acted upon
by virtue of its inner force that a being changes and endures. It
follows that there is no disposition to follow the example of Aristotle and the successors of Plato in proclaiming an eternal world in
order to save its perfection. The Stoic world is a world which comes
to birth and melts away without its perfection being affected. The
rationality of the world no longer consists in the image of an unchangeable order that is reflected in it insofar as matter permits, but
in the activity of a reason that subjects everything to its power.

The activity of reason must at the same time be viewed as a
physical and corporeal activity. Indeed, only bodies exist, for the
Stoics as well as for the sons of the earth whom Plato reprimanded
in the *Sophist;* for what exists is what is capable of acting or being
acted upon, and only bodies have this capacity. The "incorporeals,"
which they also called "intelligibles," are either wholly inactive and
impassive media, such as place, space, or the void, or they are the
expressibles which are stated by a verb and which are the events
or external aspects of the activity of a being — in a word, all that is
thought in connection with things, but not things.

Reason is a body because it acts, and the thing that is subjected
to its action or is acted upon is also a body and is called matter.[24]
An agent (reason or God) and a patient (brute matter which submits docilely to divine action) or, putting it another way, an active
body that always acts and is never acted upon together with matter
that is acted upon but never acts, such are the two principles posited
by the Stoics. One is cause, and even the sole cause to which all
others can be reduced, acting through its mobility, and the other
is the passive recipient of the action of this cause.

The Stoic dynamics, which remains Aristotelian through one of
its principles (an action is exerted without producing a reaction)
but is diametrically opposed to the theory of Aristotle through
another (a movable prime mover and corporeal being or body),
acquires full significance only by virtue of one of their strangest and
most indispensable physical doctrines, the doctrine of universal per-

[24] Diogenes Laertius vii. 139 (Arnim, II, No. 300).

meation. Two bodies can unite by mixing through juxtaposition as grains of different species are mixed together, or by blending together as metals in an alloy. But there can also be a total mixture in which the bodies spread through each other without losing any of their substance or properties and appear in varying proportions throughout the space common to both, just as incense spreads through the air or wine through the body of water into which it is mixed, even if this body is the sea as a whole.[25] Such is the manner in which the active body spreads through the passive body, reason through matter, and the soul through the body. Physical action is inconceivable apart from the categorical negation of impenetrability; it is the action of one body penetrating another and being present in all its parts. This is what gives to Stoic materialism the peculiar character that brings it close to spiritualism. The material breath (πνεῦμα) which cuts through matter and animates it is on the verge of becoming pure spirit.

Greek cosmology was always dominated by the image of a period or great year at the end of which things return to their starting point and begin a new cycle, time after time. This is especially true in the case of the Stoics. The history of the world consists of alternating periods; during one period the supreme god or Zeus, identical to fire and to the active force, has absorbed and consumed all things; during the other he animates and governs an ordered world (διακόσμησις). The world as we know it is brought to an end by a conflagration which draws everything back into the divine substance; then it begins anew, identical in every respect to what it was, with the same personages and the same events. The rigorous, eternal recurrence leaves no room for invention.[26]

Physics or cosmology is but one detail in the continuing drama. From the primitive fire (which must be imagined not as the destructive fire used on earth but rather as the bright glow in the heavens) are born through a series of transmutations all four of the

[25] Alexander of Aphrodisias *On Mixture* (ed. I. Bruns, pp. 216 ff.).
[26] Arnim, II, Nos. 596–632; see especially Alexander of Aphrodisias *Commentary on the Analytics* 180. 31 (ed. Wallies, 1891).

elements: a part of the fire is transformed into air, a part of the air into water, a part of the water into earth, and then the world comes to birth because a fiery breath or divine pneuma penetrates the watery mass. In some obscure manner (our texts offer no hints) this action creates a single world of interrelated beings, each with its distinctive quality (ἰδίως ποιόν), its irreducible individuality, which endures as long as the individual being endures. It would seem that these individualities are but fragmentations of the original pneuma since the generation of new beings through earth or water depends either on the portion of pneuma preserved since the formation of things or perhaps, in the case of man, on a spark from heaven that constitutes his soul.

The concerted action of individual beings results in the system of the world that we see: it is limited by the sphere of the fixed bodies; planets circulate in space through free and voluntary motion; the air is peopled by invisible living forms or daimons; the fixed earth is the center of the world. But it is only in appearance that the geocentric system is similar to those that had preceded it. In the first place the reasons for the unity of the world are not the same. "Plato," according to Proclus, "based the unity of the world on the unity of his model, Aristotle on the unity of matter and the determination of natural places, and the Stoics on the existence of a unifying force in the corporeal substance." [27] If the world is one, this is because the breath or soul that penetrates it retains its parts, because it possesses a tension (τόνος) analogous to the tension which any living being, and even any independent being, must have to prevent the dispersion of its parts. It is tension, the shuttling motion between the center and the periphery and between the periphery and the center, which makes the being exist. It follows that Plato's ideal form has no place here, and the same holds for Aristotle's natural place. It is through the force that is within him, through the force that is at once a thought and a reason, that God contains the world. This means that the world can exist in the heart of an infinite void without fear of being dissipated and that conversely,

[27] *Commentary on the Timaeus* 138e.

it has within itself no void since there is no natural place other than that which the force chooses for itself. Furthermore "if the world is contained by a unique soul, there must be sympathy between the parts that compose it; each animal exhibits just such sympathy, with the result that if the disposition of certain of its parts is known, the disposition of the others is easily determined. . . . If this is true, then motions can transmit their action in spite of distances, for there is but one life, and it is carried from agents to patients."[28] The universal sympathy of a world in which all things participate radically separates the world of the Stoics from the hierarchical world of Aristotle. In their circular universe the earth and all its inhabitants receive celestial influences which are not limited to the general effects of the seasons but extend to the individual destiny of each. Astrology, which became widely diffused beginning with the third century, was accepted without reservation by the Stoics. According to their theory, through a transmutation which is the reverse of the one that produced the elements, dry emanations coming from the earth and wet emanations coming from streams and seas produce diverse atmospheric phenomena and serve as food for the stars. This gives the astronomy of the Stoics its distinctive stamp. Not in the least concerned with mathematical astronomy, they discard spheres or epicycles, which had been devised to avoid introducing into the heavens anything other than circular or uniform motions; they make each planet, which consists of a condensed fire, follow its free and independent course under the influence of its own soul, and thereby introduce into the heavens motions that are not uniform; the varied, circular motion of the planet is the very proof of its animation.[29] Dynamics, on the other hand, accounts for their placing the earth at the center of the universe, for the earth is pressed from all directions by air, like a motionless grain of millet at the center of an inflated bladder; or the mass of the earth, no

[28] Proclus *Commentary on the Republic,* ed. G. Kroll, 2 vols. (Leipzig, 1899–1900), II, 258.
[29] Achilles *Isagoge* 13 (Arnim, II, No. 686).

matter how small, is equal to that of the rest of the world and therefore keeps it balanced.[30]

Thus the geocentrism of the Stoics is vastly different from Plato's. While Plato was ready to admit that his was only a mathematical hypothesis, the Stoics make theirs a dogma, closely tied in with their beliefs; Cleanthes thought that the Greeks ought to try Aristarchus of Samos for blasphemy because he held that the earth was in motion.[31] For the Stoics the world is a divine system whose parts are all divinely distributed. "It is a perfect body, but its parts are not perfect because they have a certain relation to the whole and do not exist independently." [32] Everything in the world is a product of the world.

The order of things is not eternal. Against the Peripatetics who argued in favor of the eternity of the world, Zeno marshals geological observations which indicate that the soil is constantly being leveled and the sea receding. It follows that if the world were eternal, the earth would have to be completely flat and the sea would have to have disappeared. Besides, we see every part of the universe deteriorating, including the celestial fire that has to be provided with nourishment if it is to be sustained. Why then should the whole not be destroyed? Finally, we see that the human race cannot be very old since many of the arts which are indispensable to man and which must have had their beginning at the same time as man, are still in their infancy.[33]

We have seen what the birth of the world was like. Its end, at the close of the great year determined by the return of the planets to their initial positions, consists in the universal conflagration or reabsorption of everything in the primal fire. Zeno and Chrysippus call the conflagration a purification of the world, suggesting thereby a restitution of the state of perfection and recalling the floods or

[30] *Ibid.* Nos. 555 and 572.
[31] Plutarch *Concerning the Face which Appears in the Orb of the Moon* chap. vi.
[32] Plutarch *On the Contradictions of the Stoics* chap. xliv.
[33] Philo of Alexandria *On the Incorruptibility of the World* chaps. xxiii and xxiv (Arnim, I, No. 106).

fiery blasts found in the old Semitic myths. Chrysippus takes great pains to show that this conflagration is not the death of the world, for death is the separation of the soul and the body whereas here "the soul of the world is not separated from its body but continually grows at its expense until all its substance has been absorbed." The change which he describes is in conformity with nature and not a violent revolution.

All things considered, the universe is not a somewhat imperfect, contingent, and unstable realization of a mathematical order. It is rather the effect of a cause acting in accordance with a necessary law, with the result that it is impossible for any event to happen other than as it does happen. God, the soul of Zeus, reason, the necessity of things, divine law, and finally Fate are all one for Zeno.[34] The theory of fate ($\epsilon i\mu\alpha\rho\mu\acute{e}\nu\eta$) is only a refined expression of the integral rationalism found in the Stoics. Fate, which in Greek thought was at first the wholly irrational force that apportioned their lot to men, becomes the universal "reason according to which past events have happened, present events are happening, and future events will happen." [35] It is the universal reason, mind, or will of Zeus who commands both the facts which we say are against nature, such as diseases or mutilations, and those which we say are in conformity with nature, such as health. Everything that happens is in conformity with universal nature, and we speak of things contrary to nature only in connection with the nature of a particular being separated from the whole.

Fatalism must not be confused with scientific determinism. It produced among the Stoics nothing that resembles our theory of natural laws, which appears in the vastly different doctrines of the Skeptics. The fact is that causal necessity such as we understand it is that of a relation, and a relation leaves wholly undetermined the number of phenomena that can be subject to it. The fate of the universe, on the contrary, is like an individual's fate; it applies to an individual being, the universe which has a beginning and an end.

According to the unknown Stoic who wrote a treatise attributed to Plutarch,[36] "Neither law nor reason nor anything divine could be infinite." This conception supports with the weight of its authority not only the true sciences such as astronomy and medicine, but all the modes of divination of the future (astrology, divination through dreams, etc.) to which the Stoics subscribed. Chrysippus and Diogenes of Babylon wrote summaries of their observations on such matters, and Cicero refers to their work in his treatise *On Divination*.

In short, fate is not at all the concatenation of causes and effects but rather the unique cause which is at the same time the relation of causes in the sense that it embraces in its unity all the seminal reasons that culminate in the development of each particular being. The finite world, made of *logoi* or reasons, constitutes a sort of universe of forces or, we might say, active divine thoughts, which takes the place of the Platonic world of ideas. The main *logoi,* those that govern the phenomena of the earth or sea, are popular divinities known through myths: Hestia and Poseidon. The Stoics undertake through an interpretation based on a doctrine which has been preserved by Cornutus,[37] who lived during the time of Augustus, to explain every single detail of the popular myths as an allegory of physical facts.

Fatalism nevertheless met with one difficulty, even within the system, since it seemed to deny belief in human freedom. Cicero has preserved a remnant of the complicated line of reasoning through which Chrysippus tried to resolve the conflict.[38] How can an act be free and at the same time be determined by fate? That is the way the question must be put since there can be no thought of limiting fate in any way. Chrysippus answers the question by identifying different types of causes: the rotating motion of a cylinder is explained not simply by an exterior impulsion known as the antecedent cause but by the shape of the cylinder which is the perfect

---

[36] Pseudo-Plutarch *On Fate* chap. iii.
[37] Cornutus *Outline of Greek Theology,* ed. C. Lang (1881).
[38] Cicero *On Fate* sec. 39 ff.

or principal cause; in the same way a free act, such as assent, is explained not by the apprehensive representation which is the antecedent cause but by the initiative of the mind that receives it. Thus everything seems to occur in his solution as if the power of fate extended only to the exterior circumstances or occasional causes of our acts.

VII *Stoic Theology*

The alternating rhythm of the world is of prime significance in Stoic theology. Immanence and even pantheism are words heard in connection with the Stoics, and the Christian writers missed no opportunity to ridicule the God present in the most minute parts of their universe. It is also true that their world is made of the substance of God and reabsorbed by him. But a fruitful idea must not be abused, and the truth is that in Stoicism are the rudiments of a notion of divine transcendence, completely different in nature from that of the God of Plato or Aristotle. We should note that the transcendence of God is inseparable in the thinking of Aristotle and the Platonists from the affirmation of the eternity of the world. The Platonists never tire of repeating that God is inconceivable unless he is the creator of an eternal world, and that the present existence of the world is one of the faces or conditions of divine perfection. The situation is reversed in the case of the Stoics: by virtue of the conflagration their Zeus or supreme god has a life which is to a certain degree independent of the world, and "when nature ceases to exist, it finds repose in him and surrenders completely to his thoughts." [39] Even if God is imagined as a force within things, as "a creative fire, proceeding methodically to the production of things," or as "honey seeping through the combs," the Stoics nevertheless address him as a providential being and father of men who rules everything in the world for the benefit of rational beings. He is "the omnipotent being and ruler of nature who governs all things according to the law and whom the whole universe that revolves

[39] Seneca *Letters to Lucilius* 9. 16.

around the earth obeys, going wherever he directs and submitting voluntarily to his domination." [40] The Christian writers have called attention to what seems to be an internal contradiction in the Stoic notion of God. "Although they say that the providential being is of the same substance as the being that he directs," says Origen, "they nevertheless say that he is perfect and different from that which he directs." [41]

If the God of Aristotle and the Platonists is the transcendent God of a scholarly theology, the God of the Stoics is the object of a more human piety. The Stoics examined and sanctioned all the origins of the idea of gods proposed by pious men, the notion of atmospheric phenomena and an ordered world, awareness of forces useful or harmful to man and of transcendent forces, awareness of inner motivating forces such as amorous passion or the desire for justice, and finally the myths of poets and the memory of charitable heroes. The same tendency is manifested in their proofs of the existence of the gods, which are based on the necessity of positing an architect of the world whose reason is not unlike but superior to human reason. In every respect their popular theology implies direct, special relations between God and men, whereas the Aristotelian or Platonic theology is concerned only with the general relation of God to the order of the world, not with a relation peculiar to man. The world is first and foremost "the dwelling of the gods and of men and things made for gods and men." The last consideration recalls the ridiculous extremes to which the Stoics carried their affirmation of an external finality. For instance, they attributed to fleas the function of waking us from excessively long sleep and to mice the felicitous task of forcing us to keep our affairs in order. [42]

Chrysippus, on being taken to task by his adversaries, constructed a theodicy, rather weak to be sure, to explain the presence of evil in the universe. Two arguments show that evil is indispensable in

---

[40] Cleanthes Hymn to Zeus (Arnim, I, No. 537).
[41] On the Gospel of John xiii. 21.
[42] Cf. Aetius Opinions of the Philosophers i. 6; Cicero On the Nature of the Gods chaps. xxv and xxvi, II, chap. xxvi; Stobaeus (Arnim, II, No. 527); Plutarch On the Contradictions of the Stoics 1044d.

the divinely appointed order of the universe. "Nothing is more foolish," said Chrysippus, "than to think that good could have existed if at the same time there had not been evil, for good is the contrary of evil and neither of a pair of contraries can exist without the other." According to the second argument God naturally wills good, and this is the over-all scheme of things, but to achieve good he has to resort to the use of means which in themselves are not without drawbacks: for instance, the human organism requires thin cranial bones even though its safety is endangered by their thinness. Evil then is a necessary accompaniment (παρακολούθησις) of good. A third argument is found in the words of Cleanthes' hymn to Zeus: "Nothing happens apart from thee except the acts accomplished by madmen in their folly." Here an evil moral nature or vice is due to man's freedom, which allows him to rebel against divine law, whereas in the first argument it was due to the necessity of a harmonious equilibrium. The Stoics were never able to choose between the two contradictory explanations.[43]

VIII *Psychology of the Old Stoa*

The Stoic theory of the individual soul, like the theory of the universal soul, is rationalistic, dynamistic, and spiritualistic. The Stoics say that animals have souls while plants do not, and they preserve man's pre-eminence by denying that beasts are endowed with reason. In the first place there is no soul unless there is spontaneous motion caused by an inclination initiated by a representation. Representation and inclination are the two interconnected faculties possessed not by plants but only by animals.

Animals are nevertheless bereft of reason. Their instinctive acts which are in appearance intelligent (and which attract attention, as we see in the treatise *On Animals* by Philo of Alexandria and in Plutarch's treatise *On the Cleverness of Animals*) — their forms of friendship, hostility, and political organization, for example — do not presuppose any degree of reason but derive from universal reason, which is spread throughout nature.

[43] Arnim, II, No. 1069.

Reason which is peculiar to the human soul consists in assent, which is introduced between representation and inclination or tendency. The distinguishing trait of the rational soul derives from the fact that the activity of a tendency is not engendered directly by the representation but only by the voluntary adhesion or assent of the soul to the representation; any refusal on the part of the soul prevents action.

The Stoics called that part of the soul in which representation, assent, and inclination take place the hegemonic or ruling part, or again, reflection, and it is pictured as a fiery breath that has its seat in the heart. From it come seven fiery breaths, five of which extend to the organs, and a seventh is the reproductive breath which transmits to the offspring a portion of the father's soul. The seven breaths are not really subordinate parts but the ruling soul itself spreading through the body.[44]

Concerning the origin of the soul, the early Stoics thought that the fiery breath transmitted by the father was not at first a soul but that it made the embryo live as a plant until the moment of birth; then the fiery breath, cooled by the air (the Stoics supposed that a part of the air that had entered the lungs during respiration was received by the ventricle), hardened like cast iron and became the soul of an animal.[45] The Stoics then seem to have accepted the doctrine later called traducianism. It is difficult to determine who is responsible for the opposite doctrine in which the soul is viewed as a particle of divine ether. This doctrine, found among the Stoics in the days of the Roman Empire, stresses the pre-eminence of man. The human soul is in any case pure reason, and how vice and unreason gain entrance is difficult to see.

ix Ethics of the Old Stoa

With the Stoic conception of fate, God, and the soul are associated the rules of conduct of the sage.

[44] Concerning the points of difference between Cleanthes and Chrysippus, cf. Seneca *Letters* 113. 23.

[45] Plutarch *On the Contradictions of the Stoics* chap. xli (Arnim, II, No. 806).

In our explanation of the Stoic system of ethics we shall follow the plan indicated by Diogenes Laertius (vii. 84) as being that of Chrysippus and his successors up to Posidonius.

The moralist starts from the observation of inclinations (ὁρμαί) such as those noted in man from birth or as soon as they present themselves. These inclinations, as they are received from nature, cannot be depraved. Our first inclination is toward self-preservation, as if nature had entrusted us to ourselves by giving us from the outset the feeling or consciousness of ourselves (for this inclination is inseparable from self-knowledge and does not precede it).

A living being then has from the beginning the means for distinguishing between what is in conformity with nature and what is contrary to nature, and the objects of our first inclinations — health, well-being, and everything contributing to them — are called first things according to nature (πρῶτα κατὰ φύσιν). These objects still do not merit the name of *goods,* however, for a good is by nature absolute: it is that which is sufficient unto itself and can be called useful. The Stoics would not accept a relative good, as had Aristotle when he defined the physician's good, the architect's good, etc. First things according to nature are not goods since they are relative to the living being who desires them. It is through a rational process that we manage to conceive of the good.[46] By reflecting on the general reason for our spontaneous assent to our inclinations and by comparing our inclinations, we grasp the notion of the good. Our spontaneous assent at the dawn of life was even then grounded on reason, and on right reason since it had as its aim the preservation of a being produced by nature, that is, fate or universal reason. The notion of the good is to some extent dependent on a second degree of reason which identifies our ultimate motive as the will to survive that is manifested everywhere in nature. That is why the good envisioned by universal nature is superior by far to the first objects of the inclination, which relate only to our individual natures. It can never be obtained through mere increase of first goals (for example,

[46] Cicero *On the Ends* iii. sec. 72.

by pursuing to the limit health, wealth, and other such goals). It differs in quality, not in quantity.

The proof is that praise is addressed neither to health nor to wealth but is reserved for the good. Of course not everyone admits that the good is worthy of praise in itself; Aristotle, for instance, distinguishes the virtuous act, which alone is worthy of praise, from the good or happiness that motivates it. Reflection, however, shows that the reverse is true. "The good is the object of the will; in it one takes pleasure; that in which one takes pleasure is praiseworthy." [47] To be sure Aristotle was right in saying, as common sense dictates, that a virtuous and beautiful action is alone praiseworthy; but his statement assumes completion of this line of reasoning: "What is praiseworthy is virtuous (καλόν, honestum); therefore only what is virtuous is a good." Underneath the dry dialectic we sense the profound ethical shift which consists in accepting as a good only that which we can realize through our own will by becoming indifferent to the object of our inclinations.

Virtue and the good have been identified: both are precious, praiseworthy, useful, and even indispensable. The good or happiness is no longer a divine gift that complements virtue. It has no exterior object toward which it tends; it is self-sufficient and desirable for itself; it does not draw its value from the end to which it attains, for it is itself this end. It is not directed toward an alien end, like other arts, but toward itself alone (in se tota conversa).[48] On the other hand it is not susceptible of improvement, like other arts, but perfect from the outset and complete in all its parts.

That is why virtue is, entirely internal, a stable and harmonious disposition. To this stability and constancy identical to reason, which is essentially its complete harmony, Zeno gave the name prudence (φρόνησις). If there are any other virtues, for him they are only aspects of the fundamental virtue: courage, prudence with re-

---

[47] Chrysippus in Plutarch On the Contradictions of the Stoics chap. xiii (Arnim, III, No. 29).

[48] Stobaeus Eclogae (Arnim, III, No. 208); Cicero On the Ends iii. sec. 32.

spect to what is to be endured; temperance, prudence in the choice of things; justice, prudence in the attribution of parts. Zeno[49] obviously has no thought of separating and dissociating virtues, as did Aristotle, who singled out not only virtues of men and virtues of women but also virtues of the rich and virtues of the poor. There can be no such distinction when virtue is viewed as universal reason. God himself has no virtue not shared by man. Cleanthes was probably putting more stress on the active aspect of universal reason than his teacher when he defined the main virtue as a tension (τόνος) which is courage in the case of endurance and justice in the case of distribution. Chrysippus returns to the intellectualism of Zeno and refuses to see in tension anything other than the accompaniment of virtues which in themselves are sciences, prudence being the science of things to do or not to do, courage the science of things to endure or not to endure, and so on. Though he recognizes a multiplicity of virtues, his view is by no means the same as Aristotle's, for they are all inseparably linked together. Whoever has one such virtue has them all, yet each virtue has its own sphere of action and must be learned separately.[50]

Passing from the original state of innocence, in which all inclinations are right inclinations, to the state in which inclinations are replaced by the reflective will and virtue is not so easy as our account might suggest. Those who aspire to the virtuous life are not the innocents but the perverts. The original inclinations do not persist but, deformed or exaggerated under the influence of the social conditions that deprave the child, they become passions, sorrow, fear, desire, or pleasure, which disturb the soul and stand in the way of virtue and happiness.[51] The existence of passion poses one of the most difficult problems in Stoic psychology: if the soul consists of pure reason, how can there be in it anything irrational? For passions actually go against reason inasmuch as they cause us to desire as goods or to avoid as evils that which for the reflective man

[49] Plutarch *On Moral Virtue* chap. ii.
[50] Arnim, I, No. 563, and III, Nos. 255–61.
[51] *Ibid.* III, Nos. 228–36.

is in reality neither a good nor an evil. Plato and Aristotle had been able to surmount the difficulty only by assuming one or more irrational parts in the soul; but their thesis, besides contradicting the integral rationalism of the Stoics, failed to take into account certain elements of passion. For it must be recalled that in a rational being such as man, inclination is possible only when assent or adhesion is freely given, and that what is true of inclination in general is true of exaggerated and inordinate inclination in the form of passion. There is no sorrow, for example, unless the soul adheres to the judgment that a present evil exists, and any passion thus implies a judgment of a good, present in pleasure, future in desire, or of an evil, present in suffering, future in fear. Not only the genesis but also the development of passion depends on assent; for instance, a man weeps and goes into mourning because he believes that it is fitting for him to surrender to sorrow. Assent is characteristic of a reasonable being and only of a reasonable being. It is one thing to feel physical suffering (ἄλγος) and another to experience pain (λύπη), which depends on the judgment that it is an evil. One does not explain passion by attributing it to an irrational faculty.[52]

Passion then is a reason or judgment, as Chrysippus says, but it is an "irrational reason" and one which disobeys reason. The implication is that there is still an alien element in reason, and Chrysippus attributes to it an external origin: habits developed in children to protect them against hunger and cold, pain which persuades them that any suffering is an evil, and the opinions which they hear expressed all during their training. For from poets and painters as well as their nurses, children hear only praises of pleasure and wealth.[53]

Still, our false judgments must gain admission to the soul. When Chrysippus explains exaggerated tendencies by comparing them with the force that prevents a runner from coming to a halt and then indicates that the augmentations or diminutions of a passion such as sorrow are to some extent independent of our judgment of

[52] *Ibid.* Nos. 377–420.
[53] Chalcidius *On the Timaeus* 165–66 (Arnim, III, No. 229).

objects inasmuch as sorrow is more intense in the case of a recent judgment, he is indeed introducing irrational factors into the soul. He goes even further: the initial cause of passion is a "weakness of the soul," and passion is a "weak belief"; passion also gives birth to facts that cannot possibly be likened to judgments, such as constriction of the soul in the presence of pain and expansion in the presence of joy. Finally, passions which are by nature transient and unstable become diseases of the soul, such as ambition and misanthropy, which implant themselves and become irradicable.[54]

Without denying the existence of unreason the Stoics still stressed the importance of judgment in order to show how passion depended on us. Chrysippus in particular brought to light the role of conventional judgments, such as the presumption that makes us think that it is good and just to give in to sorrow over the death of a parent. It is not through outright resistance to unleashed passion but through preventive meditation on such judgments, in accordance with reasoned maxims, that the Stoics hope to rescue us from passions.

We have seen how human reason identifies virtue and the good in spontaneous inclinations. Through the same rational process man discovers the end toward which all actions are appropriately directed. The basis of the ethical life is the type of spontaneous choice which our inclinations cause us to make with respect to things useful to our preservation. Man's end is to live by choosing through a reflective and voluntary choice the things that are in conformity with universal nature.[55] This is doubtless what Zeno meant by defining the end as a harmonious or rational life (ὁμολογουμένως).[56] To live in such a way is to live according to reason, which encounters no opposition. It is surely what Cleanthes and Chrysippus meant in proposing as an end life according to nature (ὁμολογουμένως τῇ φύσει). This, Chrysippus explains, means using scientific knowledge of things that happen naturally. Such scientific knowledge

[54] Cicero *Tusculan Disputations* iv. 125.
[55] Cicero *On the Ends* ii. 34; iii. 14.
[56] Arnim, III, No. 12.

constitutes physics: everything happens through universal reason, the will of God, or fate. Hence the end consists solely in an interior attitude of the will. Every being necessarily obeys fate, but misguided reason tries to resist and to oppose the universal good with the ghost of a particular good — health, wealth, honor. The sage on the contrary consciously submits to the events apportioned by fate; whereas the fool is forced along his course, the sage voluntarily wends his way, accepting mutilation or poverty if he knows that fate wills him mutilated or poor. *"Non pareo Deo sed assentior,"* wrote Seneca (*Letter* 97), "I do not obey God but assent to what he has decided." Stoic resignation is not a last resort but a positive, joyous acceptance of the world as it is: "We must put our will in harmony with events so that whatever happens will be to our liking." [57] To follow nature, to follow reason, to follow God — a tripartite ideal which will later be dissociated — is for the Stoics one and the same thing.

Here we come to the question of how the Stoic attitude, far from remaining something internal, invites action. This is a most important point and one that brings us to the very heart of Stoicism. The Stoic system of ethics invites action. In their teaching the founders of Stoicism stressed above all else the fulfillment of civic obligation.[58] Much later Epictetus will consider his teaching as a veritable preparation for public careers and censure young people for wanting to stay in school too long: the normal life of a man is the life of a husband, a citizen, a magistrate. Nor do the Stoics divorce the contemplative life from the practical life, as the doctrines of Aristotle and Plato at first threatened to do, and, as we shall see, finally did do. Knowledge of nature sets the stage for action.

But what kind of action is envisioned? At first glance it seems that the Stoic system of ethics contains an insurmountable difficulty which leads inevitably to the quietism of the perfect man who, willingly or not, becomes a passive witness to every event. All the Stoics agree that nothing matters except the interior disposition which is

[57] Epictetus *Discourses* ii. 14. 7.
[58] Cf. Seneca *On Leisure* (beginning).

wisdom, and that neither good nor evil is inherent in anything that happens to us. In other words, there is no reason to will one contrary rather than another, wealth rather than poverty, disease rather than health. But we can carry the analysis further. If the state of man is imperfect, then health and wealth command a higher price and are of more value to him than disease and poverty because they are more in conformity with nature or better satisfy his inclinations. If the state of man is perfect, health and disease are qualitatively different from what he seeks, namely right will or will in conformity with nature, and the latter is completely independent of both and persists in both, with the result that its value is incomparable. But it does not follow that one has no more value than the other, even in the case of a perfect man, when the two are compared. What characterizes the perfect man is that he is not attached to one more than the other, and especially that he makes no unconditional attachment. He would choose disease, for example, if he knew it to be willed by fate but, all other things being equal, would choose instead health. In a general way, without desiring them in the least as he desires the good, he considers as preferable (προηγμένα) objects in conformity with nature — health and wealth — and as non-preferable (ἀποπροηγμένα) things contrary to nature.

In this way the Stoics are then able to draw up a list of appropriate actions (καθήκοντα, *officia*) which like functions or duties are capable of safeguarding the life of a rational being as well as the lives of his fellow-creatures: bodily care, friendship and beneficence, family obligations, public charges. The accomplishment of such functions, which is neither a good nor an evil, can exist among all men and can thus give rise to a secondary system of ethics, one imposed by imperfect men on all men. This practical system of ethics (advisory or parenetic) was later developed extensively, making Stoicism a part of the common way of life. The sage and the imperfect man have exactly the same duties, with the result that the sage, no matter how perfect and happy he is, will have to end his life by suicide if he suffers to excess things contrary to his nature. Still, their conduct is the same only in appearance and externally, for whereas the imperfect man accomplishes a simple duty (καθῆκον), the sage accomplishes a perfect duty (καθηκον τέλειον) or right action (κατόρθωμα) by virtue of his conscious conformity with universal nature. Furthermore, the sage knows that his duty has only conditional value and that there are instances where it is better to renounce familial or judicial duties.[59]

Since duty or function never has a categorical form, a vast moralistic (parenetic) literature developed. Leaving aside abstract principles, writers examined and weighed individual cases, and this at times led to mere causistry. The liberties which the early Stoa took with respect to social duties were enough to recall the most radical traits of Cynicism, for example, advocacy of the community of women.[60]

Such is the Stoic theory of action, so contradictory in appearance. It is worth noting that indifference to things is an expression not of the weakness but of the absolute strength of a will which consents to manifest itself through the choice of an action but which desires neither to limit itself nor to become permanently attached to its choice.

From the very beginning the Stoic system of ethics never departs from describing man in action. It searches for no good outside the voluntary disposition and consequently can be realized wholly only through description of the being who possesses virtue, the sage. The sage is the being who retains in his soul nothing except that which is entirely ratinoal, for he is a rational principle or logos and therefore cannot err. Whatever he does will be well done, even though it may be completely insignificant, and the least of his acts will contain as much wisdom as his conduct in general. He will know neither regret nor sorrow nor fear nor anything of the kind; he will have perfect happiness; he alone will possess wealth, true majesty, true beauty — freedom; he alone will know the gods and be the true priest. Useful to himself and to others, he will be able to govern a house or a city and to have friends. All these paradoxes

[59] Cf. Arnim, III, No. 493.
[60] Sextus Empiricus *Outlines of Pyrrhonism* iii. 205.

and many others still describe all the perfect qualities of the sage.[61] To put them in proper perspective we must also note that whoever is not a sage is imperfect and that in connection with wisdom all imperfections are equal. All non-sages are equally fools; they are like madmen engulfed in unhappiness or exiles who have neither a family nor a city of their own. They may be close to the attainment of wisdom or remote from it but are nonetheless fools since the integrity of the sage concedes neither differences nor degrees. The victim of a drowning, for instance, is just as dead if he is near the surface as if he is on the bottom, and in the case of the archer a miss by an inch is the same as a miss by a mile.

It is natural and in keeping with what we have learned of Stoicism to assume that wisdom is apportioned absolutely and that it is no more susceptible of improvement than is the whole system of philosophy. The early Stoics had as their aim not what we might call ethical progress but, as Clement of Alexandria expresses it, an inner transmutation that changes the whole man into pure reason[62] and the citizen of a city into a citizen of the world — something resembling the political transformation to which Alexander subjected nations.

"Zeno," said Plutarch, "wrote an exemplary *Republic,* based on the principle that men ought not to be separated into cities and nations each of which has its own laws, inasmuch as all men are fellow-citizens with but one life and but one order of things (cosmos), but ought instead to constitute one group and be ruled by a common law. What Zeno wrote as a visionary was realized by Alexander . . . who united as in a crater all the peoples of the whole world . . . directing all men to look upon the earth as their fatherland, his army as their acropolis, virtuous people as their parents and others as aliens." [63] There is no better way of stating that the ethical system of the Stoics is that of a new age in which great monarchies which aspire to rule mankind rise upon the ruins

[61] Arnim, III, Nos. 548–656.
[62] Clement of Alexandria *Stromata* iv. 6.
[63] *On Alexander's Fortune* chap. vi.

of cities incapable of serving as bulwarks or sources of a moral life.

Reason, the universal law of nature, becomes imperious. In Aristotle the starting point was psychological or social realities — those relating to facts, passions, customs, and laws — which reason tried to temper and organize into a hierarchy; here reason assumes complete control and expels everything other than itself. "Virtue is lodged solely in reason." [64]

[64] Cicero *Academica Posteriora* i. sec. 38.

BIBLIOGRAPHY

Texts

Stoicorum veterum fragmenta, ed. H. von Arnim. 4 vols. in 3. Leipzig, 1903–05. A fourth volume containing the *Indices* was published in 1914.

Studies

I, II

P. H. Elmer More. *Hellenistic Philosophies.* Princeton, 1923.
Kaerst. *Geschichte des hellenistischen Zeitalters.* 1901.
Wilamowitz-Moellendorf. *Hellenistische Dichtung in der Zeit des Callimachos.* Vol. I, Chapter 1. Berlin, 1924.
E. Grumach. *Physis und Agathon in der alten Stoa.* Berlin, 1932.
C. Diano. *Forma ed Evento.* Venice, 1952.
A. Momigliano. "Atene nel III Secolo A. C. . . ," *Revista storica italiana,* LXXI (1959), 529.

III

Dyroff. "L'origine de la morale stoïcienne," *Archiv für die Geschichte der Philosophie,* XII.
M. Wellmann. *Die Fragmente der sikelischen Aertze.* Berlin, 1901. — "Eine pythagoreische Urkunde des IV. Jahrhunderts vor Christus," *Hermes* (1919), p. 225.
W. Jaeger. *Diokles von Karystos.* Berlin-Leipzig, 1938.
J. Moreau. *L'âme du monde de Platon aux Stoïciens.* Paris, 1939.
A. J. Festugière. "Les mémoires pythagoriques cités par Alexandre Polyhistor," *Revue des Etudes grecques* (1945), pp. 1–65.

IV

F. Ogereau. *Essai sur le système philosophique des Stoïciens.* Paris, 1885. Reprinted in 1939.
F. Ravaisson. *La métaphysique d'Aristote.* 2 vols. Paris, 1836. Vol. II. Reprinted in 1920.

G. Rodier. "Histoire extérieure et intérieure du stoïcisme," in *Etudes de philosophie grecque*. Paris (1926), pp. 219–69.

P. Barth. *Die Stoa*. Leipzig, 1908. 2d to 5th editions, 1924–1941. 6th edition, Stuttgart, 1946.

M. Pohlenz. *Die Stoa*. Göttingen, 1948–1955.

C. J. de Vogel. *Greek Philosophy*. Vol. III, pp. 44–183. Leiden, 1959.

E. Bréhier. *Chrysippe*. Paris, 1910. 2nd edition, 1951 (*Chrysippe et l'ancien stoïcisme*). — *Etudes de Philosophie antique*. Paris, 1955. Section C. — *Les Stoïciens*, Paris, 1961.

G. Verbeke. *Kleanthes van Assos*. Brussels, 1949.

R. Hirzel. *Untersuchungen über Ciceros philosophische Schriften*. 3 vols. Leipzig, 1876–83. Part II, Division 1: "Le développement de la phiolosophie stoïcienne."

R. Bevan. *Stoics and Sceptics*. Oxford, 1913. French translation, 1927.

V

V. Brochard. *De Assensione Stoici quid senserint*. 1879. — "La logique des Stoïciens," *Etudes de philosophie ancienne*, 1912, pp. 221–251.

R. Heinze. *Zur Erkenntnisslehre der Stoa*. 1886.

A. Levi. "Sulla psicologia gnoseologica degli Stoici," *Athenaeum* (July and October, 1925).

O. Hamelin. "Sur la logique des Stoïciens," *Année philosophique* (1902), p. 23.

E. Bréhier. *La théorie des incorporels dans l'ancien stoïcisme*. Paris, 1908.

A. Virieux-Reymond. *La logique et l'épistémologie des Stoïciens*. Chambéry, 1950.

V. Goldschmidt. *Le système stoïcien et l'idée de temps*. Paris, 1953.

VI, VII, VIII

Capelle. "Zur antiken Theodicee," *Archiv für die Geschichte der Philosophie*, 1903.

H. and M. Simon. *Die alte Stoa und ihr Naturbegriff*. Berlin, 1956.

L. Guillermit and J. Vuillemin. *Le sens du destin*. Neuchâtel, 1948.

P.-M. Schuhl. *Le dominateur et les possibles*. Paris, 1960.

A. Bonhoeffer. "Zur stoischen Psychologie, *Philologus*, LIV (1895).

Ganter. "Das stoische System der αἴσθησις," *Philologus*, LIII. "Zur Psychologie der Stoa," *Philologus*, LIV.

Stein. *Psychologie der Stoa*. Berlin, 1886.

G. Blin and M. Keim. "Chrysippe: Fragments de son traité sur l'âme," *Mesures*, April 15, 1939.

Przyluski. "Les Mages et les Mèdes," *Revue d'Histoire des Religions* (September-October, 1940), p. 94.

IX

Cicero. *De finibus.* Books III and IV.
Denis. *Histoire des idées et des théories morales dans l'antiquité.* Paris, 1856.
G. Rodier. "La cohérence de la morale stoïcienne." *Etudes de philosophie grecque,* Paris (1926), pp. 270–308.
A. Dyroff. *Die Ethik der alten Stoa.* Berlin, 1890.
A. Bonhoeffer. *Epiktet und die Stoa.* Stuttgart, 1890.
A. Jagu. *Zénon de Cittium, son rôle dans l'établissement de la morale stoïcienne.* Paris, 1946.
P. Milton Valente. *L'éthique stoïcienne chez Cicéron.* — *Les sources de l'éthique stoïcienne chez Cicéron.* Paris, 1956.

Special Studies in English

E. H. Blakeney (trans.). *Hymn of Cleanthes.* New York-London, 1921.
W. W. Capes. *Stoicism.* London and New York, 1880.
R. D. Hicks. *Stoic and Epicurean.* New York-London, 1910.
B. Mates. *Stoic Logic.* Berkeley, Calif., 1953.
A. C. Pearson (ed.). *Fragments of Zeno and Cleanthes.* London, 1891.
J. E. Sandys. *History of Classical Scholarship.* 3d edition, Cambridge, 1922. Vol. I.

THIRD-CENTURY EPICUREANISM

AFTER the massive system of the Stoics, it is relaxing to come to the secluded garden where Epicurus philosophizes with his friends while Zeno remains at the Porch, where he drew great crowds. Between the two minds there is no common link other than the most general traits of the age: their common detachment from the city hardly sets them apart from the old Sophist critics, and Zeno's compensatory attachment to nascent empires and cosmopolitanism is not shared by Epicurus. Both subscribe to a sensualist theory of knowledge, but Epicurus' theory is not crowned, as in the case of Zeno, by a whole dialectic grounded on reason. Both establish a close link between physics and ethics, but their views are quite different, for Epicurean physics rules out any possible reverence for what inspired in Zeno a religious respect. Both are ardent ethical propagandists, but Epicurus works through selected and tested friends. Neither has any skill as a writer, but while Zeno creates new words or significations, Epicurus, who is as prolific as Chrysippus, adopts a simple, careless style.

Incidentally, in our secluded garden in Athens we are among Greeks with good pedigrees. Epicurus is from Athens even though he was raised in Samos, and his first disciples also come from the coasts or from the neighboring islands of Ionia. Lampsacus in Troad sends Metrodorus, Polyaenus, Leontium, Colotes, and Idomeneus. From Mytilene comes Hermarchus, the first successor to Epicurus. We can imagine the welcome that must have been extended to all the worthy men by the one who boasted that he had begun to philosophize at the age of fourteen and that he wrote to Menoeceus: "The young man should not wait to philosophize nor should the old man tire of philosophizing, for it is never too early or too late to care for the soul. To say that the time for philosophizing has not yet come or that it has passed is to say that the time for desiring happiness has not yet come or no longer exists." [1]

1 *Epicurus and His Pupils*

Epicurus, born in Athens in 341 B.C., spent his youth in Samos and did not return to Athens until 323. He spent only a short while in Athens, and his retreat to Colophon seems to be linked to the hostility manifested toward him by the Macedonian teachers in Athens. We now know, thanks to the investigations of E. Bignone, the importance of the instruction which he gave in Mytilene in 310. There he engaged in a violent polemic with the Aristotelian Praxiphanes, who introduced Plato's moral asceticism into Aristotle's first doctrine (expressed in dialogues that have been lost). He returned to Athens a few years later and founded a school in 306, during the reign of Demetrius Poliorcetes. Until his death in 270, he conversed with his friends in his famous garden, which he bought for eighty minas; from his friends he drew comfort during a number of years when he seems to have been paralyzed by a cruel disease. "Of everything that wisdom lays in store for a lifetime of happiness," he wrote, thinking of his close relationship with his friends, "the possession of friendship is by far the most important." [2] And his testament, preserved by Diogenes Laertius (x. 16 ff.), shows that he was concerned mainly with the continuation of the circle of which he was the guiding spirit, for to his executors is assigned the responsibility of preserving the garden for Hermarchus and all those who will succeed him as head of the school. To Hermarchus and the philosophers of the circle he bequeaths the

---

[1] Diogenes Laertius x. 122.
[2] *Principal Doctrines* xxiii; in H. Usener (ed.), *Epicurea* (Leipzig, 1887), p. 77.

house where they are to live together. He prescribes annual commemorative ceremonies in his honor and in honor of his deceased
disciples, Metrodorus and Polyaenus. He provides for Metrodorus'
daughter and makes general recommendations concerning the needs
of all his disciples. By this time Epicurean centers were being
founded in the cities of Ionia, in Lampsacus, in Mytilene, and even
in Egypt, and the various centers tried to attract the master.[3]

It is doubtless to the flowering of these schools that we are indebted for the only direct documents through which we have knowledge of Epicurus: three didactic letters containing a summary of his
system, one to Herodotus on physics, another to Pythocles on meteorology, and the third to Menoeceus on ethics and theology. These
letters may have been written in collaboration with his principal
disciples, Hermarchus and Metrodorus, as is true of some that have
been lost.[4] Besides these letters, we have his *Principal Doctrines,*
forty aphoristic statements which summarize Epicurus' system, and
eighty aphorisms discovered in 1888.

This sickly, magnanimous man, depicted by his enemies as im-
moral, preached in these words the morality of pleasure: "What
constitutes an agreeable life is not drinking, possessing women, or
eating at sumptuous tables; it is rather sober thought which discovers the causes of all desire and all aversion and which drives
away opinions that disturb souls." [5]

He is known to have been revered by his first disciples. Familiar
to many are the beautiful verses in which, more than two hundred
years after his death, Lucretius pays homage to his genius: "He was
a god, yes, a god, this man who first discovered the way of life now
called wisdom; the man who through his art enabled us to escape
from such holocausts and such a dark night, and who set our lives
on such a calm and luminous course (v. 7)."

Serenity of the soul and enlightenment are two inseparable traits
whose fusion constitutes the originality of Epicureanism. Quietude

[3] Documents in Usener, pp. 135–7.
[4] A. Vogliano, "Nuovi testi epicurei," *Rivista di filologia* (1926), p. 37.
[5] Usener 64. 12 ff.

of the soul can be attained only through the general theory of the
universe, atomism, which alone banishes all causes of fear and
uneasiness.

II *The Epicurean Canonic*

"Epicurus uses many colorful words," said Cicero, "but he rarely
takes the trouble to be consistent." [6] The truth is that his philosophy
is built on discrete, separate facts each of which is wholly self-sufficient.

The first part of his philosophy, the canonical part, concerns the
criteria or canons of truth and is in no way similar to Stoic logic.
It is merely the enumeration of diverse types of the evidence of the
senses: passion or feeling ($\pi\acute{a}\theta$os), sensation ($a\check{\iota}\sigma\theta\eta\sigma\iota$s), prenotion
($\pi\rho\acute{o}\lambda\eta\psi\iota$s), and a fourth criterion which Diogenes attributes only
to the disciples of Epicurus but which is in fact often employed by
the master himself, imaginative or intuitive reflection ($\varphi\alpha\nu\tau\alpha\sigma\tau\iota\kappa\grave{\eta}$
$\grave{\epsilon}\pi\iota\beta o\lambda\grave{\eta}$ $\tau\hat{\eta}$s $\delta\iota\alpha\nu o\acute{\iota}\alpha$s).

The first type of evidence is passion, that is, the experiencing of
pleasure and pain. Aristippus had also made it a criterion of truth,
but in a slightly different sense inasmuch as for him only the passive
state is perceptible and its cause cannot be known with certainty.
Epicurus, on the contrary, holds that the evidence of the senses
reveals the cause of the criterion; for example, pleasure necessarily
imparts knowledge of the cause of pleasure, which is agreeable, and
suffering, a cause of suffering, which is painful.[7] By making sensation (in the passive sense of sensible impression) a second criterion
of truth, Epicurus again contradicts Aristippus since for him each
such sensation yields certain knowledge of the active cause that has
produced it. All sensations are equally true, and objects are exactly
what they appear to be; there is no reason to doubt the facts which
they convey since they are completely passive and irrational and
can neither add to nor detract from the external influence; nor is

[6] *Tusculan Disputations* v. sec. 26.
[7] Compare Sextus Empiricus *Against the Mathematicians* vii. 203 and vii. 291.

there any reason to doubt some facts rather than others, for "saying that a sensation is false is the same as saying that nothing can be perceived." [8] And when opponents of their doctrine raise objections on the basis of illusions and contradictory perceptions, they show how error is not in the representation but in a judgment contributed by reason. Confidence in the immediate evidence of the senses and distrust of everything contributed by reason are the distinctive traits of Epicurus' theory of knowledge.

The Epicureans never gave in even though their adversaries tried constantly to reduce the canonic to pure subjectivism predicated on nothing more than immediate impressions. Defense of their position seems to be the theme of the treatise *On the Impossibility of Living According to the Doctrines of Other Philosophers,* by Epicurus' immediate disciple Colotes. In this treatise, known through Plutarch's refutation (*Against Colotes*), the Epicurean attacks successively Democritus for considering sense-knowledge as bastard knowledge, Parmenides for denying the multiplicity of things, Empedocles for denying the existence of natural differences between things, Socrates for hesitating over notions as clear as the notion of man, which he tries to define, Plato for refusing to grant substantiality to tangible things, Stilpo the Megarian for supporting the old eristic thesis that nothing can be stated concerning anything, the Cyrenaics and Arcesilaus for not admitting that our representations can lead us to realities. And Plutarch has no way of replying other than by likening the Epicureans to those whom they wish to refute. From Epicurus' own texts he draws proof of the relativity of perceptions.

Sensation and passion are not the only types of immediate evidence. Any question, if it is to be asked and understood, implies that we have in advance some notion of the thing involved. Do the gods exist? Is the approaching animal a bull or a horse? Such questions all assume that we already have some notion of gods, a bull, a horse, etc., even before the present sensible impression which causes us to ask the questions. It follows that prenotions are memory

[8] Cicero *Academica Priora* ii. sec. 101 (Usener 185. 11).

images in the soul; derived from previous sensations, they have nothing in common with the general notions of the Stoics, which are the product of a rather arbitrary dialectic. It is by virtue of its origin (obvious even in the case of the gods, for instance, since the notion is born of real images received during sleep) that the pre-notion is never the notion of an imaginary thing but rather of an existing thing. This explains why Diogenes Laertius (x. 33) calls it a perception or right opinion: the prenotion implies a judgment of what obviously exists, and our past experience, of which it is to some extent the result, is just as valid as the present experience with which we compare it.

The prenotion allows us to formulate judgments or beliefs that transcend the present experience: the man that I see down there is Plato, that animal is a bull, etc. But such beliefs are valid judg-ments only if they are grounded on immediate evidence of the senses and subject to confirmation ($\epsilon \pi \iota \mu \alpha \rho \tau \acute{\nu} \rho \eta \sigma \iota s$) when I see the man or animal at closer range.

But Epicurus pretends to accumulate facts concerning not only sensible things but also invisible things ($\mathring{\alpha} \delta \eta \lambda \alpha$), such as the void, atoms, or the infinity of the universe. It is important to remember, if we are to understand clearly his canonic, that Epicurus is on the one hand the moral reformer and apostle of pleasure, the end that is grasped immediately by the will in the absence of any rational con-struct, and on the other the renovator of atomic physics, that is, a rational construction of the universe, which is far removed from immediate impressions. Here we are concerned not with the rela-tion between the two motifs, but only with the means (or crack) through which can be introduced knowledge through pure reason or thought. Besides confirmation of a belief through the evidence of the senses, Epicurus cites the case in which a belief is neither confirmed nor weakened. "Non-invalidation ($o\mathring{\nu}\kappa \ \mathring{\alpha}\nu\tau\iota\mu\alpha\rho\tau\acute{\nu}\rho\eta\sigma\iota s$) is the consequential link between what is obvious to the senses and an opinion concerning an invisible thing. For instance, Epicurus states that there is something invisible, a void, and proves it by something obvious, motion; for if there is no void, neither can there be any motion since a body in motion has no place in which to move about if everything is full." [9] It is also through the evidence of immediate experience that Lucretius proves the existence of bodies that are invisible because of their smallness: the unseen force of the wind, sounds and smells that make an impression on the senses, wetness and dryness, the gradual attrition or growth of objects — all these facts imply the existence of similar invisible corpuscles.[10] What the texts do not reveal is the exact nature of this consequential link or implication, but from the expression (*noninvalidation*) it is obvious that Epicurus is simply referring to a conception of things not contradicted by manifest experience.

The new universe of atoms constitutes a rational, closely interconnected whole. Its principles can explain in detail visible facts such as celestial and vital phenomena. Epicurus recommends to his disciples that they should always retain the "comprehensive view" since it is always possible "to discover details if the general design of things has been grasped and preserved in the memory." The necessity of a comprehensive view is one of the themes that recur most frequently in Lucretius' poem: "Once we know what is caused by the diverse elements, it is easy to discover and to see through the mind's eye what is responsible for particular meteorological phenomena." [11]

The comprehensive view of things, if it is to be convincing, would seem to require some source of evidence distinct from the sources that we have learned to recognize. For what is needed here is not the apprehension of invisible things as they are related to manifest things but the apprehension of things themselves. "If you think that atoms cannot be grasped intuitively (*injectus animi* = ἐπιβολή), you are grossly mistaken." Or again: "The mind seeks to understand what lies beyond the walls of the world in the realm of infinity, where intelligence desires to ascend and where the mind's eye (*jactus animi*) freely takes flight." [12] Now we understand, perhaps

[9] Sextus Empiricus *Against the Mathematicians* vii. 213.
[10] Lucretius *On the Nature of Things* i. 265–328.
[11] Diogenes Laertius x. 35, cf. x. 33; Lucretius iv. 532–4.
[12] Lucretius ii. 739–40; 1044–7.

not the nature, but at least the role of the fourth criterion cited by Diogenes, reflective and intellectual intuition (φανταστικὴ ἐπιβολὴ τῆς διανοίας) which, by grasping the overall scheme of the universe and transcending mere sensory intuition, enables us to witness the spectacle of the universal mechanism of atoms. Here we have another kind of evidence which, though different from the evidence of the senses, is just as immediate, and along with it — and permeating each page of Lucretius' work — a feeling of clarity and intellectual satisfaction.

Thus the canonic is indeed an enumeration of different types of evidence which, though distinct and irreducible in nature, all pretend to go beyond appearances and attain to reality.

III *The Epicurean Physics*

Under what conditions and in what manner was Epicurus persuaded to revive the physics of Democritus and with it the old Ionian images — namely the image of the plurality of worlds and the image of infinity from which their substance is drawn — which had presumably disappeared? It is certain that along with these images and through them also reappears the free Ionian spirit which stands in stark contrast with the theological rationalism which arose in Sicily and which is now represented by the Stoics.

The channel through which Democritus' system reached him is easily identified, for he was the pupil of Nausiphanes of Teos, a follower of Democritus. But Epicurus categorically disavowed him as his teacher and derided him no less than Democritus; besides, the contrast between the two is striking. Epicurus was almost a total stranger to the positive sciences, mathematics, astronomy, and music, with the result that physics was never for him an end in itself: "If we were not troubled by dread of atmospheric phenomena or by fear of death, and if ignorance of the limits of suffering and desire did not interfere with our lives, we would have no need of physics." [13]

[13] *Principal Doctrines* xi (Usener 73).

Nothing that resembles the pragmatist's view must be attributed to Epicurus, however, for his system of atomic physics rests squarely on the evidence of the senses, and the demonstration of his theorems is completely independent of the results which it might have on the moral life. A system of physics such as the Stoic or of demiurges such as in the *Timaeus* are but one aspect of a set of moral or metaphysical beliefs and cannot exist apart from such beliefs; a parallel hypothesis is meaningless. The corpuscular physics of Epicurus, on the contrary, is free of any moral implications, at least as his system can be reconstructed on the basis of Lucretius' verses. This is the system that will reappear each time the human mind adopts a vision of the universe that is equally remote, so to speak, from both anthropocentrism and theocentrism. It repels the common people (*retroque volgus abhorret ab hac*)[14] because it leaves out of account their aspirations, but it recalls ancient Ionian positivism, so disdainful of antiquated notions and so contrary to the rationalism of Magna Graecia, which was always ready to accommodate every popular belief and transform the world into a theater for man and God.

That is why we can read in its entirety the *Letter to Herodotus,* in which Epicurus summarizes for a disciple the main points of the doctrine that is to be borne in mind at all times, without ever suspecting that in his ethics he takes pleasure as the beginning and the end of the good life. Yet the negative aspect of his doctrine entails denial of most of the popular beliefs which the Stoics tried to justify: the providence of the gods, fate, divination, and omens, the immortality of the soul, and all sorts of myths that vary in credibility and concern the life of the soul outside the body. For if people realize that such beliefs are the cause of their fear and anxiety, physics can eliminate every disturbance to the soul. But his doctrine does not lead to Hedonism. Serenity, we must note, is one of the elements in Epicurus' life of pleasure because it contributes to this life; its place in the moralist's studies is therefore justified. It owes

[14] Lucretius vi. 19.

its place solely to its intrinsic rationality and its inherent intellectual value.

The axiom of Ionian cosmology was the conservation of everything: nothing is created out of nothing and nothing can return to nothingness. The notion of conservation does not apply to the world or cosmos, however, for it is considered to be only a part or a temporary aspect of the whole. The axiom of the rationalistic cosmology of Aristotle and the Platonists, on the other hand, is the conservation of the world, which is identical to the whole universe and constitutes a perfect, self-sufficient unity; and the Stoics acknowledge only the apparent destruction of the world since the same individual continues to exist throughout the conflagration. Epicurus, however, takes the Ionian axiom as his starting point: the world is a portion of the whole which separates from infinity and momentarily retains a certain order. It follows that there is no reason for the world to possess the characteristics attributed to it by the rationalists: first, there is no reason for it to be unique since an infinity of other atoms is available and thus there is an infinity of worlds; next, there is no reason for it to be self-sufficient since it is a part of the whole and atoms can pass from one world to another; finally, there is no reason for worlds to be unique and to have the same form and the same species of living beings, for vastly different species exist by virtue of the diversity of the seeds from which they are formed.

It should be noted that all these Ionian cosmological notions revived by Epicurus are independent of atomistic physics while the particular notion of the existence of atoms is linked to the general axiom of absolute conservation. It is because nothing can spring from nothing or return to nothing that any visible body must be assumed to consist of atoms, that is, of indivisible elements which form the body and into which it is resolved. These atoms are also eternal and unchangeable with respect to their function, for they serve as fixed starting points for generation and fixed terminal points for corruption. Furthermore, such natural phenomena as the force of the wind, smells, or sounds which travel through the air, evaporation, attrition, or gradual growth bear witness (through the process of non-invalidation) to their existence. The continuity of matter, apparently confirmed by the senses, is an illusion; a flock of sheep, to cite an analogous situation, when seen from a distance seems to be a motionless white spot.[15]

To understand clearly the nature of the Epicurean atom and, even more important, to avoid any possible confusion with modern atomism, we must not lose sight of one important consideration: the nature of the atom is determined by its function, which is to form diverse compounds. One of the principles underlying Epicurean physics is that just anything cannot be made from just any atoms; instead, a being of a certain species requires atoms of a certain species. Not all atoms are identical, nor are all differences between compounds to be attributed to the manner in which identical units are linked or connected; instead, to form a soul, a god, a human body, etc., atoms of a different kind must be used in each instance. One of the proofs given by Lucretius for the existence of atoms is highly significant in this context (i. 160–175): the permanence of species throughout time, he says, is an absolute law of nature. It follows that the elements used in forming the individuals that constitute each species must themselves be permanent. It would be natural to suppose that atomism is diametrically opposed to the Aristotelian idea of a stable classification of things, yet we find that Epicurus draws from it to formulate his argument, with the result that the classification of atoms into species reproduces in miniature the classification of tangible things. Thus atoms are not only the constitutive elements but the seeds of things (σπέρματα, semina rerum), and it is in fact the form of the constitutive atoms rather than their mode of composition that explains the properties of compounds.

And that is doubtless why the atom is defined not as a minimum (for all minima are equal and formless) but as an indivisible element. We have seen that Epicurus does not draw upon the impossibility of infinite division in formulating his argument, though he recognizes and uses it to prove the existence of identical minima.

[15] *Ibid.* ii. 308–32.

His real minima are similar to visible minima, that is, they are assumed to have the smallest dimension that the eye can see. Just as the visual field is composed of visible minima which serve as units of measurement, so real magnitude consists of real minima and varies according to the number of minima that it contains. The theory of minima seems to have been used by Epicurus to resolve the paradox on motion formulated by Zeno of Elea: the body in motion does not have to traverse an infinite number of divisions in going from one point to another; it merely traverses a finite number of minima by means of a finite number of indivisible leaps.[16]

The atom, given its particular properties, must have an unchangeable magnitude and shape, that is, it must be composed of minima arranged according to a definite plan. Its magnitude is never sufficient to make it visible. The number of different shapes is large but no larger than necessary to explain the properties of compounds, and the number of species of atoms, though finite, is incomprehensible (ἀπερίληπτον) since we do not even know every species of beings in our own world.

The infinite number of atoms scattered throughout the infinite void are in perpetual motion, without beginning or end, according to the Ionian hypothesis. What is the cause of their motion? It is nothing that resembles a transcendent principle of organization, such as that of the rationalistic cosmologies. It is not a supreme mind or demiurge whose action, even when eternal, is translated through periodic movements with a beginning and an end. It is rather an immanent, permanent motion determined by the nature of the atom. The cause of motion is gravity, which makes each atom, no matter what its shape or weight, move in the same direction (downward) and at the same speed. Epicurus echoes the teaching of Aristotle when he explains why all motions are the same regardless of differences between atoms: different speeds must be due to the difference in the resistance of the mediums traversed by the moving bodies; since the void offers no resistance, all speeds are equal. A distinction must be made between universal gravity, which

[16] Simplicius *In Aristotelis physica* 232a 23 (Usener 137. 9).

carries atoms downward at a very rapid but uniform speed, and the weight peculiar to each atom, which determines the relative force with which this atom collides with the others.

Magnitude, shape, gravity: these are the three properties inherent in each atomic mass. But they still do not explain why atoms combine, for they will never meet as long as they fall at the same speed and side by side. Contact between atoms, along with the collisions, rebounds, and entanglements that follow, cannot come about unless certain atoms deviate from their course. This deviation occurs spontaneously at a time and place which is completely indeterminate since it is without cause; besides, only a very slight deviation is enough to cause contact between atoms. Such is the celebrated declination (παρέγκλισις, clinamen) of atoms, which elicited so much ridicule from Epicurus' adversaries. It would seem to be a typical expedient introduced by a physicist disturbed by his inability to make the facts square with his theory. It was, as St. Augustine notes, the abandonment of the heritage of Democritus.[17]

Were the Epicureans also disturbed over the matter? We recall the peculiar pattern followed by Epicurus in introducing each of the great theses of his philosophical system. In each instance he relied on clear, discrete facts and did not bother to relate them to a common source. The Epicureans at least tried, though unsuccessfully, to present declination as something clearly inherent in each atom rather than as something primary and sensible. Here appearances are deceptive since the swerve of the atom is too small to be perceived by the senses. The argument is not invalidated, for we are dealing with a phenomenon about which there can be no doubt: free will. We sense directly the opposition between the natural motion of the body and the motion that is created by the soul, and immediately we become aware of the contrast between voluntary or free motion and motion derived from an external impulse. It follows that if declination exists in a compound such as the soul, as the evidence of the senses shows, it must exist in its component atoms.[18]

[17] Against the Academicians iii. 23.
[18] Lucretius ii. 251–93.

The Epicureans accept a purely mechanical conception of all natural processes but deny expressly their unconditioned and exception-
less necessity. In the view of their contemporaries, necessity is Stoic
fate, that is, a fixed plan of motion through which a rational, divine
will is manifested in the cosmos. Necessity in this sense is diametrically opposed to the thinking of Epicurus: "It is better to accept the
fables about the gods," he says, "than the physicists' doctrine of
fate." [19] His pronouncement should be judged in the light of his
contempt for the old fables. It is obvious, however, that Epicurus
had to accept and gloss over the flagrant contradiction inherent in
the affirmation of both declination and universal gravity.

The existing order of things which we call the world is one of
thousands of combinations produced in the infinity of time and
space. "Under the impulse of collisions and their own weight, countless elements throughout the infinity of time come together in a
thousand ways and try out every possible combination into which
they can enter, with the result that after experimenting with all
types of union and motion, they suddenly group themselves into
patterns which become the great masses which we know as the
earth, the sea, the sky, and living beings." [20] Epicurus, whose
thoughts are reproduced here by Lucretius, is obviously concerned
not so much with denying the unity and autonomy of the cosmos
as with explaining it without recourse to a providential origin. The
cosmos represents one successful result following a thousand unsuc-
cessful attempts. We should also note at this point that Epicurus'
mechanical conception of the universe is far from modern mechanism. His aim is not to show that any existing combination of
atoms is the result of laws of motion but rather that if everything
needed to produce our world happens to be brought together, the
different beings contained in the chaos will take shape through a
progressive evolution. In his explanation there is no unifying principle. One can read hundreds of verses in Lucretius' fifth book,

[19] Diogenes Laertius x. 134.
[20] Lucretius v. 422-31.

which deals with the formation of heaven and earth, and not find the slightest allusion to the doctrine of atoms. For him the important thing is to sort out what is useful in the old explanations which the Ionian physicists had to offer for celestial and terrestrial phenomena. It matters little to him whether the sun's ecliptic is explained by the fact that it is carried along more slowly than the fixed bodies in the spiraling motion of the heavens (Democritus' explanation) or by currents of air that issue from the extremities of the world's axis and chase the sun from tropic to tropic. His aim is to show that there is no intelligent soul to direct these masses of fire and to rule over celestial things. He even goes so far as to represent as possible the old supposition that a new sun is created each morning! [21] We have gone beyond geometrical astronomy, which had posited a heaven apart from atmospheric phenomena and different in nature from the earth.

Epicurus is known to have attached little importance to detailed explanations. "We need a comprehensive view," he says at the beginning of his letter to Herodotus (x. 35), "but not an equal number of particular views; the results of a comprehensive view of things must be stored in the memory; details are easily discovered if only the over-all schemes are apprehended and clearly retained in the memory." And further along (x. 79) he makes some illuminating comments about those who, although they have studied every detail of astronomy and know all about the rising and setting of the stars, eclipses, and similar things, still retain the same fear of all celestial phenomena because they are ignorant of their nature and their principal causes." Details must be disregarded if we are to go directly to the cause of all celestial phenomena. All that is necessary is that the cause explain them; it need not be their real cause. The same fact can be produced by several causes, and we need only determine its possible causes. A solar eclipse[22] can be produced not only by the interposition of the moon but also by the interposition

---

[21] *Ibid.* 660–2.
[22] *Ibid.* 751–61.

of an invisible body or even by the momentary extinction of the sun. A choice is unnecessary since any one of them is enough to banish fear of an eclipse.

Once again we see that his explanations are not even remotely related to his theory of the atom but are revivals of Ionian physics. We recall that the Ionian system also contained an outline of the history of animals and of the gradual development of human reason, the practical arts, and cities. In contrast to mythology, which depicts man as having been created by the gods and being dependent on them, the positive explanation of the Ionians stresses the role of human effort in the slow transition from animality to civilized life, yet never concedes any real progress or superiority of one over the other. The Epicureans simply annex the positive history of humanity inherited from the Ionians, as we see in the last part of Lucretius' fifth book. Epicurus must have had something similar in mind when, at the end of his *Letter to Herodotus,* he noted that "things themselves have for the most part instructed and restrained human nature," and that subsequently reason has merely identified its teachings; speech, for example, at first consists of vocal emissions that accompany man's passions and representations; each nation later agrees to use its own vocal emissions to designate objects. Justice, like speech, is also a human institution. "Among the animals that have not been able to establish conventions to prevent reciprocal injuries, there is neither justice nor injustice; and the same holds for nations that have neither been able nor seen fit to establish conventions for the same purpose." [23]

The world of Epicurus is one of the least systematic worlds imaginable. Whereas for the Stoics individual lives are aspects or forms of universal life and psychology is closely tied to cosmology, Epicurus' world has neither a soul nor the ability to produce an individual soul, which is the only soul that he recognizes. If there are souls in the world, they result from the fortuitous collision of their component atoms. This explains the singular fact that both

[23] *Principal Doctrines* xxxii (Usener 78).

Epicurus and Lucretius deal with the nature of the soul (Book III) before taking up the formation of the world and living beings (Book V) and that the study of human nature is split into two distinct parts linked by no visible tie, psychology and the history of humanity.

Epicurus' great interest in psychology is explained by the fact that the rational study of the soul dispels all the myths about destiny and, with them, one of the principal causes of the unhappiness and uneasiness of men. The soul is formed when the body is formed and dies when it dies; it does not have to think about a future which does not concern it in any way. Instead of eternal life, Lucretius proposes meditation on "immortal death," on the infinity of time during which we were not and shall no longer be.

His system of psychology is outlined in rather vague, general terms in the *Letter to Herodotus*. The soul is a body similar to breath mixed with heat but much more subtile than the breath and heat that we know; in the mixture are found all the potencies of the soul: its feelings, its motions, and its thoughts, as well as its vital potency. But the soul must be joined to the body before there can be sensation; the body enables the soul to exercise the faculty of sensation, and the soul in turn makes the body sensible; when the aggregate is destroyed, the soul disappears. It is impossible to determine whether the complex, detailed theory of the soul explained by Lucretius and attributed to the Epicureans by Plutarch (in *Against Colotes*) and by Aetius (in his *Doxography*) actually goes back to Epicurus himself. Plutarch's text suggests that he took up the broader theory because of the impossibility of attributing to the fiery breath anything other than the vital properties; judgment, memory, love, hate, and all the rest cannot be attributed to the fiery breath and must be explained through the intervention of a particular kind of atoms. It follows that the soul must be formed by the aggregation of four different kinds of atoms: atoms of breath, atoms of air, atoms of warmth, and atoms that constitute a fourth kind but have no name. They are bodies whose subtility and mobility are sufficient to explain the vivacity of thought. The introduction of the fourth unnamed substance, which according to Plutarch is "the avowal of shameful ignorance," is quite characteristic of Epicurus: each phenomenon has its own explanation; a living body is a warm body that sometimes moves, sometimes remains motionless; each of the soul's peculiarities has its origin in one of its component substances — motion from breath, motionlessness from air, heat from warmth; and different proportions of the three substances explain the diversity of temperaments, ranging from the boldness of the lion to the timidity of the stag. A fourth substance is, of course, necessary to explain the no less obvious phenomenon of thought.

A similar consideration seems to have caused Lucretius (or his mentor) to posit still another distinction, that between mind (*animus*) and soul (*anima*). Man has thoughts, inferences, desires, joys, and hates that are completely separated from the body. Since these phenomena cannot be attributed to a substance spread throughout the whole body, they must be ascribed to a mind (*animus*) which has its seat in the heart, where the motions of fear or joy are felt, and which is distinct from the soul (*anima*), spread throughout all parts of the body.

The relation between the mind-soul distinction and the four substances is not clear, and Lucretius offers no explanation. In any case, we must guard against identifying mind (*animus*) with the fourth, unnamed substance, as sometimes happens, for this would give to *animus* approximately the same role that the Stoics assigned to the ruling part of the soul; it would mean ascribing to the soul a sort of hierarchical unity, which is the polar reversal of Epicurus' intention. What is more, it would be contrary to the principal function of the nameless substance, which is to "distribute the sensitive motions through the members (iii. 245)." The atoms of the fourth substance, mixed in among the veins and the flesh and thus held together by the body as a whole, produce a local disturbance which Lucretius calls *motus sensifer*. It is the *motus sensifer* which makes the affected part of the body sensitive to stimulation, for an important tenet of the Epicureans is that sensation is produced at the very place where the stimulation must first be transmitted to the hegemonic part.

The whole theory is obviously directed toward dispersing the substance and faculties of the soul. By denying the existence of any body, Lucretius brings out once again a point that he uses various arguments to prove: the necessary dissolution of the body after death.

The problem of the mode of action of sensible phenomena on sensation is traditionally linked to the problem of the soul. Epicurus assigns to it an important place in his *Letter to Herodotus* (x. 46–53), for it is the first problem taken up after the general theorems of physics, and Lucretius devotes to it all of his fourth book. The secret of his interest is as always the practical application of his findings. Here his aim is to rule out frightening interpretations of dreams. Men interpret dreams as omens sent by the gods or see in them terrifying specters of the deceased. In contrast to these terrors, Epicurus advances a rational theory of vision: the surfaces of objects are constantly emitting simulacra (εἴδολα), very fine pellicles that can move swiftly through the air and still retain the shape of the objects from which they are constantly emanating; on colliding with the eye, they produce vision. The images of dreams and fanciful images are no different in nature, for they too are simulacra which originate in objects; they are still thinner and more subtile than those that produce vision, however, and can pass through the sense organs and come directly to the mind. The imagination therefore functions in exactly the same way as sight; it would seem that we produce our own images since we are capable of summoning up any image at will, but the truth is that the mind is constantly being assailed by thousands of simulacra, and if the desired image appears, it is because the mind is impressed only by those toward which the attention is directed. It must be added that simulacra may become deformed, waste away, lose some of their substance or become fused with each other as they move about; that is why the simulacrum of a square tower makes us see the tower as round; that is also why in dreams we see such strange monsters; thus there is a natural, reassuring explanation for objects that make us shudder. This theory of vision, like the theory of hearing and smell, is a theory of emission that contrasts sharply with Stoic thinking. Wherever the Stoics speak of pneuma spread out between the object and the sense organs or of the transmission of forces through a medium, Epicurus speaks only of motion or collision.

Epicurus never denies the existence of the gods, for this would mean denying the obvious. We see the simulacra of gods in dreams and even during wakefulness, and this prolonged, universal experience is enough to prove their existence. We have a prenotion of these gods and know that they are perfectly happy beings who live in a state of unalterable serenity. But to our prenotions we add opinions; we believe that they are concerned with the affairs of men, and that they manifest their will through omens, and our lives are filled with superstitions. To petition their help or appease them, we sacrifice victims, sometimes human victims, to the gods. Such beliefs are false since they contradict our prenotion; a perfectly calm and happy being could not have all the worries and emotions which we attribute to them. The whole Epicurean system of physics is directed toward proving that neither the world nor any of its parts nor even the history of mankind leads us to God as its cause; and Lucretius, with his pessimistic vision of things, adds that it would be impious to attribute to the will of perfect beings a world so full of imperfections and unhappiness. The gods as well as the soul must therefore be denied any cosmological or physical role. They are made of pure matter and dwell in the intermundial spaces, where they are sheltered from disturbances. They are incorruptible, for they are protected against the causes of destruction. They lead a perfectly calm and happy life, and the contemplation and meditation of their life is the only kind of piety that befits the sage — a refined paganism which doubtless is not unrelated to hero worship.

IV *Epicurean System of Ethics*

Our only important source for Epicurus' system of ethics is the short *Letter to Menoeceus*. Additional information contained in the first book of Cicero's treatise *On the Ends* is based on the teachings or treatises of his contemporaries, Zeno and Philodemus.

The *Letter* is less a systematic exposition than a collection of themes on which "the Epicurean should meditate day and night to live like a god among men."

In his ethics are two themes which are not easily reconciled. On one hand the supreme end is pleasure, for animals as well as men naturally seek pleasure and shun pain, and this from birth and without having learned it. Here is obvious proof that requires only citation, not demonstration. On the other hand the sage is the one who attains to serenity (ataraxia), calm or peace of soul by suppressing the agitation caused by the desires and fears that assail the common man: the rather haughty serenity of an intellectual who has rejected the tragic world of religions and myths, thanks to the clear vision bequeathed to him by the Ionians. No longer fearing the gods, no longer fearing death, no longer the victim of his desires, he attains to happiness.

But ataraxia is not presented as an end ($\tau\acute{\epsilon}\lambda o\varsigma$). The only end ever posited by Epicurus is pleasure, and ataraxia is therefore estimable only to the extent that it is subordinated to this end, that is, to the extent that it produces pleasure.

The relation between the two themes is at the crux of the whole problem of Epicurean ethics and is obviously hard to identify. The first of the two themes was taken up very early by his adversaries and used, in good faith or bad, to show that followers of Epicurus were men who had abandoned themselves to unrestrained desires, profligates leading the life of Sardanapalus; and they pried into the intimate life of the friends in the garden to expose their scandalous acts. But those who were better informed could not fail to recognize the moral elevation of his precepts; the Stoic Seneca, who mentions a number of them, and the Neo-Platonist Porphyry had for them the highest admiration.[24] Epicurus himself protests forcefully against what he considers a misunderstanding: "When we say that pleasure is the supreme end, we are not speaking of the pleasures of profligates and sensualists." The result was that his critics, forced to admit that he was at the same time a Hedonist in theory and sober and virtuous in practice, managed (this is Cicero's constant criticism) to accuse him of contradiction and to impugn his intelligence and the acuity of his mind more than his character and morals.

Is that really the case and was he superior to his doctrine? Epicurus views pleasure differently from the Cyrenaics and is in open controversy with them on this point. In the first place Epicurus posited only one pleasure, the one clearly perceived through the senses: corporeal pleasure, which he called pleasure of the flesh or pleasure of the belly. "I cannot conceive of the good," he said, "if I eliminate the pleasures of taste, love, sounds, visible shapes." [25] He eliminated the alleged pleasures of the mind posited by the Cyrenaics. There is doubtless a joy that belongs to the soul, but it is never anything more than remembrance or anticipation of corporeal pleasures; for instance, no joy would come from friendship if the friend were not considered as a promise of security and some sort of guarantee against suffering. Intellectual joy is the joy of the atomist whose theory eliminates dread of corporeal suffering which according to false beliefs awaits us after death.

In the second place the pleasure of the flesh is not, as the Cyrenaics thought, motion and agitation. We need only consider that man, from the beginning of his life and when his inclinations have not been perverted, seeks pleasure only when he feels a need or a pain, such as hunger or thirst; as soon as the pain disappears, he no longer seeks anything. It follows that the highest degree of pleasure as determined by nature is merely the elimination of pain. Once pain has been eliminated, pleasure may be varied but not increased;

[24] *Letters to Lucilius* 9. 21, etc.; Porphyry *Letter to Marcella* 27–30.
[25] Diogenes Laertius x. 6 (Usener 120).

a man can satisfy his hunger with a variety of foods, but the satisfaction of hunger will always be the highest pleasure to which he
can attain. Between pleasure and pain there is no indifferent state.
Such is the Epicurean sovereign good which the Christian writer
Lactantius declared to be the ideal of a patient who is expecting the
physician to cure him.[26]

In point of fact Epicurus' unexpected conception of corporeal
pleasure may well fit in with what we know of his delicate health,
and when he tells us that true pleasure is restful pleasure
(καταστηματικὴ ἡδονή), he doubtless has in mind the happy equilibrium of the body (σαρκὸς εὐατάθεια) constituted by health and the
satisfaction of natural needs. But this very ideal implies a rule of
action.

"Every pleasure," says Epicurus, "is therefore a good on account
of its own nature, but it does not follow that every pleasure is
worthy of being chosen; just as every pain is an evil, and yet every
pain must not be avoided." [27] This goes, and perhaps intentionally,
against a fundamental principle of Stoicism: "Good is always chosen
by the will." [28] This commonly accepted notion would overthrow
Hedonism unless he sanctioned the unrestrained behavior attributed
to his followers; the only other recourse was to deny what was advanced as a common sense principle. Here Epicurus is probably
following the Cyrenaics: he separates the end, which is the immediate object of the inclination, from the object of the reflective
will, just as the Cyrenaics separated the end or pleasure from happiness, which consists in a set of pleasures. Through reflection aided
by experience we must weigh the consequences of each pleasure;
then we discard pleasures which result in an excess of pains, just as
we endure suffering from which we shall derive a greater pleasure.

Reflective thought again comes into play to calm and eliminate
desires which, because they are impossible to satisfy, give rise to
new pains. Since we know that the highest degree of pleasure is

---

[26] *Divine Institutions* iii. 8. 10.
[27] Diogenes Laertius x. 129.
[28] Plutarch *On the Contradictions of the Stoics* chap. xiii.

the elimination of pain, we can define several categories of desires: natural desires which have to be satisfied, such as the desire to eat or drink; natural desires which do not have to be satisfied and which relate to objects that have a bearing only on the satisfaction of the need, such as the desire to eat a certain food (whose satisfaction will of course contribute nothing to the pleasure); desires which are neither natural nor necessary but vain, such as the desire for a crown or a statue. The sage knows that the highest degree of pleasure can be attained by the satisfaction of desires of the first type, and "with a little bread and water, he competes in happiness with Jupiter." This thought makes the sage almost independent of external circumstances since his needs are reduced to so little.[29] Desire obviously finds its rule and its limits not in a will opposed to desire but in pleasure itself, when pleasure is rightly understood.

But the Epicurean cannot fail to recognize that suffering or passion comes upon man in spite of all precaution and against his will. How can the sage maintain his serenity if the good depends on successive impressions determined by chance and our will is unable to intervene in any way? A partial answer is given in aphorisms such as these: "A strong pain is brief; a prolonged pain is weak." But most important is the comparison of present pain with the representation of past pleasures and the anticipation of future pleasures. The representation of a past pleasure is itself a pleasure, according to one Epicurean postulate which has been bitterly debated by others. Plutarch, for example, asks if remembrance of a past pleasure does not aggravate our present pain. It seems nevertheless that just such a life of remembrances and hopes was responsible for the tranquility of the aged and sickly Epicurus. On the verge of death he wrote to Idomeneus: "I am writing to you at the end of a happy day in my life. My diseases do not leave me and they cannot increase; with all that I contrast the joy that is in my soul owing to the memory of our past discussion."[30] Through an exercise of the imagination such as the one in which Epicurus invites us to participate, the sage

[29] Diogenes Laertius x. 127; Aelian *Varia historia* iv. 13 (Usener 339).
[30] Diogenes Laertius x. 22.

creates for himself lasting joys among which first place must go to those of friendship.

Conversely, the recollection of pains and especially the apprehension of pains or dread are themselves present pains. Epicurus strives to banish the fears that cause the greatest evils among men, the fear of the gods and the fear of death: the blessed gods are not to be feared, nor is death, if the soul is mortal; for then death is meaningless to us since we would have to feel it in order to suffer because of it. To appreciate fully his attitude we must realize that Epicurus had to contend not only with those who feared death as the greatest of evils but also with the pessimists who prayed for death and maintained along with Theognis that "it is better not to be born and, if born, to cross over Acheron as quickly as possible." [31] Nothingness is no more to be desired than dreaded.

We see that Epicurus' system of ethics is a series of prescriptions and practices which prevent our thoughts from straying and leading us to our detriment beyond the limits fixed by nature. We also see the close link between the two themes that we identified, for if the pursuit of pleasure is rightly defined, it implies all the intellectual practices — meditation on the natural limits of desires, the weighing of pleasures, the representation of past or future pleasures — which have as their negative counterpart the ataraxia of the soul.

From the recommended prescriptions and practices come the virtues that are inseparable from the life of pleasure, in particular prudence, "more precious than philosophy itself." [32] Prudence is nothing more than the enlightened will that we have examined. All our virtues, like prudence, are but security measures to protect us against pains. This is particularly true of justice "the fruit of which is ataraxia." [33] Justice consists in positive conventions through which men agree not to harm each other; but it is understood that each of us accepts laws for his own personal protection against injustice and that he will have no scruples about violating them if this is to

[31] *Ibid.* 126.
[32] *Ibid.* 132.
[33] Clement of Alexandria *Stromata* vi. 2 (Usener 317).

his advantage and if he can do so safely. In short, in his views on society Epicurus accepts all the conventionalism of the Sophists but without letting himself be influenced in any way be the cosmopolitanism of the Stoics. In Plutarch we see Colotes engage in a controversy with the Cynics in defense of the state, but only because a strong government offers security to the individual. Only in his characteristic way does Epicurus accept some sort of natural right: "Natural right is the expression of the advantage to be derived by men by not hurting one another." [34] It is nonetheless true that that justice varies with the country. In general the Epicurean does not refuse outright to participate in politics but tries instead, barring exceptions, "to live in seclusion" [35] and to remain an ordinary individual.

[34] *Principal Doctrines* xxxi (Usener 78); cf. Stobaeus *Florilegium* 43. 139 (Usener 320).
[35] Usener 328.

BIBLIOGRAPHY

Texts

Editions of the writings of Epicurus. *Epicurea*. Edited by Hermann Usener. Leipzig, 1887 (collection of fragments from the writings of Epicurus). — *Epicureae epistulae tres et ratae sententiae a Laertio Diogene servatae*. Edited by P. von der Mühll. Teubner edition, 1922. Cf. also *Wiener Studien*, X (1888), 191. — *Epicurus, the Extant Remains*. Translated, and with a short critical apparatus and notes by C. Bailey. Oxford, 1926. — "Trois lettres," translated by O. Hamelin. *Revue de Métaphysique*, XVIII (1910), 397. — *Doctrines et maximes*. Translated by M. Solovine. Paris, 1925. — *Lettere di Epicuro e dei suoi*. Edited by C. Diano. Florence, 1946. — *Epicure, les Epicuriens*. Texts selected by J. Brun. Paris, 1961.

Editions of the writings of Lucretius. *De rerum natura*. Text and French translation by A. Ernout. Vols. I and II, Budé Collection, 1920. — Text with French commentary by H. Bergson. Paris, 1920 (English translation by W. Baskin, under the title *The Philosophy of Poetry*, New York, 1959). — Commentary by L. Robin. Vol. I, Budé Collection, 1925; vol. II, 1926; vol. III, 1928. — Text with English commentary by W. E. Merrill. London, 1907. — Text with English commentary and translation by C. Bailey, Oxford, 1947. — "Lettres et pensées maîtresses," translated by A. Ernout. In *Le Commentaire de Lucrèce*. Vol. I, Budé Collection, 1925.

Editions of other Epicurean writings. Diogenis Oenoandensis. *Fragmenta*. Edited by A. Grilli. Milan-Varese, 1960. Cf. A. Grilli, "I frammenti dell'epicureo Diogene da Enoanda." In *Studi di Filosofia greca* (edited by Alfieri and Untersteiner, Bari, 1950), pp. 245-436. — R. Westman. "Plutarch gegen Kolotes," *Acta philosophica fennica*, Fasc. VII (Helsinki, 1955).

Special Studies

I

E. Joyau. *Epicure*. Paris, 1910.

P. Gassendi. *Syntagma philosophiae epicureae*. (*Petri Gassendi opera omnia*, ed. H. L. Habert de Montmort, Vol. III.) 1658. Cf. B. Rochot. *Les travaux de Gassendi sur Epicure et sur l'atomisme*. Paris, 1944.

C. Bailey. *The Greek Atomists and Epicurus*. Oxford, 1928.

J. von Haringer. *Epikur, Lebenskunst*. Zurich, 1947.

O. Gigon. *Epikur, von der Überwindung der Furcht*. Zurich, 1949.

E. Bignone. *L'Aristotele perduto e la formazione filosofica di Epicuro*. Florence, 1936.

Epicurea in memoriam E. Bignone. Genoa, 1959.

K. Marx. *Différence de la philosophie de la nature chez Démocrite et chez Epicure*. (*Œuvres philosophiques,* trans. Molitor, Vol. I.) Paris, 1927.

J.-P. Sartre. "Matérialisme et révolution." (*Situations,* Vol. III.) Paris, 1949. — P. Boyancé. "Epicure et M. Sartre," *Revue philosophique* (1953), p. 426.

Norman W. de Witt. *Epicurus and His Philosophy*. London, 1954. Recension by J. Brunschwig, *R. phil.* (1957), p. 386.

II

F. Thomas. *De Epicuri canonica*. Paris, 1889.

F. Merbach. *De Epicuri canonica*. Dissertation. Weida, 1909.

III

F. A. Lange. *Geschichte des Materialismus und Kritik seiner Bedeutung in der Gegenwart*. Berlin, 1866. French translation by Schleicher, Vol. I, 1910, pp. 84–150 (English translation, *History of Materialism,* new edition, 1923).

G. Bachelard. *Les intuitions atomistiques*. Paris, 1933.

IV

M. Guyau. *La Morale d'Epicure*. 2d edition. Paris, 1881.

V. Brochard. "La Morale d'Epicure." *Etudes de philosophie ancienne et moderne* (1912), p. 294.

L. Robin. "Sur la conception épicurienne du progrès." *Revue de Métaphysique* (1910). — *La pensée hellénique des origines à Epicure* (1942), p. 525.

A.-J. Festugière. *Epicure et ses dieux*. Paris, 1946.

A. Grilli. *Il problema della vita contemplativa nel mondo greco-romano*. Milan-Rome, 1953.

Studies in English

P. Merlan. *Studies in Epicurus and Aristotle*. Wiesbaden, 1960.

W. J. Oates (ed.). *The Stoic and Epicurean Philosophers*. New York, 1940.

F. Solmsen. Ἀίσθησις in *Aristotelian and Epicurean Thought*. Amsterdam, 1961.

G. K. Stradach. *The Philosophy of Epicurus*. Evanston, Ill., 1963.

E. Zeller. *The Stoics, Epicureans, and Sceptics*. Trans. O. J. Reichel. London, 1892.

SKEPTICISM AND
THE NEW ACADEMY

THE BEST possible introduction to the philosophical
currents that engaged the attention of thinkers toward the middle
of the third century is the short treatise *On Unreasonable Contempt
for Popular Opinions* by Polystratus,[1] who succeeded Hermarchus
as head of the school of Epicurus around 250 B.C. It is a protreptical
essay in which the author persuades a young man to abandon the
other schools and enter the Epicurean school.

We have seen that the Epicureans denied almost everything that
the Stoics considered as the solid basis for an ethical life: providence
of the gods, universal soul, oneness of the world and sympathy between its parts, fate and divination through signs, all interconnected
by means of dialectic. But the Stoic dogmatism was at the same
time attacked by adherents to other doctrines, the Skeptics and the
New Academicians who maintained that they were preserving the
integrity of Platonism against the invading dogmatism.

1 Polystratus the Epicurean

Polystratus writes to a young man who is about to be seduced by
an anti-dogmatic Skeptic. The young man accepts the teachings of
the Epicureans, namely the impassiveness attained through wisdom,
which can "eliminate the vain agitation that comes from dreams,

[1] Teubner edition of a Herculanum papyrus.

omens and everything that unnecessarily disturbs us" (i. *a*). But for him wisdom operates in a wholly different manner and spirit. Whereas the Epicureans sought ataraxia through a system of physics based on the evidence of the senses, Polystratus' adversaries criticize all knowledge, even the most certain, in order to unsettle the same false opinions. To do this they resort to the method most odious to an Epicurean, dialectic, which is more effective in "unsettling the opinions of others than in producing in themselves the ataraxia" of which they boast (xii. *a*). They show, by citing as evidence the diversity of opinions among men, that there is neither beauty nor ugliness, nor good nor evil, nor anything of the kind. "By complicating our lives with the complications of other men," they become incapable of identifying "the end sought by our nature and that which constitutes this end." No better definition could be given for dialectic, which consists in enabling each man to discover the uncertainty of his own opinions.

Which philosophers does Polystratus have in mind? In the text that has been preserved he mentions only "the sect of those who call themselves the impassive ones" and the Cynics, known for their conventionalism (xii. *a*), but he adds that he has already mentioned other philosophers who follow the same method.

This suggests a whole stream of thought which is distinct from both Stoicism and Epicureanism. Though in agreement with Stoicism in the use of dialectic and with Epicureanism in the denial of Stoic beliefs, the "other philosophers" are radically hostile to both dogmatisms. Their most general trait is their hostility to physics in the broad sense of the word, that is, a comprehensive conception of the world as something that can be taken for granted ($\pi i \sigma \tau \iota s$) and used to support the ethical life. This whole philosophical current would substitute for the dogmatism of the Epicureans and the Stoics a humanism which constantly leads thought away from external things that are inaccessible to us and back to the human conditions of ethical and intellectual activity. It is the widely divergent aspects of this current that we shall study in this chapter.

11 *Cynic Hedonism*

Of prime importance is the continuation of the Socratic schools, in diverse forms, during the third and second centuries. The Cyrenaic doctrine, for example, took some completely unexpected turns toward the middle of the third century.

It led in the case of Hegesias to a bleak pessimism that borders on indifference. Happiness is unattainable if it is the sum of pleasures, as Aristotle assumes, for the body is plagued by evils which create a sympathetic disturbance in the soul, and fate shatters our hopes. If it is true that pleasure is our chief end, then there is no natural end, for rarity and novelty produce pleasure while satiety entails the disappearance of pleasure. And what importance can be attached to a state of bondage or freedom, of wealth or poverty, of nobility or obscurity, since none of these promises certain pleasure? With pleasure as the end, there is no reason for us to be irritated over egoism, which is wisdom, or over offenses which necessarily result from passion; "the sinner must not be hated but instructed." His detachment leads him to the brink of suicide, and in his book *The Abstinent One* ('Αποκαρτερῶν, one who abstains from food in order to die of hunger), Hegesias develops the theme of the misfortunes of human life.[2] His argument is less the exposition of a doctrine than the statement of a series of themes, mainly pessimistic themes on the evils of life and the unhappy lot of man. It is easy to see that not one of his points was overlooked by Epicurus, who provided answers within the frame of a reformed Hedonism grounded on physics rather than on observation of human life, as in the case of Hegesias. We need only recall his condemnation of pessimism that leads to suicide, his doctrine of free will, and his aversion to those who make of chance an omnipotent goddess.

Anniceris[3] also tried to combat the discouraging consequences of Hedonism, but on humane grounds. He attributed an absolute value

[2] Diogenes Laertius ii. 93, 96; Cicero *Tusculan Disputations* i. sec. 83.
[3] Diogenes Laertius ii. 96–97.

to everything that links one individual to others: friendship, family ties, patriotism. These are the indispensable conditions for happiness. As a true observer of men he has more confidence in habit than in reason; the former is more effective than the latter in raising man above the level of public opinion. The learning of bad habits makes us weak in the face of public opinion; good habits bring us freedom.

Theodorus, a disciple of Anniceris — who was exiled from Athens and taught at the court of Ptolemy I (d. 283), who sent him as an ambassador to Lysimachus, the king of Thrace — seems to have been decidedly inclined toward Cynicism. This is the self-portrait left by the impudent Cynic:[4] a sage so independent that he has no need of friends, so superior to others that he never dreams of sacrificing himself for his country (for this would mean losing his wisdom for the sake of madmen), so far above public opinion that he does not hesitate on occasion to steal and even to commit sacrilegious thefts. He finds fault with both Hedonism and Cynicism. Since pleasure is a good for the former and an evil for the latter while pain is an evil for the former and a good for the latter, neither pleasure nor pain is important. Prudence and justice are the only goods, and the world is the only city recognized by the sage. But Theodorus, nicknamed the Atheist, is remembered especially for having denied the existence of the gods and, presumably, for having inspired Epicurus. We know nothing of his line of reasoning on the gods, but his atheism alone shows how different his cosmopolitanism must have been from the religious cosmopolitanism of the Stoics.

Such instruction as that given by Theodorus — replete with popular notions and unencumbered by a complicated technical apparatus, alien to any scientific culture and more concerned with immediate influence than with the patient search for truth — led to the development of a literary form which enjoyed great popularity: the philosophical discourse or diatribe. The diatribe resembles a sermon in which the orator presents to the listener, in an elegant

[4] *Ibid.* 97–103.

and flowery style, the fruits of his wisdom. Well known are those by one of Theodorus' pupils, Bion of Borysthenes, whose teachings were summarized by his pupil Teles and preserved by Stobaeus. But Bion, who had been the pupil of the Cynic Crates and who later, after receiving instruction under Theodorus, had heard Theophrastus, offers no well-defined systematic doctrine.[5]

With respect to its literary form Bion's diatribe is the counterpart of the didactic works of the Stoics, with their skeletal arguments and misleading terminology. But it does not have the coherence and full sentences characteristic of the discourses of the Rhetors and Sophists. It retains some of the qualities of the philosophical discussion to which it owes its origin (diatribe, in Plato's usage, designates the Socratic dialogue). Short, urgent questions are addressed directly to the hearer who is to be convinced or refuted: "Man," Poverty is supposed to say, "why do you attack me? Have I deprived you of a true good? Of temperance? Of justice? Of courage? Do you lack the necessities of life? Is the roadside not replete with beans? Are the streams not filled with water?" At times an imaginary interlocutor takes the floor and raises objections. For instance, a man bewails his lot: "You command," he says, "and I obey. You make use of many things, and I of few." But along with passages that resemble a stylized discussion are others, more oratorical, in which thought flows in images. Some of the famous passages will be repeated endlessly: "As a good actor plays well the role assigned him by the poet, so the virtuous man must play well the role assigned him by Fortune. Fortune is like a poet who sometimes assigns a main role, sometimes a secondary role, sometimes the role of a beggar." Or again, "As we leave a house whose overseer has taken away the door and the roof and plugged up the well, so I leave this poor body. When nature takes from me the eyes, ears, hands, and feet which I have borrowed, I shall not tolerate it but, just as I depart from a banquet when the time comes, without becoming angry, I shall depart from this life." Finally, Bion makes use of the edifying anecdote, the chria or apothegm, which he bor-

[5] *Ibid*. iv. 51–2.

rows from the heroes of the Cynics, particularly Diogenes and Socrates. The whole body of such literature constitutes what Eratosthenes called patchwork philosophy because it takes in discussion, anecdote, oratory, and other such types.

The diatribe includes a thousand variations on a single theme: Fortune (Tyche) has apportioned to men their lots in a sovereign manner which is to them incomprehensible and which shows no evidence of providence; happiness consists in being satisfied with one's lot ($αὐτάρκεια$) and in giving in to every circumstance just as the navigator obeys the winds; a wisdom of resignation such as this leads to impassivity, to renunciation of the attempt to understand the mystery of things or even to denial of the existence of any mystery, to renunciation of action involving things, and to a declaration of independence from things owing to the inner disposition of the soul. This was the age of the development of the worship of the goddess Tyche, who through some capricious and impersonal force was replacing the whole pantheon. Bion had learned it from his teacher, the Peripatetic Theophrastus who, before Strato, said in his *Callisthenes* that everything was ruled by chance or, as Cicero translates it, *vitam regit fortuna non sapientia*.[6] The Stoics devoted to the refutation of this disenchanted view a number of treatises that are echoed in Plutarch's *On Fortune*. Plutarch's treatise shows how prudence, man's dominant and characteristic virtue, implies that everything is not ruled by chance and that if in the lesser arts the necessity of prudence is universally admitted, the same will have to be admitted *a fortiori* in more important questions relating to happiness.[7]

Instead of accumulating proofs to support a doctrine such as this, if it is a doctrine, the Cynic Hedonists simply suggest an attitude or opinion. For example, to show that a man must not put his trust in pleasure or see in it an end, Bion repeats the theme of Crates and Hegesias. Depicting the ages of life, he shows that pains surpass pleasures when we consider all the difficulties of childhood,

[6] Cicero *Tusculan Disputations* v. 9. 24.
[7] Dümmler, *Akademika*, p. 211.

the worries of maturity, the regrets of old age and the fact that half of life is spent in the unconsciousness of sleep.[8] When trying to show how things cannot reach us, he introduces Poverty, who develops the ideal of a healthy, happy, frugal life: a meal of figs and fresh water and a bed of leaves. Wealth, on the other hand, shows what she gives to man: "The earth itself does not produce spontaneously and without my help; I am the driving force behind all things." Or if a man is to be consoled over the death of a friend: "Your friend has died; he was also born." — "Yes, but he will no longer exist." — "Ten thousand years ago he did not exist, nor at the time of the Trojan War, nor during the days of your grandparents." [9]

The diatribe, which drew together so many scattered themes, was extremely popular. It created a new style for philosophy, making it attractive to the rhetor. The image of Tyche freed it from any doctrine and made it popular. Ready also to be incorporated in any doctrine since the burden of its teaching is the same impassivity, the same detachment as the Stoics and the Epicureans believed to be attainable only at the price of a doctrine of physics or theology, it will give birth to all the popular philosophical bravura that we find in Horace the poet and Lucian or in the fabric of the doctrine of Lucretius, Philo of Alexandria, or the Stoics in the days of the Roman Empire — Musonius, Seneca, Epictetus, and even Plotinus. It is the last flower of the Socratic school, and it is traditionally considered the quintessence of ancient wisdom.

III *Pyrrho*

The men mentioned above share a clearcut, positive attitude accompanied by almost complete indifference to dogmas of whatever type. This can help us to reconstruct the doctrine of Pyrrho of Elis (365–275 B.C.), almost a contemporary of Zeno and Epicurus. His doctrine is difficult to establish. Like Socrates he wrote nothing but

[8] Stobaeus *Florilegium* 98. 72.
[9] *Ibid.* 5. 67.

stands at the head of a long line of philosophers who, generation after generation, attribute to him their own discoveries; furthermore, he too has become a legendary hero. Thus we wonder what is attributable to him in the arguments of the Skeptics against the value of knowledge and how we are to interpret the anecdotes which are related in the work *On Pyrrho* by Antigonus of Carystos and which give an exaggerated account of his indifference.

It would seem that he is to be credited with none of the technical Skeptic arguments against the value of knowledge which, as we shall see, is developed later by Aenesidemus and Sextus. If we are to rely on the statements of his immediate disciples, Nausiphanes the Democritean, later the teacher of Epicurus, and Timon of Phlius, he commanded admiration through his character and his moral worth rather than through his doctrine. Nausiphanes urges imitation of his way of life but not adherence to his theories. His enthusiastic disciple Timon in his poem *Python*[10] depicts him as follows: "How did you manage to free yourself from the vanity of the opinions of the Sophists, Pyrrho, and to break the bonds of error? You did not bother to pry into the nature of the air that surrounds Greece or the origin and destiny of things." We know that he was also universally admired, for he was named high priest by his fellow citizens of Elis and received the freedom of the city in Athens.

Our only precise information concerning his teaching is the clear summary, based on Timon,[11] preserved by Aristocles. "The man who would be happy ought first to consider what things are, then what state of mind he should adopt with reference to them, and finally what will result from this attitude. Pyrrho states that things are equal and without differences, unstable and imperceptible, and that consequently our sensations and our opinions are neither true nor false. On the second point he says that a man must have no belief but remain without opinions or inclinations and adhere rigidly to this formula: nothing is any more than it is not, it is and it is

[10] Diogenes Laertius ix. 64.
[11] In Eusebius *Evangelical Preparation* xiv 18. 2–3.

not, and it neither is nor is not. On the third point Timon says that such a state of mind will first lead to silence (ἀφασία) and then to ataraxia.

Pyrrho's school is, like all the schools of his time, a school of happiness. His starting point is not very different from the doctrines that we have just analyzed. Most men attribute their happiness or unhappiness to things themselves, to poverty or wealth, but these things make them unhappy only because they put their trust in them and because they have beliefs. If men are shown that such things are fleeting and unstable and that they are always intermingling, then any faith and any belief will disappear, and with them any affirmation and any reason for uneasiness. The instability mentioned by Pyrrho is nothing more than the instability of fortune.

There is no trace here of a criticism of knowledge such as we shall find among the Academicians. Nor is this surprising in view of the fact that Pyrrho, according to Timon's *Silloi,* is just as hostile toward dialectic as he is toward physics.[12] What he indicts is not knowledge but the very nature of things that excludes knowledge.

But the suspension of judgment (ἐποχὴ) which is the guarantee of happiness is strongly resisted by men themselves. Pyrrho shares the pessimism common to his age. He senses the universal folly that moves men and makes the crowd, according to one of Homer's lines that he admired, resemble swirling leaves.[13] His pupil Philo of Athens, who supplies us with this information, also tells us that he compared men to wasps, ants, or birds, stressing everything that draws attention to their uncertainty, their vanity, and their childishness. He would often cite this passage from Homer: "You are also dying, friend; why do you complain? Patroclus is dead, and he was worth more than you." And in *Silloi* his disciple Timon inveighed against "unhappy men, objects of shame, like so many bellies, always growling and arguing, vain, puffed up goatskins." [14] Pyrrho is no

---

[12] Diogenes Laertius ix. 65.
[13] *Ibid*. 67; *Iliad* vi. 147.
[14] Eusebius *Evangelical Preparation* xiv 18. 28.

Socrates who lives in the city and who loves men; he is a recluse who hates men.

It follows that the suspension of judgment and the ataraxia that follows it like a shadow are not attained through a simple intellectual view of the instability of things but only through prolonged training and meditation. Guidelines are provided by the formulas which Timon attributes to Pyrrho and which from this moment become a part of the Skeptic tradition. Discourse for him is a last resort: "It is through acts that one must first struggle against things." Pyrrho must have placed great stress on the practical nature of his doctrine. His harshly worded aim is to "strip men bare," and Timon, who compares his master to a god, uses a similar expression, the "baring of opinions." [15]

If in the beginning Pyrrho deviated but little from the brilliant authors of diatribes, his characteristic seriousness and austerity now set him apart from them. We surmise that the counterpart of his vision of the instability of things was not, as in their case, a vague belief in an uncertain Tyche but the certainty of a stable nature to which is linked the confidence of the sage. Indeed Timon, at the beginning of his poem *The Images* ('Ινδάλμοι), attributes to him these words: "I shall tell you what appears to me, taking as my standard this true statement, that in nature the divine and the good are eternal, and that from this fact derives the just life of man." [16]

Such religious overtones are enigmatic. Unlike the Stoic god, the god revered by Pyrrho is not a providential god of the world or even of men but only the perfectly stable being before whom the diverse and fleeting aspects of reality vanish. Do we find here, as has been suggested, an echo of the wisdom of the distant Hindus? Pyrrho must certainly have had direct contact with Hinduism since while accompanying Alexander on his voyages, he met the Hindu ascetics whom the Greeks called gymnosophists and must have been struck by their insensitivity and indifference even to torture. We

[15] Diogenes Laertius ix. 66 and 65.
[16] Sextus Empiricus *Against the Mathematicians* xi. 20.

also know that from this time on the deeds and acts of the gymnosophists have their place among edifying tales and in treatises on
popular morals, such as the treatise by Philo of Alexandria *On the
Freedom of the Sage.*

Pyrrho had many disciples, one of whom in his epitaph summed
up both the theoretical and the practical teaching of his master: "I
am Menecles the Pyrrhonian. I always find everything that is said
to be of equal worth, and I have shown mortals the path to ataraxia."

IV *Aristo*

Another aspect of the same humanism is found in Aristo of
Chios, a dissenting Stoic who had as his teacher, before Zeno, the
Academician Polemon. Adhering strictly to the Socrates of the
Phaedo and the *Memorabilia,* he abandons physics and scorns the
futile spiderwebs of dialectic. His line of argument against physics
is threefold: physics is uncertain, useless, and impious. That it is
uncertain is proven by disagreements between physicists, for instance on the size of the earth and the existence of motion. It is
useless since even when known it gives us not a single virtue, and
it is impious because it goes to the point of denying the existence
of the gods or of replacing them with abstractions such as infinity
or the one.[17] Nothing could contrast more sharply with the dogmatic physics of the Stoics, which is impregnated with morals and
religion; yet Stoic physics is what he is trying to refute; and when
he says, according to Cicero,[18] that we do not know what shape the
gods have or whether they have feelings or are animate beings, he
seems to be referring to the creative fire or the fiery bodies which
the Stoics called gods.

Aristo thus tries to restrict himself to human things and not to be
disturbed in the slightest by what may come after death. Like all
the moralists that we have just mentioned he preaches detachment

[17] Eusebius *Evangelical Preparation* xv. 62. 7.
[18] *On the Nature of the Gods* i. 37.

from things, and the sovereign good is for him the very absence of attachment to things: indifference (ἀδιαφορία).[19] He traces with rigorous logic the consequences of this principle and brings out by way of contrast the illogic of the Stoics.

We are familiar with his thinking on three points only, and in each instance he reveals himself as a critic of Stoicism: his theory of the absolute unity of virtue, his conception of moral instruction (which eliminates parenesis), and his criticism of the Stoic theory of preferables.

There is but one virtue, the knowledge (ἐπιστήμη) of good things and bad things. When we name different virtues — temperance, prudence, courage, justice — we are in reality speaking of one and the same virtue as it appears under different circumstances: temperance when we choose goods and avoid evils, prudence when we do good and abstain from evil, courage when we show daring, justice when we distribute to each according to his due. But one in possession of virtue does not have to make a new effort or have separate knowledge in each instance, for virtue is the same even though the circumstances are distinct. Virtue is like sight, which is either the sight of white things or the sight of black things, depending on circumstances, and which is still one and the same. What is the exact sense of his theory? It would seem to be closely linked to the two other points mentioned.[20]

Fortunately Seneca has indicated in detail in one of his *Letters to Lucilius* the reasons for which Aristo rejected parenesis, that is, an indefinitely fragmented ethics that takes up in succession the duties of the husband, the father, the magistrate, etc., giving in each instance advice or prescriptions. We know the importance that practical ethics of this type had from the beginning of the Stoic school; later it will at times be almost the whole of Stoicism. In it Aristo sees first of all the danger of fragmentation of the moral life, a danger which had caused him to assert the unity of virtue; the

---

[19] Cicero *Academica Priora* ii. 130.

[20] Galen *On the Doctrine of Hippocrates and Plato* vii. 2; Plutarch *On Moral Virtue* chap. ii.

task is endless since types of situations are endless and therefore cannot belong to wisdom, which is by definition complete and bounded; and Aristo does not wish to see the philosopher go into all the details and give different prescriptions to the man who is marrying, depending on whether he is marrying a maiden, a widow, or a woman without a dowry. Besides, a practice such as this is use-less, for the disciple who receives the advice is in effect like a blind man who must be guided step by step. Is it not better to give him sight in order that he may be his own guide? This is precisely the function of philosophical principles. Besides, advice is of practical worth only by virtue of the principles on which it is based since it is never heeded unless accepted as right, and since right depends on a general philosophical principle such as the principle of justice. Until general philosophical principles have been assimilated, advice is useless.

Aristo's theory brings out two very different ways of viewing moral instruction. Starting from the principle that advice cannot change the soul or free it from evil and false opinions since it affects only behavior, he concludes that change can be brought about only through what might be termed the sudden action of philo-sophical principles. Thus ethics may be considered as a guide for conduct or as a means of modifying man's inner disposition, and it is clear that the second viewpoint is the one adopted not only by Aristo but also by the others whose ethics we have just examined. Neither Aristo nor Bion nor Pyrrho gives any practical advice, and their ethics has little in common with Aristotelian ethics, which describes in detail the different ways in which men should live. But the Stoics had tried to reconcile the two viewpoints and had given parenesis a place alongside the science of ethical principles. Aristo is more intransigent.

We must examine the counterpart of his intransigence as well as the underlying reasons for the opportunism of the Stoics. Exclusive concern for the things of the soul, which is not offset by precise rules of conduct, is in fact only another form of his indifference toward parenesis. The Stoics managed to draw up rules of conduct only by justifying man's attachment to the natural objects of his inclinations: himself, body and soul, and the things that relate to himself, his family, his city, and his friends. This is their theory of *preferables,* on which is grounded the whole system of parenesis; advice is but the formulation of what is most nearly in conformity with natural inclinations. But Aristo rejects the idea of preferables, that is, the idea that if neither good nor evil is involved, one thing may be preferred over another — health over disease or wealth over poverty. Here he is in agreement with the sermonizers and their diatribes, and it is worth noting that he, too, is credited with the famous comparison of the sage and the good actor, each of whom plays the part assigned him by fate.[21] The sage must bow to circumstances, but he has no reason for choosing one action rather than another. Furthermore, it seems that Aristo's argument against preferables, preserved by Sextus,[22] is an argument *ad hominem* against the Stoics. For as we have seen, the Stoics held that things in conformity with nature — health, wealth, and the like — are preferable only under certain conditions and that, as Chrysippus puts it, the sage can choose disease if he knows that it fits into the scheme of the world's events. Aristo pretends to refute the Stoics by showing them that there are situations in which the sage must choose disease: for example, if there is a situation in which disease frees us from enslavement by a tyrant. And it would seem that he merely generalized his remark by admitting that in each case the presumed preferable is chosen or avoided by the sage according to circumstances. It should be noted that his attitude necessarily follows from the absence of any system of physics; for Aristo offers nothing that resembles a theory of natural inclinations, which alone could justify the theory of preferables; and the theory of inclinations obviously depends in turn on a comprehensive view of nature. It is not through a transcendent rule but through a design inherent in nature that the Stoics can explain the value of certain inclinations. Once this base disappears, all the rest collapses: preferables,

[21] Diogenes Laertius vii. 160.
[22] *Against the Mathematicians* ix. 63.

rules of conduct, duties. The sage seeks only to attain to the state of indifference.

This consequence leads to complete inaction, as in the case of Pyrrho (with whom our sources usually compare Aristo), in the absence of a hypothesis which Aristo seems to have formulated. According to his hypothesis the sage has a certain faculty for attributing to himself, arbitrarily and without any reason other than his own will, motives for action. This would seem to be the theory which Chrysippus has in view when he speaks of philosophers who, wishing to free the will from the constraint of external causes, ascribes to man "a certain impulsion ($\epsilon\pi\epsilon\lambda\epsilon\upsilon\sigma\tau\iota\kappa\grave{\eta}\nu$ $\kappa\acute{\iota}\nu\eta\sigma\iota\nu$) which is manifested in the case of indifferent things when it is necessary to choose one of two equal and similar courses in the absence of any motive leading to a preference of one over the other inasmuch as they offer no differences."[23] Thus unless we accept physics in the broad sense of the word, that is, unless we try to find in nature the origin, justification, and mensuration of our tendencies, as do Epicurus and the Stoics, we arrive at total inaction through an absence of motives or at the freedom of indifference.

v The New Academy in the Third Century: Arcesilaus

At the Academy the golden chain of scholarchs, after Xenocrates, Polemon, and Crates, was continued by Arcesilaus of Pitane (in Aeolia), who directed the school from 268 until 241, when he died at the age of sixty-seven. From him came a new impetus, and the new philosophical current which he initiated continued until around the middle of the first century B.C., when it underwent changes and disappeared.

This is the period of the New Academy; it is characterized mainly by a lively reaction against the new dogmatisms, against the comprehensive conceptions of the universe which are offered as the condition of wisdom, against the presumed certainties that gave them birth. Unlike the other men just mentioned, the Academician

[23] Plutarch *On the Contradictions of the Stoics* chap. xxiii.

does not retreat into a disdainful solitude and into indifference; he is a fighter who attacks and pursues his adversary. Far from giving up dialectic, he uses it to topple dogmatism.

To understand clearly the doctrine of the Academy we need to determine the difference between it, with all its traditions, and the new dogmatic schools. The young Arcesilaus had begun his studies under Theophrastus as soon as he disembarked at Athens, and when he came into contact with Crates and Polemon, he seemed to be seeing "divine beings, the remnant of the golden race of ancient humanity." Thus the struggle between Arcesilaus and Zeno is a struggle between two different minds. Arcesilaus represents the Sophistic and humanistic mind. Trained in mathematics and in music, accustomed to reading Homer daily, and familiar with Pindar, he acquired, by virtue of his endowments and education, a facility in speaking and an art of persuasion which attracted great crowds of pupils.[24] A caustic, dreaded master of sarcasm, Arcesilaus was not hampered by the ponderous style and technical terminology of the Stoics, nor did he share their somewhat forbidding seriousness. The Academicians and the Stoics must also differ sharply with respect to their conception of education. While the Stoics are indefatigable writers who put their doctrine in writing, Arcesilaus is an indefatigable debater who has a thousand devices for adapting the argument to the occasion that presents itself. He is an improvisator and accordingly would put the living word above lifeless writing; like Socrates and Pyrrho, he wrote nothing. Furthermore, from the viewpoint of politics his attitude contrasts sharply with that of the great Stoics. Like them he takes no part in civic politics, but unlike them he fails to show concern for the emergent powers. A man of considerable importance in the city on account of his personal fortune as well as his teaching, he parries the advances of Antigonus Gonatas, protector of the Stoics, and maintains only personal relations with Eumenes, King of Pergamum. In him we see no trace of Stoic cosmopolitanism.

The foregoing circumstances help to explain his resistance to the

[24] Diogenes Laertius iv. 31–7.

Stoics' vaunted pretensions to certainty, a pretension which contrasts sharply with the ordinary modesty of the Greek philosophers. His critical and analytical Greek mind rebels against the definitive synthesis that the Stoics would like to impose. Not only does Arcesilaus confront them with Socrates' maxim ("the only thing that I know is that I know nothing"), but he also rediscovers the same hostility to dogmatism in other philosophers: in Empedocles, Anaxagoras, Democritus, Heraclitus, Xenophanes, Parmenides, and Plato. These men are also the ancestors identified for him, as we saw earlier, by the Epicurean Colotes. He and his adversaries agree on a common anti-dogmatic tradition in Greek thought.[25]

"Plato from the front, Pyrrho from the back, Diodorus in between" is the composite portrait of Arcesilaus offered by Aristo. His manner is the free, sprightly manner of Plato; his conclusion is the conclusion of Pyrrho, which is that the sage must suspend judgment; but his method is the method of Diodorus the Megarian, which is the dialectic. Sextus' punctilious summary of his discussion of Zeno's theory of certainty shows, in fact, that Arcesilaus uses dialectic in the strictest sense of the word.[26] He introduces no affirmation and employs only the statements advanced by his adversaries. This point must be re-emphasized: it is by taking up their own hypothesis that he refutes the Stoics.

The Stoics make a distinction between knowledge or firm comprehension, which belongs exclusively to the sage, and vulgar opinion or weak assent, from which the sage is totally exempt. Between knowledge and opinion comes comprehension or perception, which is assent to an apprehensive representation; such perception, which is certain, may belong to either the sage or the fool. But according to the Stoics themselves such comprehension or perception is impossible since it will either be the property of the sage and, accordingly, knowledge or it will be the property of the fool and then will be opinion inasmuch as the latter must always be wrong. Besides, their definition of perception contradicts their definition of

---

[25] Plutarch *Against Colotes* 26; Cicero *Academica Priora* ii. 14.
[26] *Against the Mathematicians* vii. 150–8; cf. also Cicero *ibid*. 94–8.

assent, for they define perception as assent to a representation but say that assent can be given only to a statement or a judgment. Finally, their definition of the apprehensive representation as a true representation which cannot become false contradicts countless facts which the Stoics are the first to recognize and describe in detail, with the result that any representation presumed to be true can always be matched by another representation known to be false and so similar that the two cannot be separated. It is the second point that gives free reign to the Skeptics' line of reasoning, which will be transmitted almost unchanged until Descartes' first *Meditation*. Its details (which doubtless do not go all the way back to Arcesilaus) are known through Cicero and St. Augustine.[27] False perceptions, dreams, drunkenness, and madness give rise to false representations which the subject cannot distinguish from true representations; even in the normal state, we are forced to admit that some representations are indistinguishable from others, just as two eggs are indistinguishable; and it was a common joke to prove to the sage that he too was a victim of opinion by confronting him with twin brothers.[28] Finally, the sorites or "heaped up" syllogism is intended to prove that there are different series of representations of a given object, so that we cannot indicate with precision the limit beyond which a representation is no longer apprehensive.[29] How many grains must be added to a grain of wheat to make a heap of grains? In this familiar example Arcesilaus seems to have wanted to show the perfect continuity that exists between truth and error.

We conclude, therefore, that the Stoic sage is forced to admit either that he will have opinions or that he will suspend judgment. Since the first alternative is inadmissible inasmuch as error, frivolity, and rashness are alien to the sage, only the second alternative remains.

Suspension of judgment, as we know, caused Pyrrho to accept complete inactivity, and it caused Aristo to resort to the concept of

---

[27] St. Augustine *Against the Academicians* ii. 5. 11.
[28] Diogenes Laertius vii. 162.
[29] Sextus Empiricus *Against the Mathematicians* vii. 411.

arbitrariness. The consequence drawn by Pyrrho forms the basis for an objection soon raised (as we see through the example of Colotes) against Arcesilaus: it is impossible to live according to his principles. Arcesilaus, who is neither a contemplative man nor a recluse, finds complete inactivity unacceptable. Happiness exists only through prudence, and prudence consists in right actions. According to Sextus, for him the end is doubtless suspension of judgment, but nothing indicates that he makes it the positive condition of happiness.[30] There is then a criterion or a rule (κανών) for voluntary actions although there is no criterion of truth. The two criteria are of course inseparable in the thinking of the dogmatic philosophers, who base their whole system on the link between them; for in man, a rational being, inclination and consequently action can exist only if intelligence gives its assent. Against this, Arcesilaus seems to have assumed that man can accomplish an action without giving his assent; habitual action is just such an action, and we recall how the Sophists had stressed the role of habit. But Arcesilaus goes further and seeks a more precise criterion in what he calls rationality (εὔλογον). "Right action," he says, "will be that which, when completed, can be defended on the basis of its rationality." What is the exact meaning of his mysterious criterion of action? Verisimilitude can of course be ruled out since it has been proven conclusively that not all representations have equal value. On the other hand it must be noted that his definition of right action (that of the sage) is the same word for word as the definition given by the Stoics for appropriate action, that is, action which even the fool can accomplish by following his natural inclinations. Here the Stoics use the word εὔλογον, which Cicero renders as *probabilis*.[31] Is it not probable that Arcesilaus, following in the tradition of the teachers at the Academy, especially Polemon, wanted to adopt as his criterion natural inclinations, to which it is rational to surrender?

Only one aspect of Arcesilaus' teaching is well known, but we have many fragments of his critical examination of other Stoic doc-

[30] Sextus Empiricus *Outlines of Pyrrhonism* i. 232.
[31] Cicero *On Duties* i. 8.

trines, such as the absurd consequence which he drew from their theory of total mixture.[32] On the other hand certain texts reveal that he is willing to accept the theory of indifference, as when he argues in favor of indifference to pain and death: "That death is pain is only an opinion; when it is there, it causes no pain; it causes pain only when absent and expected." Doubtless also, it is to show that poverty is in itself neither good nor bad that he makes it appear at times as an evil and at times as a good.[33] His teaching ought, according to the Sophistic tradition, to assign an important role to virtuosity; he would criticize any thesis, no matter what it was, and was accustomed to support alternately both the affirmative and the negative side of a question, not to demonstrate the falsity of the thesis but to show the necessity of further investigation. But the literary form that found favor with him was the dialogue. According to Cicero, he was the first to revive the tradition of the philosophical dialogue, which continued through Carneades and Cicero himself, and which was subsequently taken up by Plutarch. It contrasts sharply with the new dogmatic teaching and would suffice to show the radical opposition between Arcesilaus and the dominant schools.[34]

Under these conditions there is no reason to believe that Arcesilaus set aside a part of his secret dogmatic instruction and gave it to only his most talented pupils, or that he hid anything from the public "for fear of the followers of Theodorus and of Bion the Sophist," as Diocles of Cnidus said. The tendentious teaching of Diocles, who was perhaps one of his contemporaries, has been repeated again and again by much later authors — Cicero, Sextus, and St. Augustine — who doubtless would have been pleased to see the Platonic tradition maintained without adulteration at the Academy.[35]

[32] Plutarch *Against the Stoics* chap. xxxvii.

[33] Cicero *On the Ends* v. 32; Plutarch *Consolation to Apollonius* chap. xv; Stobaeus *Florilegium* 95. 17.

[34] Cicero *Academica* frag. 20; *On the Ends* ii. 2; *On the Nature of the Gods* i. 5.

[35] Sextus Empiricus *Outlines of Pyrrhonism* i. 234; Credaro, *Lo scetticismo degli Academici*, II, 189.

VI *The New Academy in the Second Century: Carneades*

All the philosophers discussed up to this point belong to the third century B.C. The second century witnessed many events crucial to the history of the West — the Roman conquest, the conquest of Macedonia (168), the conquest of Greece (146), the conquest of Asia Minor (132) — but did not witness the birth of any original philosophers other than Carneades of Cyrene. Following the death of the scholarch Lacydes (241) and a period of obscurity during which the school was directed only by the college of the elders,[36] Carneades took charge of the Academy, sometime before 156, and continued as scholarch until his death in 129. His name is inseparable from that of Clitomachus of Carthage, who succeeded him and served as scholarch until 110 B.C.

All that is known of the life of Carneades is one celebrated event. The Roman senate, which had become the arbitrator for Greek cities, had levied against Athens a fine of five hundred talents for the devastation of the town of Oropus. The Athenian people sent to the senate to defend their cause three ambassadors, each chosen from one of the three philosophical schools: Diogenes the Stoic, Critolaus the Peripatetic, and Carneades the Academician. They were going to Rome just as, a century earlier, so many of their predecessors had gone before the diadochi. There through discussions held publicly (156 B.C.), they created a sensation: Carneades through his fiery eloquence, Critolaus through his pithy, well-rounded sentences, and Diogenes through his sober, moderate manner.

According to a classification given by Sextus, Arcesilaus and Lacydes would constitute the Second Academy, and Carneades and Clitomachus the Third Academy;[37] his classification in any case does justice to Carneades, who is one of the most profound and subtle thinkers of the Hellenistic Age. Still another circumstance

[36] Wilamowitz-Moellendorf, *Hermes*, XLV, 406.
[37] *Outlines of Pyrrhonism* i. 220.

makes access to his thought difficult. Carneades wrote nothing, and it is only through his disciples, especially Clitomachus, that we can approach him. Furthermore, the writings of his disciples have disappeared, and we know them only through Sextus Empiricus and Cicero, who borrowed from them in two treatises titled *Academica Priora* and *Academica Posteriora*. The two treatises have been imperfectly preserved, and the part in which Cicero explained Carneades' theory of knowledge has disappeared. On one crucial point of his theory there is a sharp divergence between two interpretations of his thought. Has he abandoned suspension of judgment as the ideal of wisdom? A single witness, but an important one, says that he has remained faithful to Arcesilaus' thought: his disciple and successor Clitomachus. According to the explanation given by Cicero beginning with Chapter 31 in *Academica Priora,* Clitomachus indicates that in the words of Carneades many things appear true to the sage, and he adds: "Still the sage does not give his assent to the true thing." In direct contrast to this, another disciple of Carneades, Metrodorus, who was followed by Philo and Antiochus,[38] the scholarchs of the Academy who succeeded Clitomachus, insists that Carneades has been badly understood and that he has abandoned Arcesilaus' intransigence, which made life impossible. The same interpretation, with no indication as to its source, occurs again in the writings of Sextus and the Neo-Platonist Numenius.[39] In spite of an abundance of witnesses, there is an important reason for distrusting the second interpretation: the Academy took an unexpected turn toward Stoic dogmatism after Clitomachus, and its leaders, extremely anxious to show that they had the great Carneades on their side, contrived to alter his thought.

Still, we must not hide the fact that if Clitomachus' interpretation is accepted, Carneades' theory of knowledge is more difficult to interpret. It is true that no difficulty is posed by the theses which both he and Arcesilaus uphold: the criticism of affirmations based on the senses or on custom and the criticism of reason, neither of which in

[38] Cicero *Academica Priora* ii. 78–148.
[39] In Eusebius *Evangelical Preparation* xiv. 7. 5.

all probability contained anything very original. The same holds for his argument about non-difference (ἀπαραλλαξία) with respect to representations considered as true and representations considered as false, for the argument based on the perpetual change of appearances, which prohibits attributing a permanent shape or color to an object, for the soritical argument and the argument involving the liar, for proofs based on the diversity of customs — all of which, in the second century, had become meatless bones.[40] But it is not so in the case of the positive criterion used by Carneades to complement his theory. His criterion, which he calls probability or persuasion (πίθανον), is intended not only as a practical guide to living, like Arcesilaus' *rationality,* but also — and this is completely new — as a rule for discussion in the study of beings and as a means of bringing us closer to truth: it is not only a practical but also a theoretical criterion.[41] But if probability is for him a theoretical criterion, it justifies an affirmation concerning reality; and if by definition this affirmation cannot be certain, it is an opinion. It would seem then that to use his criterion is to adhere to an uncertain opinion, and Clitomachus' adversaries would in this case be right.

We need therefore to examine more carefully the nature of his criterion. According to the exposition of Sextus,[42] Carneades' reform consists essentially in searching for the criterion, not in the relation of the representation to the object, but in the relation of the representation to the subject. In the first relation our representation may in fact be either true or false, but we cannot know anything about it since one term of the relation is missing; in the second relation some representations seem true to us while others do not seem true. On considering the first type of representations, we can try to determine the reason for their persuasiveness. We perceive that it varies in degree according to circumstances; it is weak if our sight is weak or if an object is small or far away, but if the circumstances

---

[40] Sextus Empiricus *Against the Mathematicians* vii. 143. 402 and 412; Cicero *Academica Priora* ii. 93–6 and 87; *Tusculan Disputations* i. 108.

[41] Cicero *Tusculan Disputations* 32; Sextus Empiricus *Ibid.* 436.

[42] Cicero *Ibid.* 168–76.

are reversed, the representations seem true to a rather high degree and can serve as a criterion of truth. Prolonged experience will show that even the latter can be false in extreme circumstances, but it is enough for them to be generally true since "our judgments and actions are determined by generality."

Here is something entirely new. No longer are we indiscriminately to contrast certainty with uncertainty. Instead, we are to take a middle course and to determine every degree of difference that separates the two viewpoints. It is Carneades' probability, quite distinct from Arcesilaus' clear-cut negations.

As Sextus twice states, Carneades' criterion "has breadth," [43] that is, probability has various grades. Consequently the problem of assent shifts. In the case of representation that allows apprehension of the object itself, the sage will always suspend judgment, and no one can say that he assents falsely, that is, that he wrongly believes that he is apprehending the object; but in the case, not of apprehension of the object, but of comparison of different representations on the basis of their internal characteristics, the sage can have a strong inclination to obey the representations (as Carneades is credited by Clitomachus[44] with saying) and still not think that through them he is directly apprehending a reality.

A man changes his opinion and goes from a less probable opinion to a more probable one, not by perceiving a reality not apprehended at first, but by representing to himself in a more precise and detailed fashion what he first represented to himself in only a confused fashion. For instance, he may see that a coiled rope which he was mistaking for a serpent in semi-darkness does not move and that it does not have the color of a serpent. When we go over the details of the representation (διεξωδευμένη) in this way, we give it a higher degree of probability. The probability is increased when the representation is not hindered (ἀπερίσπαστος) by another representation. For example, no matter how precise the representation that Admetus

[43] Against the Mathematicians vii. 173, 181.
[44] Ibid. 230.

has of Alcestis when Hercules brings her from Hades, he will not believe in it because he knows that she is dead.[45] In short, for what is presumed to be a direct impression of an object Carneades substitutes a critical examination of representations based on the fact, little noticed before him, that "representations are never solitary but are interlocked with other representations like the links in a chain." He substitutes a method of analysis and synthesis for what is presumed to be direct evidence of the senses.

Carneades attacks not only the theory of certainty but also the physics of the Stoic school. He could not tolerate the dogmatism that pretends to know the secret of things, and Stoic theology, with its theories of divination and fate, is a prime target of his criticism. He makes use of dialectic in his criticism, correctly deducing the consequences of the opinions accepted by the Stoics in order to call attention to their absurdity.

Take his criticism of the notion of the gods. For the Stoics the gods are blissful, animate beings of perfect virtue. If we consider each of these points, we find that a living being has sensations and that a being as perfect as a god has at least as many sensations as a man; he therefore has a sense of taste and with it sensations of sweetness and bitterness, and with these sensations, agreeable or painful states; if he has such states he is susceptible of change and therefore corruptible; he is not a god. The same holds for every sensation. Besides, is not sensation in general a change through alteration? Any being that undergoes alteration is corruptible and cannot be a god. God, say the Stoics, is a perfectly virtuous being; but according to them whoever has one virtue has them all; we must therefore attribute to the gods not only chastity but also resistance to evil; since God experiences evil, he is capable of change and therefore of corruption; he is not a god. The same could be said of every virtue.

We also find traces of another type of argumentation which is

---

[45] According to Sextus Empiricus *Outlines of Pyrrhonism* i. 227; the order of the characters differs in the exposition (following Antiochus) in *Against the Mathematicians* vii. 176 (cf. Mutschmann in *Rheinisches Museum*, 1911, p. 190).

addressed less directly to the Stoics. Carneades asks the dogmatic philosopher if God is finite or infinite, if he is an incorporeal being or a body, if he has a voice or is without a voice; and he proves successively the impossibility of each of the two alternatives. God cannot be infinite, for he would be motionless and soulless; nor finite, for he would be part of a greater whole that would dominate him. He cannot be an incorporeal being, for that which is incorporeal (in the Stoic sense of the word, that is, time or place) cannot act; nor a body, for any body is corruptible. He cannot be voiceless, for this would contradict the commonly held notion; nor endowed with a voice, for there is no reason to attribute to him one language rather than another.

Carneades' criticism of theology is important. It relegates the notion of god to the realm of impenetrable mystery. If God has life, thought, virtue, and speech, these words cannot have their human meaning. Carneades indirectly prepares for a return to a Platonist theology that is less anthropomorphic than Stoic theology.[46]

His criticism of divination is also wholly dialectical. A predicted event is either fortuitous or necessary. If it is fortuitous, how can it be foreseen? If it is necessary, it falls into the sphere of science rather than of divination. Furthermore, since along with foreknowledge it provides no protection against an evil event, divination is harmful. To grasp the true significance of his criticism one must know what Epictetus has to say later about the proper manner of approaching soothsayers: not with the desire to serve our temporal interests but with perfect confidence in divine goodness. Here again, Carneades' criticism suggests a more refined religious sentiment.[47]

Cicero in his treatise *On Fate* gives an account of Carneades' criticism of still another Stoic thesis, that of Chrysippus, who tried to reconcile fate and freedom. It is not hard for him to show, despite Chrysippus' efforts, that a consequence of the affirmation of fate is that nothing is in our power. Going even further, he takes issue with Chrysippus on the necessity of a link between the affirmation

[46] Sextus Empiricus *Against the Mathematicians* ix. 137–90.
[47] Cicero *On Divination* i. 4. 7, ii. 3. 9; Epictetus *Discourses* ii. 7.

of fate and the principle of causality. From the proposition that nothing happens without a cause, it does not follow that everything happens through fate, that is, through a scheme of interconnected causes; there can be independent causes which are injected from the outside into the scheme of things, and man's free will can be one of such causes. The significance of this criticism is essentially the same as that of the preceding criticisms; it suggests that there is an order of things that lies beyond the physicist's competence. Neither Carneades nor Arcesilaus is, like Pyrrho, a victim of despair, but both of them have the feeling that the universe is more profound and more complex than the universe that the Stoic rationalists tried to attain outright.

Finally, Carneades also breaks ground for the development of ethics by showing that the Stoic theory of preferables leads to consequences closely related to theses accepted by both Platonists and Peripatetics. Their basis for choosing between actions is the same.[48]

Clitomachus' role was mainly to preserve the purity of Carneades' thought. Stobaeus has preserved some of his sentences in which is expressed in a striking way the uncertainty of human things and the preponderant role of Fortune in human affairs. Cicero has him express forcefully the thesis that we have attributed to Carneades: we can be guided by verisimilitude and can even give our approval to representations not hindered by obstacles so long as we withhold our assent.[49]

His criticism of rhetoric, which is reported by Sextus,[50] casts an interesting light on the debate which was taking shape and which will continue during the following centuries: the debate over the relative merits of rhetoric and philosophy. The debate was meaningless so long as it involved a mode of exposition like that of the Stoics, which could not compete in any way with rhetoric. But the Academicians were orators, and pupils of the rhetors were leaving their masters to go and hear Carneades.[51] Clitomachus took the

[48] Cicero *On the Ends* iii. sec. 41.
[49] *Florilegium* 98. 67, 109. 29; *Academica Priora* ii. 103.
[50] *Against the Mathematicians* ii. 20–43.
[51] Diogenes Laertius iv. 62.

offensive in denying to rhetoric the right to exist apart from philosophy and as an independent art with a form of its own. Furthermore, since the time of Carneades, his contemporary, the Peripatetic Critolaus, had been criticizing the Stoic definition of rhetoric, the art of good speaking, which he found too formal, and instead proposed rhetoric as the art of persuasion. There can be little doubt about the place that rhetoric should have as the natural medium of the complex and subtle doctrines that we have discussed in this chapter. The mode of exposition in philosophy changed under these influences, after the end of the second century, and we shall see how the Stoics themselves were the first to become more humane.

Bibliography

I

Polystratus. *Du mépris irrationnel ou contre ceux qui s'élèvent sans raison contre les opinions du vulgaire* (ed. Wilke, Teubner, 1905); cf. Philippson, *Neue Jahrbücher für das klassische Altertum*, 1909, p. 487.

II

Wendland. *Philo und die kynisch-stoïsche Diatribe*. Berlin, 1895.
Otto Hense (ed.). *Teletis reliquiae*. Freiburg, 1889.
A. Oltramare. *Les origines de la diatribe romaine*. Lausanne, 1926.

III

V. Brochard. *Les Sceptiques grecs*. 2d edition. Paris, 1923.
A. Goedeckemayer. *Die Geschichte des griechischen Skepticismus*. Leipzig, 1905.
L. Robin. *Pyrrhon et le Scepticisme grec*. Paris, 1944.

IV

Hense. "Aristo bei Plutarch," *Rheinisches Museum*, XLV (1890).

V, VI

I. Credaro. *Lo Scetticismo degli Academici*. 2 vols. Milan, 1888–1893.
R. Hirzel. *Untersuchungen über Ciceros philosophischen Schriften*. Leipzig, 1877–83.
P. Coussin. "L'originie et l'évolution de l'EIIOXH," *Revue des Etudes grecques*, XLII (1929), 373–97. — "Les sorites de Carnéade contre le polythéisme," *Ibid*. LIV (1941), 43–57.
P. Boyancé. *Etudes sur le songe de Scipion*. Paris, 1936.
J. Croissant. "La morale de Carnéade," *Revue internationale de philosophie* (1939), pp. 545–70.

THE FIRST CENTURY B.C.

IN THE second century B.C. the scholarchs who succeeded Chrysippus and who preceded Panaetius — those from 204–
129 — show a marked tendency to modification and relaxation of
orthodox Stoicism. Sextus states, but without amplification, that the
Middle Stoa now accept as the criterion of truth, not the apprehensive representation alone, but the unhindered apprehensive representation; and they borrow from the Academicians examples of
apprehensive representations not accompanied by belief, such as
Admetus' apprehensive representation of Alcestis when she was
brought back from Hades. Here they are admitting that what constitutes certainty is less the representation itself than its relation to
the whole of which it is a part. They are doubtless contending with
Carneades, to whom Antipater of Tarsus addressed his famous
argument *ad hominem,* forcing Carneades to admit that he perceived at least one thing, namely that nothing can be perceived.[1]

Basic tenets of the Stoic conception of the world were abandoned.
For instance, Zeno of Tarsus and Diogenes of Babylon do not dare
deny the thesis of universal conflagration (which they had at first
accepted), but they suspend judgment. Boethus of Sidon, however,
marshals against it a whole series of arguments that have been preserved by Philo of Alexandria.[2] The basis for these arguments is

[1] Sextus Empiricus *Against the Mathematicians* vii. 253; Cicero *Academica Priora* ii.
109.
[2] *On the Incorruptibility of the World* chap. xv.

that the divine and perfect character of the world is incompatible with its corruptibility. In some of his most beautiful lines Lucretius (v. 1215) shows man contemplating the stars and wondering if "capable thanks to the gods of enduring forever, they may during their endless journey through the ages look with scorn on the powerful attacks of eternity." The feeling that the world is created and must disappear, far from being for the Greeks one more proof of God's might, is on the contrary a sign of his impotence. Boethus' idea is the same: there could be no cause for the corruption of the world since corruption can come neither from outside the world — from nothingness — nor from within the world that contains no source of disease (this is the teaching of the *Timaeus*). Furthermore, the world cannot be destroyed by division since it does not result from an aggregation of atoms, or by alteration of its quality since its individuality or distinctive quality remains the same after the conflagration as before (according to Stoic belief, as we have seen), or by mistake. These arguments prove that the world is indestructible. Finally, and this is the climactic argument, god remains inactive throughout the period following the conflagration, and an inactive god is a dead god. Boethus is obviously returning to a theological tradition which is much older than Stoicism and which will gradually force itself upon the supporters of Hellenism.

The Stoic system of ethics was also modified. Here is the supreme end of man as formulated by Diogenes of Babylon: "To exercise reason in the choice of things in conformity with nature and to reject things contrary to nature." In the words of Antipater it is "to live by choosing that which is in conformity with nature and by rejecting that which is contrary to nature." Rejecting Aristo's doctrine of indifference, both Diogenes and Antipater place great stress on the necessity and reasons for making choices. Cicero reports an interesting discussion between the two concerning a moral issue.[3] Suppose that a merchant brings a cargo of wheat to Rhodes during a famine, and that he knows that other ships are going to arrive. Should he conceal his information in order to sell his wheat at a

[3] Cicero *On Duties* iii. 50–5.

higher price? Diogenes maintains that the merchant should say nothing since by his silence he will be violating no established law, but Antipater maintains that his duty is to speak out since our social instinct induces us to do whatever is useful to men. The opposition here is between a pharisaism that proceeds naturally from the Old Stoic notion of functions and a broader, more liberal, more humane conception of duty which will prevail during Middle and New Stoicism. Of prime importance is the establishment of rules for everyday living, and here again Antipater reveals himself as the defender of marriage, which he looks upon as a religious duty as well as a superior type of friendship and mutual aid, and which when enfeebled is to him a dire symptom for society.[4]

We have seen Boethus introduce Platonism into physics. In the same way Antipater explicitly relates the Stoic system of ethics to Plato by finding in him the origin of the idea that only what is virtuous is a good;[5] and it is perhaps on account of a return to the ideas of Plato that one of Antipater's disciples, Heraclides of Tarsus, abandons the paradox that "all mistakes are equal."

1   The Middle Stoa: Panaetius

All the foregoing traits are manifested in the thought of Panaetius of Rhodes, one of the most striking figures of his century. And one of the most interesting symptoms of the spirit of his time is the friendship that linked him (as well as the historian Polybius) to eminent Romans of his time, Scipio Aemilianus and Laelius, at the moment when the Roman order was beginning to force itself upon everyone and seemed to consummate history by realizing the dream of a universal society. His nobility of character and his gravity, says Cicero,[6] made him worthy of such familiarity. Between 146 and 129, the year when he became the director of the school in Athens, Panaetius rarely left Scipio. Along with Polybius he went on an ex-

---

[4] Stobaeus *Florilegium* 70. 13; 73. 25.
[5] Clement of Alexandria *Stromata* v. 14.
[6] *On the Ends* iv. 33.

ploratory voyage along the western coast of Africa (146); the voyage was organized by Scipio, whom he later (142) accompanied on a voyage to Alexandria. Panaetius saw in Scipio wisdom, reserve, and ethical conduct which commanded his admiration.[7] Scipio, in turn, must have found in Stoicism an ethical guide which he considered absolutely necessary in view of the rapid growth of Rome and all the ambitions that it unleashed. "As unruly horses are entrusted to trainers," he said to Panaetius, "men who have too much confidence in their star must be taught the rule of reason and of doctrine in order that they may realize the weakness of human things and the inconstancy of fortune." [8] The old traditional education must then give way to rational instruction. Panaetius' Roman disciples are numerous and influential: Scipio's nephew Quintus Tubero, an earnest Stoic in his conduct, who wrote a treatise *On the Duties of the Judge,* in which he doubtless reconciled his juridical knowledge with the Stoic doctrine;[9] Mucius Scaevola, an augur and a jurist; Rutilius Rufus, proconsul of Asia Minor; and Aelius Stilo, a grammarian and historian who was the teacher of the scholar Varro. After his long residence in Rome, he served as director of the school in Athens from 129 to 110.

Panaetius' universe is quite different from Zeno's. He has unrestrained enthusiasm for "the divine, the very wise, the very saintly" Plato, who is "the Homer of the philosophers." [10] He no longer attaches to the tangled dialectic the same importance as did the founders of the school, and his teaching begins with physics.[11] But the unity of the cosmos becomes less rigid, for the universal conflagration that was like the symbol of the omnipotence of reason is denied, and the world — so beautiful, so perfect — will always preserve an order identical to the order that we contemplate. With the conflagration vanishes universal sympathy: "How can the in-

[7] Pliny *Natural History* v. 1; Cicero *On Duties* ii. sec. 76 (Cf. *Rheinisches Museum* LIII, p. 220).

[8] *On Duties* i. 90.

[9] Aulus Gellius *Attic Nights* i. 22. 7; xiv. 2. 30.

[10] Cicero *Tusculan Disputations* i. 32. 79.

[11] Diogenes Laertius vii. 141.

fluence of the stars spread to the moon and even to the earth across a distance that is almost infinite? Along with sympathy he rejects divination, which is based on sympathy, and he is inclined to modify to a certain degree his concept of fate.[12]

Such modifications reach to the heart of things. Panaetius is no longer a theologian but a humanist. He is interested not so much in divine reason that is immanent in things as in the civilizing activity of man, in human reason as it advances and creates arts and sciences. That is why he denies that destiny has any hold on the soul (which is for him nothing more than a fiery breath) apart from its life in the body. We are told that he even went so far as to deny the authenticity of the *Phaedo*. The soul must die since it is born, he says, and the proof that it does not exist prior to birth is the moral resemblance of children to their parents. Though the soul is corruptible since it is subject to disease, at death its ethereal part must return to the heights from which it came.[13]

Nor is it surprising that he treated the theology of the schools as idle chatter. He is doubtless responsible for the positive approach to theology transmitted to Varro by his disciple Scaevola.[14] He is actually the author of three theologies: the futile theology of poets, which puts the gods below outstanding men; the theology of philosophers, which is at odds with the beliefs that are necessary for the existence of cities (either because, as Euhemerus says, the people think that the gods are but deified men, or because the god of the philosophers, since he has neither sex nor age nor a finite body, has nothing in common with the gods whose statues are seen in cities); finally, the theology of statesmen, which maintains the traditional cult instituted in cities by the sages. Scaevola, a man of politics before all else, does not hide his predilection for the theology of statesmen.

[12] Cicero *On the Nature of the Gods* ii. 115 and 85; *On Divination* ii. 91 and i. 3; *Academica Priora* ii. 42 and 107; Philo *On the Incorruptibility of the World* chap. xv; Diogenes Laertius vii. 147 and 149.
[13] Cicero *Tusculan Disputations* i. secs. 42 and 79.
[14] Epiphanius, in H. Diels, *Doxographi graeci* (Berlin, 1879), p. 513, l. 7; Augustine *City of God* IV, 27.

In 140 B.C. Panaetius wrote a treatise *On Duty* which, according to Cicero, contains an accurate, unbiased discussion of the subject. Cicero adds that he has followed (but not translated) the treatise in the first two books of his own work, *On Duties,* "but not without making a few corrections." [15] The two books are our chief source of information about Panaetius. His ideal seems to be the conduct of the virtuous man who finds in a civilized society the means and the opportunities to satisfy and fortify the inclinations with which nature has endowed him. To live according to nature is for him "to live according to the inclinations that nature has given us." [16] Our own nature must serve as the standard. "We must of course refrain from doing anything against nature; but having taken this into consideration, let us follow our own nature; and even if we should find something better elsewhere, let us use our own nature as the standard for regulating our wills." [17] There are no more exaggerated ambitions concerning superhuman wisdom. Not that Panaetius, under the pretext of "naturalism," allows man to abandon himself to all his passions. The consciousness that we have of our humanity and of our human dignity is enough to stop us. Humanity is truly the focal point of the Ciceronian treatise. It is interesting to note the instances in which he uses the concept of humanity and to examine his meaning in each instance. For example, he tells us that there are two kinds of combat: the first, which is practiced by animals, is the direct use of force; the second is peculiar to man, and consists of just wars which are preceded by a declaration and which therefore imply respect for oaths. Or again, there are two types of societies: animal societies in which reason and language are unknown and distinctly human societies in which the two strongest bonds are reason and language (*ratio* and *oratio*). Or finally: resistance to pleasure, though unknown among beasts, is worthy of men. Cicero also says that it is "inhuman" to use eloquence, whose natural role is salvation, to destroy worthy men, and that it is quite

---

[15] Cicero *On Duties* iii. 7; ii. 60.
[16] Clement of Alexandria *Stromata* ii. 79. 14.
[17] *On Duties* ii. 110.

contrary to *humanity* to meditate at a banquet to which we have been invited or to sing on the public square.[18] In a word, humanity is all that which transforms the brutal instincts of the animal into civilized practices, ranging from politeness and good manners to the rules of justice which even enemies respect, if they are men. The ideal man, according to Panaetius, is not the primitive man of the Cynics for whom civilization creates only useless complications, for the social bond is rooted in nature itself, and it is nature that invites us to show reserve and to have respect for ourselves (*verecundia*). The arts are not the gifts of the gods, as the myths tell us, but the results of human effort, and it is through the gods that "civilized human life differs by far from the way of life of beasts." Humanity then transforms the bestial instinct but without serving as a substitute for it. There are in beasts tendencies that correspond to every virtue: a desire to see and hear and a disinterested tendency to play, corresponding to speculative virtue; and a tendency to self-preservation, corresponding to courage and temperance, which are innate social tendencies. Human virtues are merely these natural tendencies regulated by reason.[19] Man, contrary to the teachings of orthodox Stoicism, then is and remains two-sided: he exhibits both rational and irrational tendencies.

Panaetius' doctrine, which has survived only as muted echoes, seems to have been remarkably vital and vigorous. After the somewhat stifling gravity or disenchanted pessimism of the doctrines of the two preceding centuries, Panaetius' doctrine, like Carneades', gave a new impetus to Greek philosophy. The waxing intellectual life to which it contributed seems to correspond to the prodigious transformations that were being accomplished in the political world.

ii   *The Middle Stoa* (continued): *Posidonius*

The brilliant development of Stoicism took a completely new turn with the Syrian Posidonius of Apamaea (135–51 B.C.). A great

[18] *Ibid*. i. 34; i. 50; i. 105; ii. 51; i. 144.
[19] *Ibid*. ii. chap. iv.

traveler and observer of nature, he visited every Mediterranean coast, Sicily, the Adriatic coasts, Transalpine Gaul, and the coasts of Spain, where he went as far as the Atlantic and observed the phenomenon of the tides. Having taken up residence in Rhodes after 104, he served as the head of a school and at the same time had an important political function as a prytanis. He maintained constant relations with Rome; during the First Mithridatic War, when almost none of the other Near Eastern cities supported the Roman side, he went to Rome as an ambassador to seek support for Rhodes. Pompey was his personal friend and visited him several times in Rhodes; recollections of their conversations have been preserved by Cicero, Pliny the Elder, and Plutarch. It is there that Pompey heard him defend philosophy against the usurpations of the rhetor, Hermagoras, on the basis that the philosopher must reserve to himself general theses while the orator must be satisfied with hypotheses.[20] He was also the friend and teacher of Cicero, who came to hear him in 77 b.c. Like Panaetius, Posidonius was a loyal supporter of Rome. Their common link was the historian Polybius, who saw in Roman domination the conclusion of history; Panaetius was his friend, and Posidonius continued his history.

His philosophical works, like his scientific, mathematical, historical and geographic works, have all disappeared. Nothing remains of his work which by its breadth is comparable to nothing less than Aristotle's encyclopedia. To reconstruct his thought we must turn to the second book of Cicero's treatise *On the Nature of the Gods,* the first book of *Tusculan Disputations* and the treatise *On Divination.* Galen gives an account of his polemic against Chrysippus on the nature of the passions. Seneca in *Natural Questions* made use of a meteorological work by Asclepiodotus of Nicea, whose ideas go back to Posidonius. Strabo often cites him in his *Geography,* and Cleomedes' *Theory of Circular Motion* is inspired

[20] Cicero *Tusculan Disputations* ii. 26, 61; Pliny *Natural History* vii. 30; Plutarch *Life of Pompey* 42 (cf. H. von Arnim, *Leben und Werke des Dion von Prusa* (1898), p. 93).

by him. Finally, Proclus adds to our knowledge of his mathematical thought in his *Commentaries on Euclid*.

All this is quite fragmentary, and the important question of the historical significance of the work of Posidonius is still controversial, especially since Heinze in his work on Xenocrates (1892) and Norden in his commentary on the sixth book in Vergil's *Aeneid* (1903) claim to have detected the influence of Posidonius on the eschatological myth in the *Aeneid* and the myth at the end of Plutarch's treatise *Concerning the Face which Appears in the Orb of the Moon*. The myths, especially the first, which represents the purified soul rising toward the celestial regions, are essentially Platonic, and the same is true of Scipio's dream in which Cicero depicts the soul contemplating the order of the world after death. Besides, Posidonius broke with Stoicism, much more decisively than Panaetius, when he returned to the Platonic theory of the soul. All this has suggested the hypothesis that Posidonius was a devout thinker, the author of a synthesis of Stoicism and Platonism, and the true initiator of Neo-Platonism. There have been attempts to start from this hypothesis and to see vestiges of Posidonius' thought wherever we find the type of mystical asceticism which was prevalent at the end of antiquity and implies a certain conception of the soul and of the world: a soul composed of two elements, one pure and the other impure, and a world made in the image of the soul. The impure element defiles the pure element, which must free itself from impurity; the mind, which is in the impure region of the world, must attain the pure region (heaven or God). Typical examples include numerous ascetic passages in the works of Philo of Alexandria (whose treatise *On the Creation of the World* is supposed to reflect the influence of Posidonius' *Commentary on the Timaeus*), similar passages in the works of Seneca, and the cosmological notions of *On the Universe* which is found in the Aristotelian corpus.

But if we restrict ourselves to undisputed facts, we must refrain from making Posidonius responsible for the beliefs that will insinuate themselves in diverse forms into works dating from the beginning of the Christian era.

The Posidonian image of the universe stands out clearly in the second book of Cicero's *On the Nature of the Gods,* if we accept Reinhardt's exemplary critical analysis of the treatise. Reinhardt has shown, by comparing this book with the corresponding passages in Sextus Empiricus, that Cicero used two Stoic treatises that are quite different in character: the first, the exposition of a scholarly theory, consists of a collection of syllogisms that are repeated in several forms; the second, based largely on intuition and experience, differs in style from the first and makes no use of syllogisms. Whenever Cicero draws on the second treatise, as in Chapters 17–22 and 39–60, which together constitute a unified treatise on providence, no corresponding text is to be found in Sextus. In these chapters providence is not proven as the corollary of principles but is apprehended through a direct vision of the over-all scheme of the ascending scale of beings, from inorganic entities to organic entities to man. Exotic details make the picture very vivid. Similarly, in Chapters 11, 15, and 16, it is easy to see that providence is explained, not on the basis of reason (in the manner of the Old Stoa), but on the basis of a physical agent, warmth, which is manifested particularly in the stars. Finally, in Chapters 32–37, we find the same comprehensive view of the hierarchy of grades of living things, ranging from the particular life of plants to the universal life of the earth that gave it birth. As Reinhardt aptly phrases it, in Old Stoicism "reason is organic, and what is organic is rational." The divine fire is no longer primarily a rational force but a vital force (*vis vitalis,* says Seneca; ζοτικὴ δύναμις).

Posidonius' physics would therefore be primarily a dynamism stressing the exuberance of life and the structural ordering of living beings. This would explain the full significance of the definition of the world attributed to Posidonius by Diogenes Laertius (vii. 138): a system comprising the sky, the earth, and the natures that are in them. What matters most in such a system is the articulated unity of the world, which embraces a flexible and rich variety of hierarchically structured beings. That is why we are inclined to believe the testimony of Philo of Alexandria (notwithstanding a contradictory text by the doxographer, Aetius), who says that Posidonius abandoned the doctrine of the universal conflagration and supported the doctrine of the eternity of the world.[21]

The same trait characterizes his theology. Where the Old Stoa sought to identify, Posidonius seems to have tried to make distinctions. According to Aetius[22] he separated Zeus, nature, and fate and subordinated each concept to the preceding one: Zeus is force in its unity, destiny the same force viewed from its multiple aspects, and nature a power emanating from Zeus and binding together the multiple forces of fate. This triad or trinity shows up again in Cicero in connection with the origin of divination in his treatise *On Divination,* inspired by the five books written by Posidonius on the same subject. Divination can come either from God, when God vaticinates through the mouth of an inspired prophet, or from fate in the case of astrology whose rules are derived from observation, or from nature when the soul is freed from the body and has prophetic dreams, as in sleep. Thus the soul enters into direct relations with God through mystical states of ecstasy, and fate enables man through observation to deduce the laws responsible for the universal harmony of the cosmos.

The same tendency is also reflected in the psychology of Posidonius. Contrary to the opinion held by Chrysippus, he believes that it is impossible to explain passion without separating and arranging into a hierarchy the faculties of the soul discovered by Plato. Galen has preserved the details of his criticism of Chrysippus. Passion is the unreasonable exaggeration of a tendency. He first raises this question: What would be the origin of this unreasonable exaggeration if there were only reason in man? Pleasure, it is said, is but the opinion of a good; but then the sages, being acquainted with happiness, ought to feel pleasure. It is true that pleasure, according to Zeno, is the recent opinion of a good; if pleasure depends on time, however, then its cause is something

---

[21] Philo *On the Incorruptibility of the World* II, 497 (ed. Mangey); Aetius *Placita* ii. 9. 3.

[22] *Placita* (Diels, *Doxographi graeci,* p. 324, l. 4).

other than the purely intellectual fact of opinion. Chrysippus can tell us nothing about the cause of passion, which he attributes to a disease of the soul without discovering the cause of the disease. He says that to experience passion one must have an uncommon weakness, but this is false since there are as many gradations among the passions as there are gradations leading up to wisdom. Finally, passion would have to be the same whenever opinion of good and evil is the same; this is not true, however, and habit or vice causes passions to be stronger when opinion remains the same. The real cause of passions is that there are within us two parts: a daimon that has the same nature as God; and a bad, bestial, irrational, ungodly part. Contrary to what Chrysippus says, some inclinations are bad in themselves. Our corporeal temperament itself predisposes us to certain passions, and it is not through arguments that we can mitigate or combat them. We can act upon what is irrational only through irrational means. For example, certain musical rhythms unleash anger or desire.

Everywhere Posidonius seems to have had as his aim the revelation of the articulated unity of nature. "The good geographer," he says, "must consider terrestrial things in relation to celestial things." In his search for dynamic relations he follows Aristotle and does not concern himself with the presumed mystery of things. Within the total structure, from the location of zones determined by mathematical astronomy he tries to deduce climatic conditions and their influence on the human body. For instance, in contrast to physical geography which treats the fact as if it were a tale, he accepts the account of Pytheas of Massalia who had observed one country where the shortest day in winter lasted four hours and the longest in summer eighteen hours. The same spirit, at once experimental and mathematical, is evidenced in his theory of tides; he observes their daily, monthly, and annual variations and, after making still other calculations, attributes them to the influence of the moon in conjunction with the action of the sun.

Posidonius' preference for the sciences carries over naturally to the arts which constitute civilization and which he looks upon as the fruit of the highest wisdom of mankind. Criticizing his ideas on this point, Seneca asks: "How can one admire both Diogenes and Daedalus?" [23] His question shows how far above the petty asceticism of the Cynics is the philosophy of Posidonius, who tries to achieve a comprehensive view of man and nature in their most intricate manifestation. He follows the role of wisdom throughout the whole history of mankind: the wise men ruled during the golden age, then they had to become legislators and invent laws to combat the growing vices of men; then they invented the arts that facilitate daily living, such as the art of construction; they discovered metals and their uses, the agricultural arts, and the flour mill; Anacharsis invented the potter's wheel and Democritus the kiln. Seneca is somewhat offended by the lack of elevation of such wisdom. For Posidonius it is obvious that nothing is inseparable and that human reason ought to be equally practical and theoretical. Besides, such great discoveries are actually borrowed from nature: metals were first smelted by a forest fire, and wheat was first ground by human teeth. Others are eager to stress the opposition between art and nature, but no such opposition exists.

Posidonius applies the same idea to the history of civilization. In his sequel to Polybius, in fifty-two books dealing with the events that took place from 145 B.C. to 86 B.C., he looks upon Roman civilization as a continuation of the preceding Etruscan and Greek civilizations but shows that it has brought them to perfection.

History, like geography, ethics, and physics, is for Posidonius evidence of a dynamic continuity which the philosopher must seek everywhere to reveal.

III The Epicureans

Epicureanism also participated in the philosophical renaissance that followed the Roman conquest. A host of names proves that Epicureanism played a conspicuous role in the Roman world: Apollodorus who died in 81 B.C., Phaedrus whom Cicero heard at Athens

[23] Letter to Lucilius, 90.

in 79, Zeno of Sidon who was an old man in 76, Philodemus of Gadara who was a friend of Cicero's and whose works were found during the excavation of Herculaneum, and finally Lucretius (93–51).

The Epicureans had to defend themselves against the other schools. In his treatise *On Signs* Philodemus gives an account of a discussion between the Stoic Dionysius and the Epicureans Zeno, Bromius, and Demetrius Lacon. Epicurus uses signs to pass from phenomena to the invisible realities, the void and atoms; motion, for example, is the sign of the void. To this Dionysius objects that one has no right to pass from transient phenomena to such eternal and unchangeable realities as the void and atoms; if the argument is based on an analogy with what is observed (for instance, if the immutability of atoms is deduced from the immutability of species), only identical cases can be cited and the result is sterile, or the degree of resemblance must be indicated, and this gives free reign to arbitrariness. Zeno replies by defending Epicurean induction, "passing from like to like." His reasoning is that the invisible (ἄδηλον) is invisible only because of its smallness while the conditions of existence are the same on a small scale as those that we observe on a large scale; for example, having observed that every motion has a common characteristic, namely that it can be produced only if obstacles are removed, we rightly conclude that the same is true of hidden motions. Bromius, in turn, readily acknowledges that many facts must be collected, particularly similar but different facts which allow us to single out the circumstance that serves as their common link (τὸ συνεδρεῦον ἀχωρίστως); and Demetrius adds that conclusions must be drawn only on the basis of cases that have met every test and ruled out the slightest possibility of a contradictory affirmation.

Their interesting discussion, from which we have sifted out only two essential points, implies confidence in an unchangeable nature from which inductive conclusions draw support. The Epicurean recognizes stable concepts or "common immutable characteristics."

Or again: "A certain thing is the characteristic concept of a certain other thing, as when we say that the body has mass and resistance or that man is a rational animal." [24]

The same mixture of rationalism and empiricism appears in Demetrius Lacon's reply to the Skeptics who were trying to show the impossibility of demonstration on the ground that the demonstration itself has to be demonstrated: "We establish a particular conclusive demonstration, for instance that there are atoms and the void, and show that it is valid; now we have in it proof of generic demonstration, for wherever we find a species belonging to a genus, we find the genus to which the species belongs." [25] The same trait always makes us sympathetic to the intellectual attitude of the Epicureans: their contempt for verbalism and dialectic, and their readiness to leap *in medias res*.

Philodemus' book *On Rhetoric* gives the Epicureans' reply to the question then in vogue: Is rhetoric an art? It was especially important to determine whether the instruction that was being given in the Sophist schools could be put to practical use before popular assemblies and before tribunes. Epicurus had already said that "seduced by the noise of balanced and contrasting sentences with the same cadence, the young people pay a salary to the Sophists but soon learn that they have lost their money." Then it is an art, but an art that is useless in politics. But on this point there were discussions within the school, and Philodemus has harsh criticism for two Epicureans from Rhodes who try to find in Epicurus proof that rhetoric is not an art.

His treatise *On Music,* in which he discusses the opinions of the Stoic Diogenes of Babylon, is also of great interest. Here the Stoic is depicted as a typical conservative who defends music on the basis of its close ties with traditional Greek civilization, its relation to piety and worship of the gods, and the way in which it calms passions and draws men together. The Epicurean is on the contrary a

---

[24] Cf. especially the Teubner edition of περὶ σημείων, cols. 20, 28, 29, and 34.
[25] Sextus Empiricus *Against the Mathematicians* viii. 348.

typical rationalist, a free thinker who will not bow to usage and custom and who answers, for example, that music adds nothing to the gravity of the thoughts in a poem.

In his little treatise *On Anger,* which makes use of Chrysippus' description of this form of passion, he separates vain anger from natural anger or indignation, which only fools do not experience and which is inevitable even in the sage.[26]

We have already seen the length to which Philodemus went in order to defend Epicurean orthodoxy against the heterodoxies of the school which he calls the Sophists and against whom he wrote a special treatise. In a short fragment of this treatise which has recently been studied, he indicates the famous quadruple Epicurean remedy (*tetrapharmakon*) for all evils: "God is not to be feared, death is not frightful, the good is easy to attain, danger is easy to tolerate." His is the sort of formulary which Epicurus had inspired his disciples to produce.[27]

Finally, this is the age that witnessed the birth of Lucretius' remarkable poem *On the Nature of Things,* which extols the serenity of a mind calmed by the Epicurean vision of nature. Lucretius' words of praise are proof of the enthusiastic welcome accorded to Epicurus' ideas by the best minds in Rome. The poem is marked by a gravity of accent that contrasts with the dialectical agility of the other Greek schools, with the virtuosity that must have found little favor in Rome. Does everything in the vast poem owe its origin to Epicurus? Certainly not. Many of the technical details in his explanation of atmospheric phenomena in the fourth book hark back to Posidonius or to Theophrastus. At times he also borrows directly from Empedocles and supplies allegorical interpretations rarely found among the Epicureans. Furthermore, the mood is not completely Epicurean, and Lucretius' serenity is tinged with pessimism. Epicurus is not the source of the history of mankind which is placed at the end of the fifth book and which views civilization as a downfall rather than an advancement. The feeling of

[26] Edited by Wilcke (Teubner, 1914).
[27] Vogliano, *Rivista di filologia* (1926).

irremediable decadence, voiced a thousand times, cannot have its source in Epicurus. Consider also the third book on the mortality of the soul: Lucretius has shown by a host of arguments that the soul is mortal, and this would be enough for an Epicurean; but the last part is addressed in its entirety to those who are still beset by uneasiness even though they have accepted his thesis. Lucretius still wants to protect us against the horror of nothingness through meditation on "immortal death." His celebrated discourse on nature employs no Epicurean arguments, but it stresses the eternal monotony of things (*eadem sunt omnia semper*), suggesting in this way disgust with life rather than intrepidity in the face of death. Here Lucretius utilizes much more so than Epicurus the pessimistic themes that we found in the old diatribes.

IV *The End of the New Academy*

The crisis that affected every school during the first half of the first century B.C. also affected the Academy. The two scholarchs who succeeded Clitomachus, Philo of Larissa (110–85) and Antiochus of Ascalon (85–69), agreed with neither their predecessors nor each other on the signification to be given to the Academic doctrine. We can reconstruct the debate from Cicero's *Academica*. Cicero, who knew Philo at Rome between 88 and 85, and who was a pupil of Antiochus in Athens in 79, wrote his first treatise, *Academica Priora,* in 46 B.C. The first book in his treatise, *Catulus,* now lost, contained an exposition of Carneades' theory; the second, *Lucullus,* which has been preserved, contains Lucullus' exposition of Antiochus' doctrine, followed by Cicero's refutation, in which he conforms to the teaching of Philo of Larissa. The following year he wrote a second edition of the same treatise, *Academica Posteriora;* the first of the four books — and the only one that has survived — contains an exposition (in words attributed to Varro) of Antiochus' doctrine.

To understand clearly the subject of the debate, we must move ahead in time and examine first the contents of the first book in

Academica Posteriora. In it Varro-Antiochus sets forth a most unusual historical thesis: the true successors to Plato and the Academicians are not Arcesilaus and Carneades but the Stoics, and the Academic tradition will be renewed by a return to Stoicism, rightly understood and purged of its inconsistencies. Zeno of Citium, who received it through Polemon, simply changed a few names; by giving the name *preferables* to wealth and health, which Plato called goods, he changed nothing concerning standards of conduct; even while rejecting the incorporeality of the soul, he preserved what is essential in Platonic physics — the duality of an agent and a patient; finally, he accepts certainty, along with Plato, even while basing it on the senses. Antiochus is here the founder of a syncretistic dogmatism that wipes out all minor differences; he is contributing in his own way to the reconciliation, observable in Panaetius and Posidonius, of Platonism and Stoicism.

Cicero relates that in 87 B.C. Lucullus, praetor in Alexandria, had among his familiars Antiochus and his friend Heraclitus of Tyre. Two books by Philo had been brought to Alexandria. Antiochus read them, became upset, and asked Heraclitus if he had ever heard Philo or any Academician say such things. It was at this moment that Heraclitus started to write a book, titled *Sosus,* in which he took issue with his teacher.

It would seem that Antiochus' irritation must have resulted from his singular historical thesis. In his reply to Lucullus and Varro, Cicero, who represents Philo, confronts them with another historical truth: the Skeptic tradition that began with the physicists Anaxagoras and Empedocles and continued through Socrates whom Antiochus tried to separate from Plato, through Plato himself and through the Cyrenaics.[28] As for Philo, the Neo-Platonist Numenius relates that he changed his mind and after cultivating and exaggerating the dogmas of Clitomachus, became a dogmatist "on the basis of the obvious proofs provided by passive impressions and their reciprocal concordance." [29] Was Philo then following the path

[28] *Academica Priora* ii. 72–6; *Academica Posteriora* 43–6.
[29] Eusebius *Evangelical Preparation* xiv. 712.

that led to Antiochus' dogmatism? In the same sentence, according to Sextus,[30] Philo says that things are apprehensible and that they are inapprehensible. Cicero indicates that he destroys the Zenonian definition of the apprehensive representation and nevertheless refuses at the same time to admit that anything can be understood.[31] Finally, he acknowledges that some things are clearly impressed on the mind (*perspicua*) even as he denies that these things are perceived. Antiochus knew him well since he studied with him much longer than anyone else. Was he wrong in accusing Zeno of contradicting himself? The contradiction may be only apparent, for he could have acknowledged the irresistible evidence of the senses without acknowledging the Stoic criterion. This is exactly what Sextus' text means: if one wishes to use the Stoic criterion (that is, a representation which not only corresponds to the object but which is also capable of being distinguished from any object other than itself), then nothing is apprehensible; but if one accepts the spontaneity of nature, some things are apprehensible, and these are Cicero's *perspicua*. Philo is then one of the philosophers who, according to the Skeptic Aenesidemus, were dogmatic about many things but did not want to base their affirmations on the apprehensive representation. Stobaeus[32] has in fact preserved under his name the outline of an ethical doctrine that is not very different in design from the Stoic doctrine.

Thus we see that Academic thought tended to culminate in rigid dogmas.

[30] *Outlines of Pyrrhonism* i. 235.
[31] *Academica Priora* ii. sec. 34.
[32] *Eclogae* ii. 40.

BIBLIOGRAPHY

Texts

Editions of the writings of Panaetius. Fragments have been edited by M. van
Straaten, *Panaetii Rhodii fragmenta* (Leiden, 1952) and by H. N.
Fowler, *Panaetii et Hecatonis librorum fragmenta* (Bonn, 1885).

Editions of the writings of Posidonius. Fragments have been edited by J.
Blake, *Posidonii Rhodii reliquiae doctrinae* (Leiden, 1810), and by C.
Müller, *Fragmenta historicorum graecorum* (1849).

Editions of the writings of Philodemus. Editions of fragments of Philodemus are included in the Teubner Library. In addition, his περὶ Θεῶν
ἀγωγῆς has been edited by Diels, *Preuss. Akademie der Wissenschaften* A1916), Nos. 4 and 6. Cf. Philippson, *Hermes,* LIII, 358, and
LIV, 216.

For editions of the works of Lucretius, see the bibliography for Chapter III.

Studies

I

A. Schmekel. *Die Philosophie der mittleren Stoa in ihrem geschichtlichen
Zusammenhange.* Berlin, 1892.

A. Besançon. *Les adversaires de l'Hellénisme à Rome.* Paris, 1910, chap. v.

B. N. Tatakis. *Panétius de Rhodes.* Paris, 1931.

M. Pohlenz. *Antikes Führertum, Cicero De officiis und das Lebensideal des
Panaitios.* Leipzig, 1934.

M. van Straaten. *Panétius, sa vie, ses écrits, sa doctrine.* Amsterdam, 1946.

E. Bréhier. "Sur une des origines de l'humanisme moderne," *Etudes de
philosophie antique,* (Paris, 1955), p. 131.

A. Grilli. "Studi paneziani." *Studi italiani di Filologia classica,* XXIX, No. 1
(1957); cf. *Revue philosophique,* 1960, p. 233.

P.-M. Schuhl. "Panaitios et la philosophie active," *Revue philosophique*
(1960), pp. 233 ff.

II

K. Reinhardt. *Poseidonios.* Munich, 1921. — *Kosmos und Sympathie.* Munich,
1926. — *Poseidonios über Ursprung und Entartung.* Heidelberg, 1928. —
Article "Poseidonios" in Pauly-Wissowa *Realenzyklopaedie.*

J. Heinemann. *Poseidonios metaphysische Schriften.* Vol. I, Breslau, 1921. Vol. II, 1928.

W. Jaeger. "Nemesios von Emesa," *Quellenforschungen zum Neuplatonismus und seinen Anfängen bei Poseidonios.* Berlin, 1914.

M. Pohlenz. "De Posidonii περὶ παθῶν," *Fleckeisens Jahrbücher für class. Philologie.* Supplementband XXIV, 1898.

W. Capelle. "Die Schrift von der Welt," *Neue Jahrbücher für d. kl. A.*, XV (1905), 55.

W. Capelle. "Die griechische Erdkunde und Poseidonios," *Ibid.*, XXXIII (1920), 305.

E. Bréhier. "Poseidonios d'Apamée théoricien de la géométrie," *Rev. Et. gr.,* 1914.—*Etudes de philosophie antique.* Paris, 1955, pp. 117–30.

J. F. Dobson. *The Poseidonios Myth.* London, 1918.

M. Laffranque. "Poseidonios d'Apamée et les mines d'Ibérie," *Pallas,* V (Toulouse, 1957). Cf. *Rev. philos.* (1958), p. 377.— *Poseidonios d'Apamée* (in preparation).

III, IV

V. de Falco. *L'epicureo Demetrio Lacone.* Naples, 1923.

C. Giussani. *Studi lucreziani.* Turin, 1906.

B. C. Martha. *Le Poème de Lucrèce.* Paris, 1896.

G. Della Valle. "Tito Lucrezio Caro e l'epicureismo campano," *Atti dell" Accademia pontaniana,* XLII (Naples, 1933).

Epicurea in memoriam E. Bignone. Genoa, 1959.

P. Boyancé. *Lucrèce et l'epicurisme.* Paris, 1963.

Studies in English

E. V. Arnold. *Roman Stoicism.* Cambridge, 1911.

E. R. Bevan. *Stoics and Sceptics.* Oxford, 1913.

L. Edelstein. "The Philosophical System of Posidonius," *American Journal of Philosophy,* LVII (1936).

G. A. Gordon. *A Bibliography of Lucretius.* London, 1962.

R. D. Hicks. *Stoic and Epicurean.* New York, 1910.

J. R. Mattingly. "Cosmogony and Stereometry in Posidonian Physics," in *Osiris,* III (Brussels, 1957), pp. 558–83.

F. Solmsen. *Cleanthes or Posidonius? The Basis of Stoic Physics.* Amsterdam, 1961.

A. D. Winspear. *Lucretius and Scientific Thought.* Montreal, 1963.

THE FIRST TWO CENTURIES A.D.

NOTHING is harder to disentangle than the history of intellectual thought during the first two centuries A.D., which witnessed the brief but brilliant resurgence — under Seneca, Epictetus, and Marcus Aurelius — and subsequent disappearance of the great post-Aristotelian dogmatisms. The two centuries also witnessed the rebirth of Athenian idealism as it had existed during the fifth and fourth centuries B.C. in the systems of Plato and Aristotle. Philo of Alexandria at the beginning of the first century A.D., Plutarch of Chaeronea (49–120), then the commentators on Plato, particularly Albinus (about the middle of the second century), and the commentators on Aristotle were its new exponents. At the same time a Pythagorean literature, impregnated with Platonism, came into existence. But alongside the great philosophical schools, how many new trends of thought took shape and penetrated the mainstream of civilization! The interpenetration of Hellenism and the Near East was continuous. The Alexandrian Jews, including Philo, were the first to make their influence felt. Then came Christianity, which produced simultaneously the great Gnostic systems and the apologists Justin, Tatian, and Irenaeus. Less conspicuous but no less active were the Eastern religions, particularly Mithraism, which had not only their forms of worship and mysteries but also comprehensive views of the world and of human destiny.

It is only through abstraction that such trends can be studied separately, for they all belong to one and the same intellectual civilization. The common characteristics of this civilization are worth noting. In the first place, the creative period has come to an end, and instead of advancing what had been done by Plato, Aristotle, and Chrysippus, men write commentaries on their works, which are studied assiduously and used as the basis for an infinite variety of exercises. No one feels the need to revise the conception of the universe and the cosmos; the fruit of long experience and patient reasoning, it has become a stable image and now serves as a point of departure. A finite and unique world, geocentrism, the opposition between the world as the seat of change and corruption and incorruptible heaven, the intermediate regions of the air, the variable influence of the stars on the destinies of earthlings — such are the beliefs common to almost everyone and which will not be revised for long years to come. No deep philosophical curiosity exists; consequently, if we exempt the practical arts of medicine (Galen), mechanics (Hero of Alexandria), and even alchemy, there is no scientific curiosity. In fact, the practical arts are generally extolled as being simple expedients developed through experience and completely independent of the theoretical sciences. Galen doubtless wants the physician to be a philosopher; what he intends, however, is not for the physician to have his own theories but to adopt for his physiology the Aristotelian or the Stoic system of physics. Sextus Empiricus and the so-called empirical school of physicians, on the other hand, are very careful to restrict the method of the physician to mere observation. The theoretical sciences of mathematics, music, and astronomy are of no use in the practical arts other than as instruments for speculating on the universe, and their place in education is questioned. Their development as independent sciences is viewed with alarm and they are generally relegated to a subordinate role: to provide a basis for an understanding and conception of the system of the cosmos, but nothing more than that. The whole cycle of liberal education (παιδεία ἐγκύκλιος) is at most the slave of philosophy or an introduction to philosophy: Theo of Smyrna wrote a treatise (*ca.* 125) on the mathematical knowledge required for reading Plato, and Philo of Alexandria used arithmetic only to lay the foundation for numerical symbolism.

We have identified one general trait of the first two centuries A.D.: an inert comprehension resulting from the imposition of existing images and the blockage of any attempt to rise to intellectual heights. It follows that in a certain sense philosophy no longer provides anything more than topics for study, and these topics are so overworked that freshness can be achieved only through virtuosity of form. Will philosophy degenerate into mere rhetoric? The danger is always present. How many times was it felt by Epictetus, who constantly censures his pupils because of their tendency to display mere rhetorical skill and to neglect deep emotions! How many times does Seneca sacrifice thought to euphony and the pursuit of clever phrases! And a man like Maximus of Tyre expounds eloquently on either the negative or the affirmative side of the most serious philosophical subjects, on practical issues or on the role of the sciences in philosophy.[1] The result is that in the constant struggle between philosophers and the Sophists, or professors who lecture on rhetoric, the Sophists are on the verge of winning. Aelius Aristides (117–177), who inveighs against Plato's condemnation of rhetoric in the *Gorgias,* places the formal education of the rhetor far above that of the philosopher.[2]

The superficial treatment of ideas is matched by moral and religious preoccupations that are fundamentally the same in every school. Now the philosopher is looked upon as a guide, a comforter or a moral counselor. Philosophy is a school of peace and serenity. The pursuit of truth and knowledge are of value only to the extent that they contribute to the tranquility of the soul and its happiness. "Philosophy, along with the desire for wisdom," says Albinus in his *Manual of Platonist Philosophy,* "is the deliverance of the soul and its conversion outside the body, with the result that we are turned toward intelligible things and true beings." What matters in the

[1] *Discourses* v and vi, xx and xxi.
[2] A. Boulanger, *Aelius Aristide* (1923).

pursuit of truth is the attainment of the object of truth which alone produces happiness, not the method through which it is pursued. It matters less, as we have already seen with respect to Stoicism, to discover a new truth than to transform the mind and its view or judgment of things. Such a result is achieved not so much through instruction as through vivid impressions.

I Stoicism in the Days of the Empire

What literary forms does Stoicism take at the time of the Empire? We find Stoic writings that resemble ethical catechisms (discourses by Musonius), sermons on philosophical subjects (Dio Chrysostom), letters or essays designed as spiritual guides (Seneca), lectures on spiritual growth (Epictetus), and works directed toward self-examination (Marcus Aurelius). But underneath such literary works are countless anonymous contributions by men who came to grips with the growing vices of Roman society, where the have-nots thought only of living at the expense of the rich and on public funds, and chose moral reformation as their mission. Sometimes we witness the birth of such a vocation: for instance, the merchant Damasippus who after failing in business became a Stoic and said, according to Horace,[3] "no longer having a business of my own, I concern myself with the business of others." Dio Chrysostom, the brilliant worldly lecturer, when brought to ruin as a result of his being exiled under Domitian in A.D. 83, took up the Cynic's staff and went from town to town to preach the good word. Young men identified themselves with the most celebrated figures and established veritable centers of propaganda. It was through the influence of Dio that the Stoic cause was espoused by Favorinus of Arles, whose discourse on the exile[4] was recently discovered on a papyrus, and the satirist Persius[5] tells us about the enthusiasm generated among young people by Cornutus, whose short allegory on Stoic theology

[3] *Satires* book ii, iii. 18.
[4] Cf. Cumont, *Journal des Savants* (1931), p. 370, and Collart, *Revue de l'Association Guillaume Budé* (1932).
[5] *Satire* v.

has survived. Lucian relates the role played in his town by Demonax, the Stoic whose soothing words settled disputes in private as well as in public. We know how many young Romans were sent to study with Epictetus on the distant shores of Nicopolis and how hard it was for him to make them leave the protection of the school and enter into public life. We need only read Lucian's *Hermotimus* to see the force of the attraction exerted on others by philosophers who offered moral guidance; around them were clustered white-haired disciples who never tired of learning.

With such multiple ramifications it was natural for Stoicism at times to appear in the world of politics. Stoicism was looked upon with suspicion, especially by bad emperors. Among the accusations made by Nero's freedman Tigellinus against Augustus' grandson Rubellius Plautus, whom Tigellinus depicted as a pretender to the throne, was the imputation of Stoicism: "He is a member of the arrogant sect of the Stoics, instigators of public disturbances and disorder." Rubellius, who was then (A.D. 62) in Syria, had with him as moral counselors the philosophers Coeranus and Musonius; and on learning that soldiers had been sent to put him to death, against the advice of a freedman who urged him to resist, they counseled him to choose "instead of an uncertain and tremulous life the security of easy death." Later (A.D. 65), following Piso's conspiracy, the measures ordered by Nero included banishment of Musonius and Cornutus; Musonius was suspected of having taught philosophy to the young people.[6] These examples show that generally there was covert opposition rather than overt resistance; Stoicism had not become, nor had it ever been, a political party. The celebrated Stoic Thrasea was not a politician; his son-in-law Helvidius Priscus, then a praetor, was accused of refusing to pay homage to the emperor and to champion the cause of democracy. In this new assault against philosophers during the reign of Vespasian, all philosophers except Musonius were expelled from Rome (A.D. 71); Musonius, who had been recalled to Rome under Galba, was not

---

[6] Boissier, *L'Opposition sous les Césars* chap. ii; Tacitus *Annals* xiv. 57 and 59; xv. 71.

worried. It was at this time that Dio Chrysostom, still a rhetor and still untouched by Cynicism, delivered his speeches *Against Philosophers,* "the pests that infect cities and governments." Later (A.D. 85) the suspicious Domitian put the Sophist Maternus to death because he had delivered a scholarly oration against tyrants, Rusticus Arulinus "because he was philosophizing and looked upon Thrasea as a saint," and Herennius Senecion because he had compiled a life of Helvidius Priscus.[7]

Has any trace of Stoicism, once prevalent throughout the Roman Empire, been preserved in Roman law? Historically, the distinctive trait of Roman law is doubtless its almost complete independence from religion and morality as well as the notion of the sovereignty of the state, which is truly alien to Greek thought. It follows that even though theoretical treatises such as Cicero's *Laws* are inspired by Stoicism, and even though in Ulpian we can find the Stoic definition of justice ("the constant and perpetual will to distribute to each what is his"), Stoicism played a role that has since been obliterated. Legal historians do not even agree that the notion of natural law goes back to Stoicism, and several of them attribute to it an exclusively Roman origin.[8]

The teaching of the Stoics assumes several distinct forms. First, technical instruction in schools, very dry and scholastic, is based on the reading and annotation of the works of earlier Stoic masters, particularly Chrysippus, whose doctrine was transmitted to Aulus Gellius by the Athenian Stoics in the first half of the second century A.D. He indicates the divisions of philosophy, particularly dialectic and ethics, which are simply a restatement of the traditional divisions, and stresses the formalization of syllogisms.[9] In the writings of Philo of Alexandria and Epictetus we find many allusions to such scholastic instruction; Epictetus repeatedly censures teachers of philosophy for limiting themselves to the interpretation of Chrysippus and for being mere philologists. It is worth

[7] Dio Cassius *Roman History* 66. 12–19; 67. 13.
[8] Hildenbrand, *Geschichte und System der Rechts und Staatsphilosophie,* I, 600, in contrast to Voigt, *Romische Rechtsgeschichte,* I, 237 ff.
[9] Aulus Gellius *Attic Nights* i. 2; ii. 8.

noting that the only Stoics who are read are the Old Stoa: the most recent names cited by Epictetus are Archedemus, Antipater, and Crinis; Panaetius and Posidonius go unnoticed and, with them, the new humanistic and Platonist direction that the school had taken. Epictetus is closer to Zeno than to Panaetius.[10]

There was a livelier, more active form of teaching. It used every procedure from public speeches, addressed to everyone in the rhetorical style, to personal consultation adapted to each particular case. Plutarch speaks of the astonishment of people who, accustomed to hear with the same feeling philosophers in schools, tragedians in theaters, and Sophists in assemblies (that is, accustomed to find verbal pyrotechnics), are surprised to find that at the end of the course they do not put aside their ideas along with their notebooks. Especially "when the philosopher singles them out and warns them candidly of their shortcomings, they find him out of place . . . they fail to realize that for true philosophers seriousness and jesting, smiles and harshness, and especially the arguments addressed to each of them individually are of the utmost importance." [11] Between the set moral lectures typified by the sermons of Dio Chrysostom and personal advice such as that offered by Seneca to his friend Serenus in *On the Tranquility of the Soul,* are intermediate procedures of every type, but the type that stands out in the environment of the school is the diatribe. The teacher (or a pupil) has just completed a technical lesson and given permission for questioning. Then begins an improvisation, untrammeled by any technical requirements, in a style that is often brilliant and imaginative, replete with anecdotes, and tinged with indignation or irony. Such is the procedure that the philosopher Taurus used in Athens, according to Aulus Gellius (i. 26), and such is the procedure used by Epictetus, whose pupil Arrian edited his diatribes. A summary of the lesson or of a technical commentary just made by a disciple is sometimes included in Arrian's texts, and we are indebted to him for

[10] Philo *On Agriculture* sec. 139 (ed. Cohn); Epictetus *Discourses* i. 17. 13; iii. 2. 13.
[11] Plutarch *On the Right Way of Hearing* chap. xii.

some of the rarest and most valuable technical information about the Old Stoa. The tone of his summaries contrasts sharply with the tone of the master's diatribes.[12]

II *Musonius Rufus*

A few of Musonius Rufus' moral pronouncements, edited by one of his pupils, have been preserved by Stobaeus in his *Florilegium:* for example, a sermon *On Food* (17. 43) in which he makes abstinence in eating and drinking the rule of conduct for temperance and recommends vegetarianism as practiced by the Pythagoreans, and a sermon *On Shelter* (1. 64) in which he prescribes simplicity in dress and in architecture. Elsewhere (19. 16) he advises philosophers not to complain about insults, which (as we see in reading Epictetus) must have been numerous (56. 20). He answers those who feel that the vocation of the philosopher is incompatible with marriage by citing a long list of great philosophers who were married — Pythagoras, Socrates, Crates, etc. — and by praising marriage: "to destroy it is to destroy the family and the city; to destroy it is to destroy the whole human race (67. 20)." He spells out the obligations entailed by marriage and warns against incontinence. Elsewhere (75. 15) he shows great concern over the diminution of the number of children in Roman families, "the worst thing that could happen to the city," and inveighs specifically against the abominable practice, apparently still prevalent, of exposing children. A young man desirous of studying philosophy against the explicit orders of his parents asked him if there were not instances in which a son could disobey. In his reply he recommends complete and strict obedience and at the same time shows the young man that his parents cannot and do not wish to prevent him from being a philosopher, which does not mean wearing a long beard and a short coat but being just and temperate. Finally, also worth noting are his reflections on exile, which deprives us of no true good.[13]

[12] For example, in *Discourses* ii. 1 the lesson is summarized in secs. 1–7; the rest is the diatribe.

[13] Stobaeus 69. 23; 70. 14; 75. 15; 84. 21.

His style is simple: short, independent items that reflect the same inspiration but are not systematized or encumbered by a technical apparatus. Musonius has the greatest confidence in education based on his principles: it produces good kings as well as good citizens; the teacher of ethics is indispensable; it is fitting to eat, drink, and sleep under the supervision of a worthy man (56. 19). He has the highest respect for his vocation and therefore seeks to discourage rather than to encourage others to become moral educators: "It is better for most of the young men who say that they wish to philosophize not to approach philosophy; their approach is a task for philosophy." And he points up the contrast between the student who applauds and praises the worldly philosopher and the student who listens to the true philosopher, who makes him aware of sin and leads him to repentance.[14] To complete the portrait we must add that Musonius knew the rebuffs that are occasioned by the untimely exercise of wisdom. According to Tacitus, who relates the anecdote, when Musonius was sent by Vitellius in A.D. 69 to negotiate with the Flavian army which was at the gates of Rome, he had to endure the gibes and even the abuse of the soldiers.[15]

III Seneca

Less candid was Seneca, first Nero's tutor and later his minister. Born in Cordova in 4 B.C., he was the son of a rhetor, many of whose exercises in composition and oratory are extant, and received an exemplary education in the home of his aunt, whose husband, Vitrasius Pollio, was the prefect of Egypt for sixteen years. He was exiled to Corsica in A.D. 41 following a court scandal, and in 43 he wrote his flattering Consolation to a powerful minister (Ad Polybium de consolatione). In 49 he was recalled by Agrippina who entrusted him with the education of Nero, whom he served as minister from 54 to 61, when he fell into disfavor. He lived in retirement from 62 to 65 when, on Nero's orders, he took his own life.

[14] Aulus Gellius Attic Nights ii. 1.
[15] Tacitus Histories iii. 71.

From 41 to 62 he wrote ten dialogues on ethics (the word *dialogi* is a translation of the Greek *diatribes* and shows immediately the literary type to which they belong) and the essay *On Benefits* (*De beneficiis, ca.* 59). Toward the end of his life (62), after his retirement, he wrote *Natural Questions,* a popular sketch of astronomy and meteorology, drawn largely from Asclepiodotus, a pupil of Posidonius, and the famous *Letters to Lucilius.* Lucilius, the procurator of Sicily, plays only a very minor part in the 124 letters, for they are not so much a moral guide as a literary form chosen under the influence of a collection of Epicurus' writings which he had just read and which he cites repeatedly in the twenty-nine letters. The epistolary form was more appropriate for a man always concerned with the ordering of his ideas.[16]

He pictures himself as a very liberal Stoic: the Old Stoa "are not masters but guides." They are not to be followed but supported; their ideas ought to be treated as a patrimony subject to continuous betterment. Thus he does not hesitate to class Epicurus among the *prudentiores* who offer counsel or to place him beside Zeno and Socrates and say that these are among the philosophers who have exercised a greater influence by their example and character than through their words and teaching.[17] Seneca then reveals that he is not interested in the systematic side of philosophy and that he has much more confidence in personal influences than in the influence of doctrines. In other words, he mistrusts too much knowledge and futile curiosity: "To want to know more than what is essential is a form of intemperance." One should study the liberal arts, mathematics, and astronomy, but only so long as the mind can produce nothing superior. And after explaining a few subtle arguments of the Stoics, he adds: "The course of wisdom is simpler and more direct." [18]

This gives us a clue to his attitude toward physics. He feels that knowledge of the world and the heavens "elevates the soul and

[16] Cf. Bourgery, *Revue de philologie* (1911), p. 40; Pichon, *Journal des Savants* (May, 1912).
[17] *Letters to Lucilius* 45. 4; 80. 1; 64. 7; 22. 5; 6. 6.
[18] *Ibid.* 88. 36; 106. 11.

transports it to the level of the objects that it contemplates." His physical investigations, *Natural Questions,* are compilations, doubtless like his lost books *The Religion of the Egyptians* and *India.* In connection with a section on fish in his study of natural history, he launches into a diatribe against extravagance in eating, just as he criticizes the alimentary use of ice in connection with a study of the formation of snow. His theology is also directed solely toward moral edification. "Do you want to be pleasing to God? Be good; to worship him is to imitate him; he requires not sacrifices but a pious and upright will." He has the Stoic devotion to God — a beneficent God, an inner God who bears witness to our acts, God the father, God the judge — but ignores completely the study of God's nature and relation to the world. He also puts to the service of edification the divine origin of the human soul (a particle of the divine that has fallen and entered the body) but shows little concern over what the soul is or where it is.[19]

Seneca is truly in his element when he comes to the subtile and infinitely detailed description of vices or moral diseases that he wishes to cure. He is a penetrating and pessimistic observer: "It is a gathering of wild beasts," he writes concerning the society of his time. "The difference is that whereas beasts treat each other kindly and abstain from biting each other, men tear each other apart." [20] The sage does not become irritated over a vice common to all but looks upon men as indulgently as the doctor looks upon his patients; counterbalancing this will be an awareness of the extreme fragility of human things, where the only certainty is death.[21] Thus Seneca obligingly develops every facet of moral evil, particularly the distaste for life and action that robs his friend Serenus of calm: "remorse over a deed undertaken, fear of undertaking anything, vacillation of the mind that finds no outlet because it can neither subdue nor obey its desires. This accounts for boredom and discontent." [22]

[19] See, successively, *Ibid.* 117. 19; 95. 10; *Natural Questions* iv. 13; v. 15; *Letters* 95, 115; 44. 49; *On Service* ii. 29; *Letters* 41.2; 66. 12; 31. 11; 92. 30; *Natural Questions* vii. 25.

[20] *On Anger* ii. 8–10.

[21] *Letters* 90. 11.

[22] *On Tranquillity* chap. ii.

IV   *Epictetus*

Seneca generally addresses himself to mature men who have been tested by circumstances and whom he wishes to heal. Epictetus is the teacher of young men whose wills are still to be shaped; they are often rich young men who will follow public careers and who must be protected against the multifold dangers of servility, flattery, and sudden reversals of fortune. In countless ways he repeats to them the same truth: good and evil are inherent only in that which depends on man himself, that is, in his judgment and will; depending on whether they are healthy and uncorrupted or depraved, they will produce all the happiness or unhappiness of which man is susceptible. True freedom is liberation from false opinions. His age was the age when the ranks of the *ingenuus,* the man who numbered only freemen among his ancestors, were thinning, while freedmen and their families were beginning to assume a more important role. Epictetus had himself been a slave before becoming a freedman.[23] His emancipation from slavery is transformed into a moral attitude when he says: "The philosophical doctrine allows those who are downcast to lift up their heads and to look the rich and the powerful straight in the eye." [24] Many times he expresses the notion that manual work is not degrading, and to one of his disciples who feared poverty, he cites the example of beggars, slaves, and workers.

Inner freedom consists in "the use of representations." [25] Any action, among animals as well as among men, follows a representation; animals, like men, use representations as a basis for acting. But beasts are not aware of using them whereas man is, and that is because he can use them for good or for evil, rightly or wrongly. "My ancestors, my near relations, my friends, my reputation, my residence, none of this is mine." — "What then is yours?" — "The

[23] Denis, *Histoire des théories et des idées morales dans l'antiquité* (Paris, 1856), II, 80.

[24] *Discourses* iii. 26. 35.

[25] A. Bonhoeffer, *Die Ethik des stoikers Epiktet* (Stuttgart, 1894), p. 73; *Discourses* iii. 20. 7; i. 9. 8; i. 16. 12; i. 10. 7; iv. 4. 4.

use of my representations. No one can force me to think what I do not think." [26]

To his sense of freedom is linked a deep-seated religious feeling that stems primarily from the recognition of a special relation between man and God. If man is free it is because he is one of the most important components in the system of nature, and because all other things are made to complement him; and since he is one of the main components, he is not a work of God like the other things, but a particle of God, who gave him over to himself instead of allowing him to be dependent.[27] But it must be clearly understood that the apotheosis of man is less a raw datum than an ideal to be realized and a belief to be used as a guide.

v Marcus Aurelius

Daily self-examination is an exercise in morality recommended by Seneca, who attributed the practice to the Pythagorean Sextius. Each night before falling asleep one must ask: "Which evil have I overcome today? Which vice have I resisted? In what respect am I better?" [28] It is surely to the practice of introspection that we owe the thoughts addressed by Marcus Aurelius *To Himself*. What mattered most to the emperor, preoccupied with political worries and his campaigns against the barbarians, was to protect himself against discouragement. His writings convey a feeling of boundless energy. The feeling of anguish upon awaking, disturbing thoughts that come upon him, criticism by others of what he thinks to be good, the constraints of the court and of society, the feeling of emptiness, monotony and pettiness, the vagaries of the flesh, the violence of anger, the horror of the nothingness that awaits the soul after death — such are the dangers against which he battles through intense meditation. In general he does not think highly of the remedies proposed by philosophy; he knows the uncertainty of

---

[26] *Discourses* iii. 24. 68.
[27] *Ibid*. ii. 8.
[28] *On Anger* iii. 3. 6.

physics and does not wish to link morality to a particular notion about the world and the gods; he knows the vain ostentation of public lessons; and because he knows how ineffective and inhumane it is, he substitutes politeness for harsh criticism.[29] Similarly, he has little use for the all-inclusive affirmations of Stoicism. That death is a state of indifference is not his usual consolatory theme, for he believes rather that through death the individual is returned to the universe and diffused throughout it, that death is an emancipation, and that it enables us to escape from the danger of intellectual decrepitude.[30]

Indeed, his basic theme is everywhere the link between the individual and the universe: only this gives meaning to life, which is itself so unstable and fleeting. The affirmation of the essential goodness of the world complements and transcends ordinary belief in providence. "Even if the gods are in no way concerned over me, I know that I am a rational being, that I have two fatherlands, Rome in my role as Marcus Aurelius and the world in my role as a man, and that the only good is that which is of benefit to these two fatherlands." It is clear that even here the essential religious affirmation persists: the moral act is like the flowering of universal nature in man; man must produce unknowingly, just as a tree yields its fruit.[31]

After Marcus Aurelius Stoicism declines into obscurity, though of course philosophers from other schools know it, utilize it, explain it, and criticize it. The teaching of Plotinus includes the criticism of many Stoic theories, particularly in physics, and Aristotle's commentators frequently contrast Stoicism with the teachings of their master. In addition, consolations, diatribes, and exercises on moral conduct drawn up by the moralists of the school, along with similar works by Cynic writers, become the common property of all. Christians and pagans alike have recourse to their vast storehouse of moral consolation, but the Stoics have nothing to do with its strik-

[29] Ibid. 6. 40; 76. 5; 5. 6.
[30] To Himself 64. 17; 75. 21; 4. 10.
[31] Ibid. 16. 18; 55. 13–22; 71. 4.

ing and lasting usefulness. We have seen how the Stoics in the days of the Empire refused to be bound by a technical dogma, and how before them Epictetus seemed to tender his acceptance only as a matter of form. Now we shall see how the dogma, almost lifeless by this time, is attacked by the Skeptics even as it gives way to Platonism.

VI *Skepticism*

Our knowledge of the external history of Skepticism is vague. Between the two most illustrious Skeptics, Aenesidemus who probably lived during the first century B.C. and Sextus Empiricus whose work probably dates from the second half of the second century A.D., we find other Skeptics, among them Agrippa, whose dates are indeterminate.

Aenesidemus' work is fairly well known through a summary of his *Pyrrhonian Discourses* preserved in his *Library* (cod. 212) by the Byzantine Photius. Here Aenesidemus is intent upon setting himself apart from the Academicians of his time (doubtless Philo of Larissa) who are Stoics even though they are combatting Stoicism and who dogmatize about virtue and vice, being and non-being. The aim of the book is to show that the Pyrrhonian sage attains to happiness by realizing that he perceives nothing with certainty either through sensation or through thought, and that in this way he frees himself from the vexations and cares that harass the adepts of other sects. Skepticism, too, is then a school of happiness and of ataraxia. The *Discourses* followed in detail the dogmatic philosophies, even going to great lengths to give the opposing arguments with respect to the principles of physics (agent and patient, generation and corruption, motion and sensation), the method of physics (trying to determine whether phenomena are signs of hidden realities and whether a causal relation can be identified), and finally the principles of ethics (good and evil, virtues, the supreme end of man).

Sextus has preserved a few details from their line of reasoning.

For example, according to Aenesidemus generation is impossible: one body is incapable of producing another since it must either remain in itself (and consequently produce only itself) or join with another body, for if one body by being joined to another could produce a third, then by the same logic the third by uniting with either of the first two could produce a fourth, and so on indefinitely. The incorporeal (in the Stoic sense of the word: space, place, or time) can produce only the incorporeal since it is by definition incapable of acting or being acted upon. Just as a plane tree cannot produce a horse, so body cannot produce the incorporeal or the incorporeal body. We see that generation (implicit in this whole line of reasoning) is always compared to the production of a living being.[32]

We also know his eight arguments or tropes against causes.[33] Are causes to be found in the invisible world? How could the visible world *testify* (according to the wording of the Epicurean dogmatism) in support of an invisible world completely different from itself — one that is not ephemeral but unchangeable and eternal? By what right can the cause of such multiple phenomena be reduced to the unity of a single substance (like the atom)? How can the order of the world be attributed (in the manner of Epicurus) to causes that act blindly? How is it possible to pattern (still following the example of the Epicureans) the actions and passions of invisible things on visible things? Why boast (as they do) of adhering to general impressions acknowledged by all when their hypotheses concerning the elements are quite exceptional? What right have they to restrict hidden causes, such as the causes of meteorological phenomena, to those that fit in which their hypotheses? Why do they contradict both appearances and their own hypotheses by admitting such causes as declination? The brunt of his criticism is obviously directed toward Epicureanism.

With respect to signs, Aenedisemus cites the Stoic definition, "signs are visible antecedents which are known by all and which are intended to reveal a hidden consequent," and asks why the things

[32] *Against the Mathematicians* ix. 218–226.
[33] Sextus Empiricus *Outlines of Pyrrhonism* i. 180–5.

signified are not the same for all. Why, for example, are redness and dampness of the skin and rapidity of the pulse symptoms of different things according to different doctors? [34]

Finally, we know the ten tropes or general frames in which Aenedisemus accumulated arguments against sensible knowledge. The first concludes, on the basis of the difference between the organs of different animals and between the organs of animals and man, that each species must have its own particular sensations. Sextus probably acted on his own initiative in developing the superiority of the animal over man (62–77), which represents a telling blow against Stoicism. The second concludes that because men differ with respect to their bodies and souls, they must also differ with respect to their sensations. The third shows how different kinds of sensations are at variance with each other; our several senses judge the same object differently, and objects can have either more or fewer qualities than those we perceive. The fourth shows how sensations of the same kind can differ according to circumstances (delusion of madness or dream, age, passion, etc.). The fifth, sixth, seventh, eighth, and ninth show how an object varies in appearance, depending on its location or distance, its mixture in varying degrees with other objects, its magnitude, its relation to the perceiver and to other objects, and its rarity. Last of all, the tenth reveals how indefinitely variable are the beliefs, laws, and customs of men. [35]

The five tropes attributed by Sextus to more recent Skeptics and by Diogenes Laertius to Agrippa are completely different in nature from Aenesidemus' tropes: discordance, which bases suspension of judgment on disagreement among philosophers themselves and between them and the common people; the infinite regress, through which an affirmation must be based on proof, this proof on still another proof and so on *ad infinitum;* relativity, which shows that our judgment depends not on what things are but on their relation either to us or to one another; the unproven hypothesis, which

[34] Sextus Empiricus *Against the Mathematicians* viii. 215.
[35] Sextus Empiricus i. 31–163; Philo *On Inebriety* sections 171 ff. (ed. Cohn); Diogenes Laertius ix. 79–88.

serves as a starting point for those who try to avoid the infinite regress; the diallelos, which shows that escape from the second or third trope leads to a circular demonstration in which the sensible is proved by the intelligible, which in its turn is established by the sensible. The five tropes do not deal specifically with the senses but rather with rational problems and modes of proof. The same is true of the two tropes cited later by Sextus. They give the dogmatic philosopher the choice of positing initial affirmations that cannot be proven or of deducing them from other affirmations and falling into the infinite regress or the diallelos.[36]

In view of the many arguments accumulated by Aenesidemus, it is surprising to learn through Sextus that Skepticism is for him the road that leads to Heracliteanism. In his name Sextus describes a complete system of physics based on the principle that air, like the weather and night, is susceptible to two types of changes, qualitative (such as change of color) and local, and that man is endowed with thought which, through the intermediary of the senses, seems true. The contrast between this dogmatism and Skeptic doubt poses a problem that has not been resolved despite the kinship that had always been acknowledged on the part of the Skeptics between their system and the system of Heraclitus.

Sextus Empiricus' *Outlines of Pyrrhonism* and his vast work in eleven volumes, *Against the Mathematicians* — the first six on the liberal arts, mathematics, grammar, rhetoric, geometry, arithmetic, and music, and the last five on philosophical dogmatism — are a summation of Skepticism and an arsenal in which he assembled and classified all the arguments of the school. Because of the stress placed on divergences between philosophers by the adherents to the school, these works include the copious and valuable historical data which we have frequently utilized. But the line of reasoning is often barren, monotonous, and exhausting on account of its verbalism and dryness. Sextus, who enlightens us on many points, would add little to our understanding of his personal contribution to Skepticism if we did not find, alongside and apart from the stream of argu-

[36] Sextus Empiricus i. 166–77; 178–9; Diogenes Laertius ix. 88–9.

ments, a positive idea of an empirical method of knowledge that traces the outlines of a true inductive logic. Sextus often stresses the fact that as soon as we stop trying to attain to reality, our judgments based on appearances are sufficient in daily life. "Skeptics do not destroy appearances," says Sextus;[37] and so long as honey tastes sweet, we know (without having to determine whether or not it has the quality of sweetness) whether or not to eat it. Skeptics, too, have a criterion, that of "daily observation," which has a quadruple form: we can use nature as a guide, or we can let the necessity of passions be our guide, or we can pattern our conduct on the tradition of laws and customs, or finally, we can use the technical procedures of the arts. In each instance the mind is set free and subjected in the least possible degree to the constraint of things. Hence the positive theory of the sign, which is essentially that of a physician (Sextus belonged to the methodical sect of physicians[38]) accustomed to observation. In his words: "We do not contradict common sense and we do not revolutionize life, as we are slanderously accused of doing; if we eliminated every type of sign, we would be contradicting life and men." There are in fact two types of signs, the indicative sign used by the dogmatists who pretend to identify through appearances things hidden from us by nature, such as the gods and atoms, and the commemorative sign that simply reminds us of something else frequently observed along with what we are actually observing. "There is an observable sequence through which man recalls something else that was observed after, before, or along with what he perceives at a particular moment." In this sense the notion of consequence distinguishes man from the beast.[39]

Thus in philosophy we find traces of some of the practical and positive techniques employed by unrelated arts. As in the case of the Stoics, these independent arts, though not defined as such, were looked upon as an inferior degree of a pseudo-science that had no right to existence.

[37] *Outlines of Pyrrhonism* i. 19–21.
[38] Cf. *Against the Mathematicians* i. 260, and *Outlines of Pyrrhonism* i. 236.
[39] *Letters to Lucilius* 92. 25.

VII *The Renascence of Platonism*

For many reasons, beginning with the second century A.D., Stoicism succumbed to Platonism. First, the change doubtless involved a social factor. Philostratus' fictional *Life of Apollonius of Tyana* (v. 32–35) brings together in the presence of Vespasian the Stoic Euphrates, who as a friend of liberty and democracy advises the emperor to abdicate, and the hero of the book, the Pythagorean and Platonist Apollonius of Tyana, who as a conservative and friend of imperialism sees in the regime the guarantee of prosperity and local liberties. Euphrates, the representative of "philosophy according to nature," is confronted by the representative of the philosophy that lays claim to "divine inspiration." The Neo-Platonists were recruited from the privileged, cultivated classes. Among them there is no place for a slave who might aspire to be a philosopher, no trace of popular success such as that which the Stoic masters had known. The natural setting of Neo-Platonist thought might take several forms: a circle of distinguished men in a small town such as we find in the works of Plutarch of Chaeronea; a closed circle of cultivated men such as Plotinus' school in Rome in the third century; or enlightened pagans who toward the end of the fifth and sixth centuries come together to keep alive the tradition of Hellenism. The refined politeness of the Platonists depicted by Lucian contrasts sharply with the coarseness attributed by him to other philosophers.[40] Here philosophy requires a slow, laborious initiation and, at its highest levels, bears a closer resemblance to confidences to be hidden from the common people than to common-sense truths.

The setting is different, but so is the universe and the conception of destiny. "In such a brief span," says Seneca of the Stoic sage, "he amasses eternal wealth." [41] To the unity of the ethical life, perfectly concentrated within itself, corresponds the vision of a universe which is at each moment necessary and perfect and in which events

[40] *Banquet* chaps. xxxvii–xxxix on Ion the Platonist.
[41] *Letters to Lucilius* 92. 25.

point to a reality that is always the same. The will needs only to relax in order for uneasiness to present itself; then destiny does not seem to be accomplished at each moment but gradually, in the course of time. With this conception of destiny the vision of the universe is transformed, its unity destroyed; for the interdependence of beings is substituted the hierarchy of the forms of being, from the most perfect to the least perfect, through which the soul passes in ascending from a less perfect region to a purer region. The result is the renascence of all the myths concerning the soul, and the universe has the unique role of serving as a theater for their re-enactment.

Platonism is therefore no longer a humanism, that is, a vision of the universe in which man and human action are seen in a social, human setting that is the focal point of philosophical concern. The Stoics held that God had a peculiar relation to man and that man had a purpose in the universe. Quite different is a vision of reality in which the universal order or the world has value in itself and not because it is for the use of rational beings; man as such transfers his pre-eminence to the pure mind into which he seeks to be transformed, that is, the mind that contemplates the universal order. The rational man is in some ways inferior to animals and plants. "Let no one be astounded," says Plutarch, "if irrational beasts follow nature better than rational beings; from this viewpoint, animals are even inferior to plants, to which nature has given neither representation nor inclination to permit deviation against nature." [42]

VIII *Philo of Alexandria*

Clear-cut formulations of Neo-Platonism appear in the writings of Philo of Alexandria (40 B.C.–A.D. 40). He was an influential member of the rich and flourishing Jewish community in Alexandria, and toward the end of his life was a member of the embassy that presented to Caligula the grievances of the community against the Roman governor of Egypt. Greek culture had been assimilated by

[42] *On the Love of Offspring* chap. i.

the community long before; the Bible was read only in Greek translations, and literate young men studied the sciences and Greek philosophy. Here as elsewhere in the Jewish world, however, reading and commenting on the Bible still constituted the basis for speculation. But the Bible was explained just as Homer had long been explained by the Greeks: by the allegorical method. The result was that everything in the Bible became the history of a soul that moved closer to God or farther away from him as it moved toward or away from the body. The first chapter of the Book of Genesis, for example, is from start to finish, according to the Alexandrian interpreters, the account of a purified mind created by God and surrounded by virtues; God fashions in the image of his creation a more terrestrial mind (Adam) and gives it necessary support in the form of sensation (Eve); through the intermediary of sensation mind allows itself to be perverted and depraved by pleasure (the serpent); the rest of the Book of Genesis is the account of the diverse ways through which man again becomes a pure spirit; specifically, the patriarchs signify the three possible modes of man's return: through ascetic training (Jacob), through instruction (Abraham), or through spontaneous and natural grace (Isaac). Through this method Philo brings into his commentary every philosophical theme of his time, and his vast work is a veritable museum in which we find a jumbled assortment of consolatory discourses, diatribes, questions of the type asked by the Stoics (Can the sage become intoxicated?), and parts of lectures on dialectics or physics.

From the amalgam it is nevertheless possible to single out a few ideas. Most important is the idea of a transcendent God who deals with the world only through intermediaries. According to Philo the intermediary is characterized less by its nature than by its function; it is by seeing its purpose that one can determine what it is. It follows that the intermediary is separated into a host of different beings: the son of God, the Logos or Word in whom God sees the model of the world and whom he uses as a model to create the world; the whole series of powers ranging from the beneficent or creative power to the power that punishes and chastises; wisdom

with which he unites himself through a mysterious union to produce the world; and even the fiery or ethereal angels and daimons
that execute divine orders. All these intermediaries are also the
means through which the soul returns to God. The return, which
depends on our awareness of the fragility and nothingness of sensible things (which Philo reveals by utilizing Aenesidemus' tropes),
brings us to God only by virtue of the intermediaries; in this sense
the sage who has arrived at the state of pure spirit and the world
in which the divine order is reflected are both our intermediaries.
In a word, the Philonic method draws together and builds into a
hierarchy every possible form and degree of worship that binds the
soul to God; Abraham, under the name of Abram, was an astrolo-
ger before he attained to a purer form of piety.

Philo's doctrine is not without ambiguity. In it we find all the
piety of a Jew who thinks that God maintains constant, multiple,
and individual relations with man, sustaining him, succoring him,
and punishing him: the Semitic piety which, as we have seen, was
readily adopted by the Stoics. But there is also in his doctrine the
idea of a transcendent God who shares no relation with man, who
is reached only by pure spirits, spirits that have broken loose from
the world and themselves and attained to a state of ecstasy. Thus
we find in the Philonic doctrine the two forms of theology and of
transcendence mentioned above.

Henceforth the great issue in Neo-Platonism and in Neo-Pythag-
oreanism (if we ignore devotion or the relations between man
and God) is that of attaining, in itself and outside any relation between the world and man, the transcendent reality or the intelligible; here again, to a very narrow extent to be sure, we find Hellenism in its purest form. The Stoic theory of the Logos or Word and
of God succoring man, which will reappear among the Christians,
had little importance among the pagans.

IX *The Neo-Pythagoreans*

Pythagoreanism was revived under rather obscure conditions. In the time of Augustus lived the Sextii, whose ethical standards involving self-examination are cited and praised by Seneca.[43] Practical and ascetic ethics also inspired the *Cebetis Tabula,* a moral allegory in which the dominant idea, as in the case of Philo, is that repentance causes man to break away from pleasure. Similar in spirit and impregnated with Platonism are all the Pythagorean fragments preserved by Stobaeus in his *Florilegium.* Mere summaries of Plato's ethics written in the Dorian dialect, their main thought is this: "The man who follows the gods is happy, while the man who follows mortal things is unhappy (103. 26)." To such asceticism are linked precise images concerning the destiny of the soul after death: it ascends once again to heaven from which it descended to animate the body. Such images were prevalent after the first century B.C. For example, we find them among the Jewish community of the Essenes as well as in Plutarch.[44]

Upon the foundation of ascetic morality was raised a fanciful arithmetic that sought to determine the nature of transcendent reality through numbers and their properties. One of the Pythagoreans, Moderatus of Gades, a contemporary of Plutarch, tells us that the theory of matter expounded by Plato in his *Timaeus* was first taught by the Pythagoreans, who transmitted it to Plato. One part of his whimsical account is true: the metaphysical arithmetic of Moderatus is but a numerical translation of Plato's metaphysics, based on a commentary of the *Parmenides.*[45] According to Moderatus, the diverse forms of reality represent diverse degrees of expansion of the primitive One; next to the primal One that transcends being or essence is a second One, real or intelligible being, that is, ideas; then comes a third One, the soul, which participates in ideas; below

---

[43] *Letters to Lucilius* 59, 64 and 73.
[44] Cf. Franz Cumont, *Académie des Inscriptions,* session of May 2, 1936.
[45] See Simplicius *Commentary on the Physics,* ed. Diels, p. 230.

the trinity of Ones is the dyad or matter, which does not participate
in ideas but is shaped in their image. This view of the universe will
become the dominant view of Neo-Platonism. As for numbers,
Moderatus realizes that they provide only a convenient symbolism
and do not penetrate to the essence of things. "Being unable to
transmit the first principles clearly through speech, the Pythagoreans
have recourse to numbers to explain them. *One* is the name chosen
to explain the principle of union or conspiracy, *two* the principle
of alteration, divisibility or change." [46] In short, the Pythagorean
recognizes numbers not as the starting point for an independent
science but as a method of gaining access to non-sensible reality.
Such is the Pythagoreanism described by Moderatus in his commentary on the section in the *Timaeus* on numerical proportions in
the soul.[47] Such is also the Pythagoreanism found so frequently in
the works of Philo, who utilizes the *Timaeus,* and of Nicomachus
of Gerasa in his *Arithmetic Theology.*

x *Plutarch of Chaeronea*

That the works of Plato found growing favor during the first
two centuries A.D. is amply attested. His works, especially the *Timaeus,* are explained in numerous commentaries. One question frequently discussed is this: Is it simply for the sake of expediency
that Plato in his exposition represents the world as begotten rather
than eternal? To refute those who support the interpretation that
Plato actually believed in the eternity of the world, Philo cites
passages in which Plato speaks of God as a father, creator ($\pi o\iota\eta\tau\eta\varsigma$)
or demiurge and also the interpretation given by Aristotle.[48] Plu-
tarch[49] deals instead with the creation of the soul and concludes,
in the same sense, that the soul was created before the body since
the Platonic argument against atheists, which is based on the fact
that the soul exists before the body, would otherwise be invalidated.

[46] Porphyry *Life of Pythagoras* 48–9.
[47] Proclus *Commentary on the Timaeus,* pp. 144 ff.
[48] *On the Incorruptibility of the World* chap. iv.
[49] *On the Production of the Soul according to the Timaeus.*

But the opposite interpretation — that of the eternity of the world — finally won out everywhere except among Christian thinkers acquainted with the *Timaeus*.

Myths concerning destiny were also widely imitated. Plutarch wrote several imitations. In one such myth, souls after death ascend toward heaven, first crossing a celestial Styx and reaching the moon, where those that are neither bad nor impure reside; there follows a second death and, just as the soul had separated from the body on earth, the mind separates from the soul, leaving it on the moon and ascending through the celestial spheres. The same general plan recurs with infinite variations.[50] No trace of a subterranean Hades is to be found in the myths; the world in its entirety serves as a theater for the drama of the soul.

Plutarch's Platonism is linked to a strong national reaction in favor of Greek religious traditions and at the same time to a rather violent criticism of the great post-Aristotelian dogmatisms. In his writings we find, along with an apology for the Delphic oracle, a protestation against the rationalist interpretation of the gods: against both the interpretation that reduces the gods to faculties and passions of the soul and Stoicism that treats them as natural forces.[51] Plutarch is the man who, as theologian, priest, and philosopher all in one, wishes to give up none of the Greek heritage and at the same time to add to it all the wealth of the Egyptian cults of Isis.

XI *Gaius, Albinus, Apuleius, and Numenius*

Several manuscripts have preserved, under the name of Alcinous, an *Introduction to the Dogmas of Plato*. As Freudenthal has shown, the work is actually by Albinus, the Platonist who studied with Gaius in Athens and later (A.D. 152) taught Galen in Smyrna. Sinko, on the other hand, has shown that Apuleius, who lived in Athens around A.D. 140, used the same lectures as Albinus as the basis for his treatise *On the Dogma of Plato* — that is, he relied on the

---

[50] *Concerning the Face which Appears in the Orb of the Moon* (end).
[51] *Amatorius* chap. xii.

teachings of Gaius. Both works show how Gaius contrived to fit Plato's teachings into the traditional frame of logic, physics, and ethics; in them we find an eternal world and a transcendent god whose nature is determined by double negations (neither bad nor good, neither qualified nor unqualified) in the manner of the One in Plato's *Parmenides,* and who is known either through the method of abstraction or through the method of analogy.

From extant fragments of the works of late second-century Platonists — Severus, Atticus, Harpocration, Cronius, and especially Numenius — we can conclude that the broad outlines of the Neo-Platonist representation of the world were firmly established. Numenius wrote a book during the time of the Antonines to refute the thesis of Antiochus, who compared Plato to the Stoics, and to reassert the autonomy of Platonism which, like Philo, he linked to Moses.[52] We know his theory of the three gods: at the summit, supreme mind (or the Good in Itself), creator of the intelligible world; underneath, the demiurge or the creator of the sensible world; and finally the world or the third god. This is merely one interpretation of the *Timaeus.*[53] Through Proclus[54] we also know of Numenius' belief in a celestial Hades and of his description of the arrival and departure of souls.

XII *Renascence of Aristotelianism*

Much less popular than Platonism and much less susceptible of incorporation in the general beliefs of the age, Aristotelianism owes its revival to the preference shown by second-century thinkers for the ancient doctrines. The Peripatetics, since Andronicus, who edited Aristotle's works about 50 B.C., had tended to search for the exact meaning of the master's words rather than to explore nature according to his method. The result was a series of commentaries of which the first, those of Adrastus (during the time of Hadrian)

[52] *On the Difference between the Academicians and Plato,* cited by Eusebius in *Evangelical Preparation* xiv. 5 ff.

[53] In the work *On the Good,* known also through references in Eusebius.

[54] *Commentary on The Republic* ii. 96 (ed. Kroll).

have been lost; the oldest extant commentaries are those of Alexander of Aphrodisias on the *Metaphysics, Prior Analytics, Topics, Sophistical Refutations,* and, finally, *On Sensation* and *Meteorology,* together with the treatises *On the Soul* and *On Fate,* were the subjects of commentaries prepared near the end of the second century B.C. Later the study of Aristotle and his commentators became obligatory in every philosophical school. Frequently the reading of a commentary on Aristotle served as a point of departure for Plotinus (for instance, *Enneads* iv. 6). The result was that even though the Peripatetic school was disappearing in the face of the great success enjoyed by Platonism, commentaries on Aristotle continued to appear until the end of antiquity. The celebrated book by Plotinus' pupil Porphyry, *Isagoge,* widely known in the Middle Ages through Boethius' Latin translation, is an introduction to the study of Aristotle's *Categories.* The best known commentators are Themistius (second half of the fourth century) and especially Simplicius, whose commentaries on the *Categories, Physics,* and the treatise *On the Heavens* contain a wealth of information.[55] These commentaries are loosely connected with others written in Syriac and later in Arabic, with others written by Byzantine commentators linked to Johannes Philoponus (early sixth century), and with still others written in the West, beginning with the thirteenth century.

The unbroken tradition established by the commentaries on Aristotle has a historical importance that can hardly be exaggerated. Through it were transmitted certain methods of posing philosophical problems and certain methods of classifying ideas, and Western thought still reflects its impact. A good illustration is provided by the discussion that began with Theophrastus and continued throughout the Middle Ages concerning the nature of the intellect and of intellectual knowledge as portrayed in an obscure chapter in Aristotle.[56]

[55] The Greek commentaries have been edited by the Academy of Berlin: *Commentaria in Aristotelem graeca, edita consilio et auctoritate Academiae regiae borussicae* (23 vols. and 3 suppls.; Berlin, 1882–1909).

[56] See E. Bréhier, *The Hellenic Age,* trans. Joseph Thomas (Chicago, 1964), p. 217.

According to Themistius, Theophrastus interpreted the master's doctrine in this way: intellectual knowledge is the discovery of intelligible forms enclosed in sensible things by a passive mind that is stimulated to activity by an active mind. He posed the following three difficulties concerning the doctrine: "We do not know whether the passive mind is acquired or inherent; furthermore, we know nothing about its passivity; for if intellectual knowledge has its origin in sensation, the passive mind must receive the action of the body; but how could the passive mind receive action if it is incorporeal? And how could it be the master of thought since nothing can be acted upon by itself? Finally, if a mind is nothing in actuality but everything potentially, in what way does it differ from prime matter? With respect to the eternally actual mind, the difficulties are no less imposing, for we can explain neither its entrance into the soul nor, if it is inherent in the soul, the occurrence of forgetting, error, and deceit." [57]

Through Alexander of Aphrodisias[58] we know how Aristocles, his master, tried to resolve such difficulties. The solution was suggested to him by the Stoics (for a long time people confused Aristocles and Aristotle, and the matter was obscured even more by the fact that the ideas of the former were attributed to the latter). Aristocles first grants that what Aristotle calls the material or potential mind is a mind that evolves naturally with age, like all our other faculties, and permits us to engage in the activity of abstraction. This activity, which is inherent in the soul, is nevertheless possible only by virtue of an intellect that has its source outside the soul: pure thought or divine mind which is spread throughout matter, like a substance within a substance, and which penetrates everything and resides in every conceivable body. When the actual mind finds a favorable corporeal mixture, it acts through it as through an instrument, and we are said to be thinking. Our material or potential mind, like all our other faculties, is then but a

[57] According to Themistius *In de anima paraphrasis,* ed. R. Heinze (Berlin, 1899), pp. 117, 310 ff.

[58] *De anima liber* (ed. J. Bruns), pp. 110 ff. But compare P. Moraux, *Alexandre d'Aphrodise exégète de la noétique d'Aristote* (Liège and Paris, 1942).

certain organic combination which can serve as the instrument of thought.

Aristocles' theory provides an answer to Theophrastus' objections, but Alexander thinks that it deviates too far from the master's theory. He therefore proceeds to identify four minds or intellects. The first is potential or hylic mind, which is the capacity to receive forms. It is analogous to a blank tablet or rather to "the character that it has of being blank," and it differs from prime matter in that it does not become this or that particular thing and is not acted upon like matter. The second is acquired intellect or intellect as a disposition created when the forms of matter are separated through abstraction and the universal apprehended. It is the totality of the thoughts that are always at our disposition, just as the knowledge possessed by the scholar is always at his disposition even though he does not actually think about it at all times. Finally, actual intellect is actual thought in which the subject is identical with its object.

The three intellects already mentioned described the three phases of intellectual activity, from potency to disposition and from disposition to act. The fourth is the active mind, the principle that makes potential mind become actual. It must as a consequence be intelligible in actuality by virtue of its own nature, separate and without mixture. In the active mind Alexander no longer recognizes a faculty of the soul but the pure act, the thought of thought — in a word, Aristotle's God. God within us is the agent responsible for the operation of our intellect. Ours is not the vision of God but rather, we might say, vision through God. Thanks to Alexander, in the case of the Peripatetics as well as the Platonists, meditation on the nature of intellectual knowledge and its object brings us not to science but to theology.

Bibliography

Texts

Musonii Rufi fragmenta ostendit O. Hense. Teubner edition. 1905.

Seneca. *Editio princeps of prose works,* 1475; T. F. Gronovius, 1649–58; Ruhkopf, 1797–1811; F. Haase, 1852, 1872–98.

Epictetus. Works edited by J. Schweighäuser (5 vols., 1799–1800) and by H. Schenkl (1894, new edition, 1916). Text with English translation by W. A. Oldfather, Loeb Library, 1926.

Marcus Aurelius. Critical edition of *Meditations* by J. Stich. Teubner edition. Leipzig, 1882. 2d edition, 1903.

Philo of Alexandria. Works edited by T. Mangey (2 vols., London, 1742); L. Cohn, P. Wendland, and S. Reiter (7 vols., Berlin, 1896–1930); and F. H. Colson and G. H. Whitaker (9 vols., with English translation, Loeb Series, London, 1929 *et seq.*).

Plutarch of Chaeronea. *Editio princeps* by H. Stephanus, 1572. Complete editions by J. J. Reiske, 1774–1782; J. G. Hutten, 1791–1804; T. Döhner and F. Dübner, 1846–1855. Loeb edition of *Lives,* with English translalation. 11 vols. 1914–1926. See also *Roman Questions,* edited by P. Holland. London, 1892; and *The Roman Questions of Plutarch,* text and commentary, edited by H. J. Rose, Oxford, 1924.

Albinus. *Epitome,* edited with French translation by P. Louis. Paris, 1945. See also H. Cary *et al., The Works of Plato.* Vol. VI, 1852.

Alexander of Aphrodisia. The Greek commentaries on Aristotle have been edited by the Academy of Berlin. Alexander's works are printed in Vols. I–III and in Vol. II of the supplement in *Commentaria in Aristotelem Graeca.* 23 vols. and 3 suppls. Berlin, 1882–1909.

Studies

I, II

F. Robiou. *De l'Influence du stoïcisme à l'époque des Flaviens et des Antonins.* Rennes, 1852.

G. Boissier. *La Fin du paganisme.* 2 vols. Paris, 1891.

Denis. *Historie des théories et des idées morales dans l'antiquité.* Paris, 1856.

T. Zielinski. "Science grecque et science romaine," *Scientia,* XXVII (January, 1933).

F. Cumont. *Lux perpetua.* Paris, 1949.

J. Gagé. "La propagande sérapiste et la lutte des empereurs flaviens avec les philosophes (Stoïciens et Syniques)," *Revue philosophique* (1959), pp. 73–100.

III

B. C. Martha. *Les Moralistes sous l'Empire romain*. Paris, 1894. — *Etudes morales sur l'antiquité*. Paris, 1889.
R. Waltz. *La Vie politique de Sénèque*. Paris, 1909.
E. Albertini. *La Composition dans les ouvrages philosophiques de Sénèque*. Paris, 1923.
F. Préchac. "Sénèque, lecture royale sous le dernier Valois," *Bulletin Budé* (March, 1950), pp. 185–205.

IV

L. Weber. "La Morale d'Epictète et les besoins présents de l'enseignement moral," *Revue de Métaphysique* (1905).
A. Bonhoeffer. *Epiktet und die Stoa*. Stuttgart, 1890. — *Die Ethik des Stoïkers Epiktet*. Stuttgart, 1894 — *Epiktet und das neue Testament*. Giessen, 1911.
J. Bruns. *De Schola Epicteti*. Kiel, 1897.
T. Collardeau. *Etude sur Epictète*. Paris, 1903.
V. Courdaveaux (trans.). *Les Entretiens d'Epictète*. Paris, 1908.
Souilhe (trans.). *Les Entretiens*. Paris (Budé Collection).
A. Jagu. *Epictète et Platon*. Paris, 1946.
B. L. Hymans. Ἄσκησις. *Notes on Epictetus' Educational System*. Assen, 1959.

V

E. Renan. *Marcus Antoninus et la fin du monde antique*. Paris, 1882. Eng. tran. by W. P. Dickson. London, 1886.
J. Stich (ed.). *Meditations*. Teubner edition. Leipzig, 1882. 2d edition, 1903.
Pensées de Marc-Aurèle. Translated by Couat. Bordeaux, 1904. Also edited and translated by Trannoy. Budé Collection. Paris, 1925.

VI

V. Brochard. *Les Sceptiques grecs*. Paris, 1887. 2d edition, 1923.
Goedeckemeyer. *Die Geschichte des griechischen Skepticimus*. Leipzig, 1905.
L. Robin. *Pyrrhon et le scepticisme grec*. Paris, 1944.
Sextus Empiricus. *Oeuvres Choisies,* translated by J. Grenier and G. Goron. Paris, 1948.
E. Bréhier. "Les tropes d'Enésidème," *Revue des Etudes anciennes*, XX (1918), 69 ff.; and *Etudes de Philosophie ancienne* (1955), p. 185.

K. Deichgraeber. *Die griechische Empirikerschule.* Berlin, 1930.

M. dal Pra. *Lo scetticismo greco.* Milan, 1950.

J. Grenier. "L'exigence d'intelligibilité du sceptique grec," *Revue philosophique* (1957), p. 357.

VIII

Philo. *Allégories des Saintes Lois.* Edited and translated by E. Bréhier. Paris, 1908.

E. Bréhier. *Les Idées philosophiques et religieuses de Philon d'Alexandrie.* Paris, 1907. 2d edition, 1924.

Philo. *La migration d'Abraham.* Translated by R. Cadiou. Paris, 1957. Also editions by Wendland and by Colson-Whitaker (Loeb Series, London, 1939).

E. R. Goodenough. *By Light, Light.* New Haven, 1935. — *The Politics of Philo Judaeus, Practice and Theory.* New Haven, 1938. — *An Introduction to Philo Judaeus.* New Haven, 1940. 2d ed. Oxford, 1962.

H. Wolfson. *Philo.* Cambridge, Mass., 1948.

J. Daniélou. *Philon d'Alexandrie.* Paris, 1958.

IX

J. Carcopino. *Etudes Romaines,* vol. I. *La basilique pythagoricienne de la Porte majeure.* Paris, 1926. — *De Pythagore aux apôtres.* Paris, 1956.

X

B. Latzarus. *Les Idées religieuses de Plutarque.* Paris, 1920.

E. R. Volkmann. *Leben, Schriften und Philosophie des Plutarch von Chaeronaea.* Berlin, 1869, 1873.

O. Gréard. *De la Morale de Plutarque.* Paris, 1865.

E. Guimet. *Plutarque et l'Egypte.* Paris, 1898.

Plutarch. *Dialogues.* Edited by R. Flacelière. Paris, 1937–1947. — *Sur les oracles de la Pythie.* Paris, 1937 — *Sur l'E de Delphes.* Paris, 1941. — *Sur la disparition des oracles.* Paris, 1947. Cf. *Le Banquet des Sept Sages,* edited by Defradas, Paris, 1954; and *De la musique,* edited by F. Lasserre, Olten and Lausanne, 1954.

D. Babut. *Plutarque et le stoïcisme* (in preparation).

XI

Freudenthal. *Hellenistische Studien.* 1879. III, p. 322.

T. Sinko. *De Apulaei et Albini doctrinae platonicae adumbratione* (Dissertat. philol. Acad. litt. Cracov., XLI, 129). Cracow, 1905.

P. Vallette. *L'Apologie d'Apulée.* Paris, 1908.

P. Monceaux. *Apulée, roman et magie.* Paris, 1888. — *Les Africains; étude sur la littérature latine d'Afrique. Les Païens.* Paris, 1894.

R. Le Corre. "Le prologue d'Albinus," *Revue philosophique* (1956), p. 28.

C.-J. de Vogel. *La théorie de l'intellect d'après Aristote et ses commentateurs.* Edited by Barbotin. Paris, 1953.

O. Hamelin. "La théorie de l'ἄπειρον chez Platon et dans la tradition platonicienne," *Revue philosophique* (1959), p. 21.

XII

Paul Moraux. *Alexandre d'Aphrodise exégète de la noétique d'Aristote.* Liège and Paris, 1942.

P. Thillet. *Le De fato d'Alexandre d'Aphrodise* (in preparation).

Works in English

N. Bentwich. *Philo-Judaeus of Alexandria.* Philadelphia, 1910.

T. H. Billings. *The Platonism of Philo Judaeus.* Chicago, 1919.

F. W. Bussell. *Marcus Aurelius and the Later Stoics.* Edinburgh, 1910.

J. Drummond. *Philo Judaeus.* 2 vols. London, 1888.

H. Kennedy. *Philo's Contribution to Religion.* London, 1919.

R. Marchu. "Recent Literature on Philo (1924-1934)," *Jewish Studies in Memory of G. A. Kohut* (New York, 1935).

Marcus Aurelius. *The Meditations of the Emperor Marcus Aurelius.* Edited with trans. and commentary by A. Farquharson. 2 vols. Oxford, 1944.

Seneca. *The Stoic Philosophy of Seneca,* trans. and intro. by M. Hadas. Garden City, N. Y., 1958. *Seneca's Letters to Lucilius,* trans. by E. P. Barker. Oxford, 1932.

H. D. Sedgwick. *Marcus Aurelius.* New Haven, 1921.

P. B. Watson. *M. Aurelius Antoninus.* New York, 1884.

R. E. Witt. *Albinus and the History of Middle Platonism.* Cambridge, 1937.

H. Wolfson. *Philo: Foundations of Religious Philosophy in Judaism, Christianity and Islam.* 2 vols. Cambridge, Mass., 1947.

NEO-PLATONISM

As WE have already seen, Neo-Platonism is essentially a means of approaching an intelligible reality and a construction or description of this reality. Our worst mistake would be to believe that the main function of the intelligible reality is to explain the sensible world rather than to enable us to return to the One or the Good beyond being. In Neo-Platonism what matters most is passage from a sphere where knowledge and happiness are impossible to one where they are possible, and the resemblance that permits passage from one sphere to the other (the sensible world is the image of the intelligible world) is important not so much because it explains our world as because it makes possible our return to the supreme source of being. The gods, according to the ancient myths, are indifferent to the world of men; in the same way Plotinus' intelligible reality remains aloof and is not acquainted with our world. His view, subtilized to the extreme, is the mythological view.

During the third century and the two following centuries, paganism made an attempt to seize the structure and articulations of intelligible reality. The philosophy of the age is in a sense a description of the metaphysical landscapes through which the soul is transported as it undergoes what might be described as spiritual training.

One of the initiators of Neo-Platonism was Ammonius Saccas, who taught at Alexandria, at least from 232 to 243, and who revealed the true meaning of philosophy to Plotinus, then aged twenty-eight. We have but scant information about him: he wrote nothing, and aside from Plotinus, his only known disciples were the philologist Longinus, Herennius, and a man named Origen who cannot be positively identified with the Christian writer by the same name, even though he belongs to the same period. Nothing is known about what was taught in his school. Not until the fifth century do we hear the ideas of Ammonius mentioned (by Nemesius and Hierocles), and there is no definite proof that even here the reference is to Ammonius Saccas. It is therefore impossible for us to identify the role of his beloved master in the intellectual development of Plotinus.

1 *Plotinus*

Plotinus (205–270), the pupil of Ammonius from 232 to 243, left him to accompany the emperor Gordian on his expedition against the Persians. In 245 he was in Rome, where he remained until his death. There he was surrounded by enthusiastic disciples, among them Porphyry, who was his secretary. It was at the insistence of his disciples, it seems, that he decided belatedly (255) to write and to publish. He wrote hastily and without revising, entrusting to Porphyry the task of making necessary corrections. Such was the origin of the fifty-four treatises composed according to the sequence indicated by Porphyry in his *Life of Plotinus* and arranged by him, after Plotinus' death, in one comprehensive work consisting of six *Enneads* or groups of nine. The treatises seem to reproduce faithfully his oral instruction. They do not give a consistent, progressive explanation of his doctrine but are rather a series of lectures in which are elucidated particular points: the worth of astrology, the way in which the soul descends into the body and is united with it, and the problem of memory in different kinds of souls ranging from the human soul to the world soul. Each point is studied as a function of a constant and comprehensive vision of the universe.

Such a vision of the universe is not peculiar to Plotinus. We saw it emerge vaguely in Posidonius when he identified and classified the concepts of the Old Stoa: God, fate, nature. We saw it clearly outlined in Moderatus' theory of the triple unity. What is its explanation? We saw how the Stoics (whose thesis is explicitly adopted by Plotinus) insisted that the degree of reality of beings — ranging from the pile of stones whose parts are simply juxtaposed to the living being whose parts are all held together by the soul's tension and even to a collective body such as a chorus or an army — depended on the degree of unity between their parts. We can conceive of a unity that increases to the point where the parts of a being fuse and become almost inseparable. For instance, we cannot speak in the same sense of the parts of a living body and of the parts of a science; in a living body the parts are solidary but are locally separated, whereas in a science a part is a theorem and each theorem contains potentially every other theorem. Thus we see how an additional degree of unification takes us from the corporeal to the spiritual.

But every imperfect reality or union of parts implies a more complete unity beyond itself. Mutual sympathy between the parts of a living body or the parts of the world implies a superior, more perfect unity, namely the unity of the soul that contains the parts, and the theorems that constitute a science by their unity imply the unity of a mind that apprehends them. In the absence of the higher unity everything disperses, crumbles, and loses its being. Nothing is other than through the One. Aristotle was wrong in saying that being and the One are always interchangeable, for in reality being is always subordinated to the One, which is the principle of being. But there is one condition: the higher unity must not be purely formal and empty but must contain all the reality that will evolve through it. For example, every single detail of a living body is contained in the soul as a set of inseparable seminal principles, and nothing can exist in the absence of the soul. The condition posited by Plotinus suggests the importance of the method through which he pursues intelligibility: that of explaining a particular aspect of reality by relating it to a more perfect unity.[1]

[1] *Enneads* vi. 9.

Plotinus nevertheless abandons entirely the Stoic theory whose formulas he sometimes uses. It will be recalled that according to the Stoics unification was due to an activity characteristic of the agent that penetrated matter and through its tension held together its parts. Plotinus holds that any unity is always more or less like the unity of a science. In a science the mind is one because it contemplates one and the same object; what introduces unity into the lower reality is the contemplation of the higher principle.[2] Saying that the One is the principle of being is then the same as saying that the only true reality is contemplation. Not only is mind contemplation of its object, but also nature is contemplation — tacit, silent, unconscious contemplation — of the intelligible model that it strives to imitate. An animal, a plant, or just any object has its form (in the Aristotelian sense) only to the degree that it contemplates the ideal model reflected in it. Thus the higher principle remains in its own place, immobile, undiminished, and unimpaired; no part of itself or of its activity passes into the lower reality since it acts, like things of beauty, only by filling things with its light and its reflection according to the capacity of each to receive them.

Still, to understand clearly his system we must keep in mind the fixed image of a unique cosmos — a finite, eternal cosmos with an order always identical to itself — which obsessed Plotinus and all his contemporaries, for only in the light of this image does his metaphysical doctrine make sense. The datum is the unity of the sensible world, and all intelligible realities on which it depends are but the same world, shrunken and to some degree dematerialized. The whole metaphysical system of Plotinus loses much of its meaning unless we accept, along with the oneness of the world, its unity, the sympathy of its parts, its eternity, and geocentrism.[3]

The first of Plotinus' principles or hypostases is the indivisible One or the First of all being. It is nothing since there is in it nothing distinct, and it is all since it is the potency of all things. It is

[2] *Ibid*. iii. 8.
[3] *Ibid*. ii. 1.

like the One in Plato's *Parmenides*; we can at one breath attribute all qualities to it and at the next deny it has any qualities at all. In fact, it is from the *Parmenides* that Plotinus borrows the principle of his theory of the One; but he borrows also from the sixth book of the *Republic,* and the One is also the Good since it gives being to each being. It is itself "beyond essence" since to be, according to Plato, is necessarily to be something. The First, the Good, or the One is a hypostasis, not an essence or a substance. The word hypostasis signifies any existent, whether determined or not; the word essence or substance (οὐσία) also designates an existent or a hypostasis, but an existent determined by positive attributes and in possession of a form. That is why care must be exercised to avoid mistaking the attributes of First, One, or Good for positive properties or forms of the One. They are terms that may be applied to subordinate hypostases. It is First because prior to any other reality, One as a unifying principle, Good in the sense of an end; but such expressions do not express what it is since in a strict sense it is nothing, not even one, not even a good, nothing but a superessential nothingness.[4]

Why does not this One remain unique? Why does not reality remain eternally shrunken? The reason is that any perfect thing, like a living being that has achieved maturity, produces its likeness — unconsciously, involuntarily, as a spring discharges a stream of excess water or as a light diffuses its rays. The living being, the spring, the light lose nothing as they expand, and they retain the fullness of their reality. This has been called (on the basis of a traditional but not wholly appropriate metaphor) the theory of emanation, but it would be better to follow the practice of Plotinus and to speak of the *procession,* production, or advancement of something derived from a principle. But each derived being seeks to remain as close as possible to the source from which it receives the fullness of its reality, and almost as soon as it begins its procession, it turns backward in order to contemplate its source. *Retroversion* or the act of turning backward gives birth (an eternal and non-temporal

[4] *Ibid.* vi. 9; v. 1. 6; vi. 8.

birth, of course) to the second hypostasis, which is at once Being, Mind, and Intelligible World.[5]

The systematic unity of Plotinian thought should not be exaggerated in the description of the second hypostasis, which can be viewed from different angles. First, as it appears in the intelligible world, it is the One somewhat expanded and multiplied: reality, indistinct in the One, is diffused as a hierarchical multiplicity of genera and species that emerge through a sort of dialectic (Platonic division) and spiritual motion, starting from the highest genera. It must be clearly understood that the motion is eternally completed, that the hierarchy of intelligibles is eternally fixed, and that only our thought moves as it ascends the hierarchy.[6] Care must also be exercised to guard against exaggerating the multiplicity of the intelligible world. In such a systematic unity each being contains every other being and everything is contained by everything. Plotinus reminds us that Platonic dialectic does not proceed through additions, like Aristotelian logic, and simply adding specific differences in order to define the species; it proceeds instead through division, and this means that the genus is a concrete whole selected for division into species in much the same way that we might divide the world into sky and sublunar regions. Progression from genus to species is not an enrichment but rather a passing from the whole to parts which still preserve the richness of the whole.[7]

One important consequence issues from Plotinus' line of reasoning. The Aristotelian intelligible designated only genera and species, and the individual realized in the sensible world therefore contained all the characteristics of its specific form, to which were added an indeterminate number of other characteristics attributable to its realization in matter and responsible for its true individuality. It is possible to think "man" but not "Socrates," whose individuality is attributable to the myriad accidents that have befallen the specific form of man during his realization. Thus according to Aristotle,

[5] *Ibid*. v. 1. 6; v. 2; v. 3. 13 ff.; v. 4.
[6] *Ibid*. iv. 1–2.
[7] *Ibid*. i. 3; iii. 2. 1–2; v. 9.

in certain respects the sensible world would be greater than the intelligible world! Plotinus holds on the contrary that the individual exists in the intelligible world, or that there are "ideas of individuals." [8] Plotinus does not concede in any general way that form must receive additional positive characteristics — for example, defensive organs or sense organs that are of use to the sensible animal but not to the intelligible animal — when realized in the sensible being. One might ask: "Why does the intelligible lion need claws since he does not have to defend himself? Why does the living intelligible being need sense organs in a region where there is nothing sensible?" To such questions he replies: "In order that everything may be, in order that the intelligible world may contain all possible richness." Sensation in the living material being is not, as the Stoics say, a simple impression of matter on matter; it retains something spiritual and immaterial that guarantees its intelligible origin. And Plotinus refuses to explain the production of the sense organs by a happy coincidence, an attentive providence, or anything of the kind. For him they are but a degraded imitation of a higher reality.[9]

The second hypostasis is therefore a veritable world, complete and perfect, and not simply an abstract diagram of the sensible world.

The second hypostasis is also being or essence, that is, the concrete or positive content that makes a thing an object of knowledge. The first hypostasis was above being and had to be denied any positive characteristic; the second is being itself, that is, everything that causes reality to have a form that makes it knowable.

Finally, the second hypostasis is mind. Plotinus here introduces changes that astonished his contemporaries, particularly Porphyry at the time of his entrance into the school. Mind is that which knows being or essence. Now it would seem that we make a distinction between being or the known intelligible and the knowing mind: between being that is actual reality and mind whose poten-

[8] *Ibid.* v. 7.
[9] *Ibid.* vi. 7. 1–2.

tialities are actualized when it apprehends being. Platonism even forces us to posit the intelligible before mind, whereas Aristotle and Anaxagoras, unable to define the intelligible, discard it and take as their principle mind. If a Platonist accepted mind as the second principle, this was because he posited the intelligible as the first principle just as did Plato, who in the *Timaeus* described the mind of the demiurge contemplating, outside itself and above itself, the ideal models of which things are imitations. But Plotinus breaks with this tradition. Appropriating for his own use Aristotle's well-known formula, "In science the known thing is identical to the knowing subject," he refuses to grant that intelligibles are outside mind. He is probably faithful to Plato when he posits above mind a transcendent reality contemplated by mind, but his reality, which is the One, is no longer the intelligible. Why such a profound change? We should first recall that if the *Timaeus* subordinated the demiurgic mind to ideal models, the *Republic* in turn made the Good the common principle of the knowing agent and the known subject, just as the sun is the common principle of visible things and visual sensation; mind and the intelligible, the knowing agent and the known subject, are accordingly on the same level. Thus Plotinus, too, pretended to follow Plato. But above and beyond this, the contrary thesis seems to him to introduce into philosophy all the difficulties of the theory of knowledge of the post-Aristotelian dogmatists. If the intelligible were outside mind, then we would have to imagine a mind which is devoid of actual thought and on which intelligibles are impressed on impact, just as sensible things are impressed on the sense organs; this mind would be imperfect, unable eternally to apprehend its object, unable to attain to certainty with respect to the object of which it would possess only an image. The hypostatic Mind must therefore discover in itself all the richness of the intelligible world. Self-knowledge gives it not only categorical certainty of its existence (like the Augustinian or Cartesian *cogito*) but also certainty of its content. Here its knowledge has its end, just as it has its beginning.[10]

[10] *Ibid*. v. 5. 1–2; iii. 8. 8.

Here, too, it would seem that Plotinus achieves unity in his speculations concerning the second hypostasis: Mind is vision of the One and, for this very reason, self-knowledge and knowledge of the intelligible world. The intelligible world must not be visualized as an inert being which is not at the same time a thought. We must remember that being is contemplation. The most profound conception of the world that can be formulated is this: it is a society of intellects or rational minds, each of which contemplates all others as it contemplates itself, with the result that all minds form but a single Intellect or unique Mind.

As the One produces Mind, so Mind produces a third hypostasis which is Soul. The Plotinian theory of the soul is still more complex than the theory of Mind. To grasp clearly its significance we must do as Plotinus constantly does and contrast Aristotle's theory of the soul with the not wholly discordant speculations of the Platonists and Stoics. Here we have what seemed at the time to be one of the main points of disagreement between Aristotle and Plato. Aristotle in a sense expunged the soul from his image of the universe; the primary moving principles of the heavens are minds; the soul appears only in living sublunar bodies, as bodily form, and is a wholly intellectual concept formulated by a physiologist in search of the principle of corporeal functions; the soul as the seat of destiny has disappeared. Against this the *Phaedrus, Timaeus,* and *Laws* as well as the Stoics offer a universal soul that rules the sensible world; individual souls — the souls of stars and the souls of men — are consubstantial with it and are but fragments of it. Here we have not a difference in terminology but a radically different conception of the universe and destiny. In the first place the universe is envisioned as a living being, and consequently the general motions within it (the circular motions of the stars) are due, not to the peculiar quality of a quintessence whose nature it is to move in circles, but to the influence of a soul that rules the fiery elements which constitute the sky, making it go against its own nature and execute instead the circular motion, the turning backward upon itself, which is in imitation of its own motion.[11] Nothing horrifies the Platonist so much as the Aristotelian quintessence, for as a defender of the substantial unity of the cosmos and the sympathy of its parts, he rightly sees in it the negation of his thesis. The Platonist also has a radically different conception of destiny: individual souls govern details just as the universal soul governs the operation of all things, and their destinies are accordingly a part of the total plan. Plotinus chooses to develop the old image of the diatribes: the world is a theater in which providence assigns to each his role.[12]

Only by keeping in mind Plotinus' vision of the world and his conception of the cosmic function of souls can we understand the nature of his third hypostasis. For the soul is but the intelligible world, further divided and further expanded, though still not diluted in a material way. This is true because it has the property of being entirely in every part of the living body that it animates[13] and at the same time of exerting its influence in space by delineating the divisions of the world, like the universal soul in the *Timaeus*. Soul is in a word the intermediary between the intelligible world and the sensible world. It proceeds from the first, turning back toward it to contemplate it eternally, and it shapes and organizes the second. Still, the two functions differ only in appearance since in reality, as we shall see, the soul organizes only because it contemplates, though an influence that emanates from it spontaneously; it is as if figures conceived by a geometrician could take shape independently.[14] Soul does not have an active, providential function to accompany its contemplative function; purely contemplative and aloof, it acts.

With the triad of hypostases the series of divine realities impervious to evil comes to an end. Does the triad constitute a theology? Plotinus never pronounces the name of God (except in a dubious

[11] *Ibid.* ii. 2; ii. 1.
[12] *Ibid.* iii. 2 and 3.
[13] *Ibid.* vi. 4 and 5.
[14] Description of the action of nature, *Enneads* iii. 8. 4.

text) in connection with the first principle. The word appears frequently in his writings only in connection with the ruling souls of the world or of the stars; for him only these are rightly called gods, and he speaks of them in his defense of Hellenic polytheism. Furthermore, Plotinus took pains to separate religious practices from speculations on principles. He speaks at length of astrological divination, of prayer, and of the worship of statues in order to show that the efficacy of religious practices, which he does not deny, results not from the action of a god on the world in response to such practices (as if the blissful stars could concern themselves with human follies) but from the sympathy that binds together the parts of the world: any act of worship is like an incantation that produces its effect so long as it is well executed. Between religion that tends to become mere ritual and the soul's access to intelligible realities, there is no connection. It is important to note in this context the degree to which his theory of hypostases differs from the Philonian theory of intermediaries with which it is often wrongly compared. The Philonian intermediary, the Word that punishes or rewards, in a certain sense anticipates the needs of the human soul and has as its sole concern the welfare of man; the Plotinian hypostasis has no desire to do good, no intention of saving men. Here again we see the opposition, which manifests itself in countless forms, between Semitic devotion and Hellenic intellectualism. With Plotinus each hypostasis is but a higher degree of contraction or unification of the world, and the highest degree is absolute unity.

Still, there is one restriction: in the One, the ineffable reality devoid of positive characters, Plotinus discerns an infinitude and an indetermination that make it something other than the simple abstract principle of the world's unity. In the treatise that he wrote *On the Freedom and the Will of the One* (vi. 8), we see the emergence in the ultimate Principle of a positive and independent life. It is not only the independence (αὐτάρκεια) possessed by the intelligible world or the sensible world, that is, the faculty of being self-sufficient without having recourse to anything external (this is the independence of an essence, but the world is bound to its own essence and cannot relinquish it); the independence of the ultimate Principle is absolute freedom: the fact of being able to be whatever it wishes without being bound to any essence; of being able to undergo metamorphosis indefinitely without stopping at any form. Here we have something new and something not found in Plato, who had spoken of a supreme principle, which was limit, measure, and fixed ratio and which as a consequence was always viewed in relation to the order of which it was the principle. Plotinus' infinite One is absolute freedom: reality that is what it is through itself, with respect to itself, and for itself.[15] Platonism characteristically makes ultimate reality independent of the Forms through which the mind defines being, but with the result that it can be reached only through methods independent of intellectual methods since the intellect can deal only with definite, limited being.

Below the triad of divine hypostases Plotinus posits still another hypostasis: matter. Whereas Aristotle defines matter in terms of form and always makes it something relative, Plotinus makes it an absolute reality. Whereas Aristotle considers matter (except for prime matter) as indeterminate only with respect to a form (bronze with respect to a statue) even though it can be determinate in itself, Plotinus recognizes only completely indeterminate — and even indeterminable — matter. This is because form does not make matter more determinate through its mode of existence in matter; when form departs, matter is left as indeterminate as it was before its discovery. Matter is impassive and impoverished; it is the absolute poverty of the myth in the *Banquet*. There is accordingly no true union between form and matter but rather a fleeting reflection of form in matter, and the reflection affects matter no more than light affects the air that it fills.[16]

The incapacity for receiving, possessing, and preserving form and order, the impossibility of saying *I* and having a positive attribute, is evil in itself and is the root of all the evils that exist in the sensible world. The fact is that evil is not a simple imperfection, for if it were, then we would have to say that Mind is bad since it is inferior to the One. Vice, foibles, everything that seems to be bad in itself is an evil only because the soul has come into contact with matter and is immersed in becoming as a result of this contact; it achieves purity not by dominating matter but by fleeing from matter. If matter nevertheless exists, this is because every degree of reality must be exhausted; it is not independent of the One but is its last reflection, before the total darkness of nothingness.[17]

In Plotinus' account of the origin of evil we find two distinct theodicies. In the theodicy just outlined, evil is matter and the sensible existent is a reflection in a reflection; one can escape from evil by returning to realities. The second theodicy is developed in his later writings and is quite different from the first: the logos or reason, which is a principle of harmony, impartially rules the world, and each being in the world has a place and a role that make it contribute to the harmony of the whole; each being suffers or endures whatever is appropriate in its case, and its suffering (like that of the tortoise that moves too slowly to escape the advancing chorus and is trod upon) may be an evil for it, if considered in isolation and apart from the whole, but not for the universe.[18] Here we see two disparate theses: on the one hand a pessimistic theodicy that accepts as a remedy for evil nothing short of flight from the world into supersensible reality, and on the other a progressive and optimistic theodicy that accepts the Stoic remedy of voluntary assent. But are the two theses contradictory?

The ugliness of the sensible world, which is fleeting, evanescent, and indeterminate in contrast to the beauty of the cosmos, which is ordered, harmonious, and ruled by eternal laws: such is the asceticism of the *Phaedo* in contrast to the admiration expressed in the *Timaeus* for the art of the demiurge. The two attitudes are distinct but not contradictory, for they correspond to the dissociation of the sensible world into its real factors; we look downward on the one

[17] *Ibid*. i. 8.
[18] *Ibid*. iii. 2 and 3.

hand toward the indetermination of matter and upward on the other toward the universal soul and the supersensible region. The beauty that we admire in a thing, said Plotinus in his first treatise *On Beauty* (i. 6), is not a simple arrangement of the parts of a particular thing but the reflection of a supersensible idea; consequently, it is the intelligible world which we actually admire in the sensible world and to which we gain access through a necessary dialectic that separates order from disorder.

This distinction will facilitate comprehension of the difficult question of the destiny of individual souls. We recall that Plotinus assumes that all souls are characterized by a certain unity inasmuch as all are derived from the supreme Mind. The universal soul has prepared for each soul an abode which corresponds to its nature and which it must govern during the time set by the order of things. The soul governs the body, as we recall, only because it contemplates the intelligible order; turned back toward the intelligible world and through its retroversion being itself mind, the soul maintains contact with mind while its reflection illuminates and vivifies the body. But because the bond between souls is slacker than the bond between minds, the soul can turn around toward its reflection and, instead of contemplating its model, see its own reflection. Like Narcissus, who was attracted by his own image and drowned in the attempt to embrace it, the soul rushes toward its reflection and falls prey to the changes of the sensible world; from this time onward it is subjected to myriad anxieties relating to its body and the false goods that elude it. Such is the *descent* of the soul, and its destiny in the future life depends, through a kind of immanent justice, on the sin committed through its descent.[19]

The aim of philosophical education is the restoration of the soul to its original state of contemplation. Here we come to a complex doctrine that can be clearly understood only on the basis of a distinction between the soul and the self. In reality the order of the world implies that the intellectual part of the soul (the part that contemplates mind) is eternally turned backward toward the intelligible

[19] *Ibid.* iv. 9; iv. 3. 2–8; iv. 8; iv. 3. 9–10.

world since from the soul's contemplation is derived the very existence of the body that it governs. My self descends toward the reflection projected by my soul instead of remaining at the level of my
own mind; the self is the intermediate soul which is between the
intellectual soul and its reflection and which can go now toward
one, now toward the other, while the higher part of the soul remains aloft. Destiny and history can influence the rigidly structured world of Plotinus only if what he often calls the soul, and
what we call the self, passes from one region to another. The destiny of the soul (or the self) is the change that takes place within
it when it is successively impregnated with all the metaphysical
landscapes through which it passes.[20]

Each level of reality is matched by a way of life open to the soul.
At the lowest level is life in the sensible world, in the form of either
a life of pleasure in which the soul is completely passive or an active life in which standards are set by the social virtues that govern
action. Higher up is the reflective life in which the soul communes
with itself, reasoning and passing judgment; it is pre-eminently at
the intermediate level that the soul is its own master. Going beyond
discursive thought that proceeds through demonstration, the soul
reaches intuitive or intellectual thought and rises to the level of
mind, that is, to the level of essences that presuppose nothing
higher and are intuitive data. But the soul can at times go even
higher, up to the ultimate Principle, in which case intellectual vision
or intuition plays no part since only what is determinate can be apprehended. Here we are dealing rather with an ineffable type of
contact in which we cannot even speak of a knowing subject and
a known object, in which the duality itself vanishes and unification is complete, and in which knowledge matters less than enjoyment. Only those who have experienced the state can give testimony
of it, but they are few in number and their experiences rare. Plotinus is reported by Porphyry to have said that he reached such a
state only four times. Furthermore, those who have experienced it
can speak of it only from memory since at the moment of experi-

[20] *Ibid.* 8. 8.

encing it they lose all awareness of themselves. Superior to mind and thought, the state of ecstasy is the highest degree to which we can attain.[21]

II *Neo-Platonism and Oriental Religions*

Neo-Platonism had a very complex history during the two and one-half centuries that followed the death of Plotinus, both because of his doctrines, which were often given conflicting interpretations by the numerous teachers who interpreted them, and because of religious and political factors.

With respect to religion, Neo-Platonism gradually merged with paganism, which came to an end as Christianity gained ascendancy. As we have seen, the teaching of Plotinus contained a religious doctrine distinct from his philosophical doctrine. It has two distinctive traits: the divinity of the celestial beings or stars and a set of religious practices — prayers, evocations of souls, magical incantations — whose efficacy results almost mechanically from the strict observance of prescribed rites. These are not Plotinus' own discoveries, of course, but common ideas which he incorporated in his philosophy. In the second and third centuries worship of the sun in diverse forms spread, infiltrating even the mysteries of Mithraism, which numbered as many adherents at this time as did the official cult of Deus Sol [22] instituted in 270 by the emperor Aurelian. In the official cult Aurelian tried to bring together all the religions of the empire and to make it possible for the Syrian worshipers of Baal, the Greeks, and the Latins to participate in the new religion without sacrificing anything of their personal preferences. Nearly a century later, in 362, the emperor Julian, a practitioner of the Mithraic mysteries, also tried to reorganize an official pagan religion around the cult of the Sun. And how indeed can the religious veneration inspired in the Neo-Platonists by the cosmos be understood apart from the religious substructure which they recog-

---

[21] Porphyry *Life of Plotinus* chap. xxiii; vi. 7. 33 ff.
[22] Homo, *Essai sur le règne de l'empereur Aurélien*, p. 270.

nize rather than create? While the philosopher legitimatizes the cult
through the totality of his speculations, figurative monuments make
it appeal to the imagination. For example, a magic sphere that dates
from the second or third century contains a collection of symbols
of cosmic divinities: a figure of the sun, seated, is surrounded by an
aureole consisting of seven rays, a triangle symbolizing generation,
and five intersecting circles indicating the five elements identified by
Aristotle.[23] Many of the same details are found in a hymn to the
sun by Proclus. In Mythraism, moreover, the cult of the sun is linked
to a view of human destiny identical to Plotinus' view. In Mithraic
bas-reliefs "the radiant sun continuously sends particles of fire down
through seven rays and into the body that he calls to life. Conversely, when death has dissolved the elements of which a human
being is composed, the sun draws them upward to himself." [24]
Belief in the transformation of the soul into a celestial being after
death or in life under the influence of mystical rites predominates
in second-century mystery religions. In the mysteries of the Great
Mother, Apuleius indicates that the initiated, called to rebirth and a
new life, successively clothes himself in twelve garments during
nocturnal initiation ceremonies, and in the morning, dressed in
"celestial garments," is honored as a god by the whole community.[25]
The Neo-Platonists try on occasion to combat such beliefs by
popularizing their own. Take Sallustius' little work *On the Gods
and the World;* addressed to the common people and purportedly
based solely on common sense and myths known by all, the work
obviously reflects the writer's concern for clarity and might pass
for the catechism of the Neo-Platonists. A fundamental tenet of
their religion, and one that contrasts with the new Christian beliefs, is that the world is eternal and now has the order that it has
always had. To acknowledge creation is to acknowledge that the
stars are not divine beings, and the Neo-Platonists, from Porphyry

---

[23] Delatte, *Bulletin de correspondance hellénique* (1913), p. 253.

[24] Cumont, *Astrology and Religion among the Greeks and Romans* (1912), p. 188.

[25] Apuleius *Metamorphoses* viii; Reitzenstein, *Die hellenistische Mysterien,* pp. 26, 30, 31.

to Proclus, never tire of repeating the same argument against creation: the creation of the world is a necessary and consequently an eternal result of the nature of God who could be inactive only if imperfect.

A second trait of Plotinus' religion is the extraordinary power attributed to rites, which radically transform any religious practice into a magical act.[26] Here again is a trait common to his age, for although magical incantations in the form of either curses or love charms are never written on tablets in any age, in the second century we find more ways of foreseeing the future than ever before. These circumstances explain charlatanism such as that practiced by Alexander of Abonuteichos, whose odious machinations were exposed by Lucian in his *Alexander*. Plotinus himself depicts the sensible world as a vast network of magical influences and offers philosophy as the only means of escaping from these influences. We also know the success enjoyed by Philostratus' novel (*ca.* 220) in which the Pythagorean Apollonius of Tyana is initiated into all the magical practices of the Orient. In *Alexander* Lucian tells us that the charlatan considered as his worst enemies "the Epicureans and the Christians." The fact is that from the end of the third century the state regarded such superstitions as a threat to the public welfare and took numerous measures against them.[27] After A.D. 296 a law prohibited astrology, and under Constantine private divination was outlawed in 319, while the exact legal conditions under which divination could be practiced were defined in 321; later came a new law against divination (358), the prohibition of sacrifices (368), a suit against magicians and philosophers (370), and still stronger laws under Theodosius, to say nothing of numerous edicts against paganism in general, which continued until the fifth century. All of this shows the popularity of the ideas and practices that the Neo-Platonists had incorporated in their philosophy. The lives of philosophers — Porphyry's life of Plotinus, Eunapius' *Lives of the Sophists* (*ca.* 375), Marinus' life of Proclus (*ca.* 490), Damascius' life of Isi-

---

[26] *Enneads* iv. 4. 38 ff.
[27] A. Maury, *La Magie et l'astrologie* (3d ed. 1864), pp. 94–150.

dorus (*ca.* 511) — show that superstitious beliefs were being received more and more enthusiastically in some quarters and that the most absurd tales were being told about the magical power of a black stone or a statue. It must be added that the desire on the part of the public authority to bring about a reform was not related to the absurdity of such beliefs but rather to the fear that they engendered, for everyone — Christians and pagans, the uneducated and the educated — feared them because they believed in their power. Skeptics and Epicureans like those mentioned by Lucian were rare. In a universe ruled by sympathetic magic there can be no place for even the most elementary knowledge of the laws of mechanics, and a mechanistic conception of the universe was further from the minds of the people than it had ever been. In their universe there is no action other than a radiation of some sort which is not affected by distance, and any mechanical transmission of forces is ignored or avoided. For Plotinus the material medium between the eye and the visible object, far from serving to transmit light, can only be an obstacle to its influence.[28] He does not grant the mechanical transmission of impressions from sense organs to the seat of the soul, and he forcefully rejects any attempt to liken natural action to the action of a lever. How can the mechanical production of a quality like color be understood?[29] Far from being exceptional, the natural action of things on one another is but a particular instance of universal magic.

Divinity of the stars, eternity of the world, belief in magic, the belief that souls are of divine origin and are destined to return to the gods — such are the tenets of a faith traditionally called *Hellenism* and contrasted with Christianity. Hellenism had its sacred books: the *Chaldean Oracles,* which are reputed to be very ancient and which date at least from the third century, since Porphyry makes use of them. The *Oracles* are actually a simple versified account of Platonism. Proclus held the work in such high esteem that he was accustomed to say that he would have no regret about seeing all other books destroyed if only the *Oracles* and Plato's *Timaeus*

---

[28] *Enneads* iv. 5.
[29] *Ibid.* 7. 6; iii. 8. 2. 5.

were preserved. Hellenism also had its creed, and there was even a most unusual schism between philosophers and theurgists, who would abandon all philosophical speculation and reduce Hellenism to a ritual practice. Theurgy is knowledge of the practices necessary to invoke the divine influence wherever and whenever desired. Like alchemy, widely practiced in the same period, the art of theurgy rests on belief in the unity of beings, which accounts for their sympathy.[30] The theurgic viewpoint is clearly presented in the treatise titled *On the Mysteries of the Egyptians;* wrongly attributed to Iamblichus, the treatise is actually an Egyptian priest's reply to the *Letter to Anebo* in which Porphyry directed several criticisms against the Egyptian religion. Its inspiration and date (early fourth century) identify it with the Hermetic writings that teach the essential dogmas of Platonism in the name of Hermes, who corresponds to the Egyptian god Thoth.[31]

The philosophers speak respectfully of the theurgists but choose as their mission speculation concerning the supersensible reality that is above the magic of the sensible world. Their aim is always to define within their hierarchy the forms of the supersensible reality. Though all of them have the same problem and, by and large, the same method of procession and retroversion, there are variations in their thinking and, consequently, distinct schools of thought. The main trends owe their origin to Porphyry, to the Syrian Iamblichus (d. 329), to Proclus (414–484), who made the Academy in Athens burst forth in a last shower of light, and finally to Damascius (early sixth century), the last Alexandrian master.

III   *Porphyry*

Porphyry of Tyre (233–305), after becoming acquainted with Plotinus in Rome in 263, devoted himself to spreading the ideas of his master. He edited Plotinus' works, prefaced by an account

[30] J. Bidez, "Liturgie des mystères chez les néoplatoniciens," *Bulletin de l'Académie royale de Belgique* (Letters) (1919), p. 415.
[31] Cf. W. Scott (ed.), *Hermetica*, 4 vols. (Oxford, 1924–1936).

of his life (298), and wrote an *Introduction to Intelligibles* in which he used the *Enneads* to give a comprehensive view of the nature of the soul and of the intelligible world. In the *Introduction to Intelligibles* he stresses the impassivity of the soul, even in sensation (Section 18), and its independence of the body, but it seems that personally he inclined toward a Pythagorean type of asceticism and allegorical theology. His treatise *On Abstinence from Animal Foods,* addressed to a certain Firmus who had given up the practice of vegetarianism and written to defend the practice, contains unusually rich and valuable details (because of the authors discussed, particularly Aristotle's successor Theophrastus) concerning blood sacrifices; they find favor only with the wicked daimons who wish to be worshiped and who corrupt even the philosophers' opinions about the gods. Porphyry's *Letter to Marcella,* written to a widow who was the mother of seven children and whom he married, is imbued with traditional piety and reflects his concept of a god like Epictetus' "witness and observer of all our actions and all our words." Practical theology takes first place in the treatise *On the Philosophy to be Derived from the Oracles,* written before he met Plotinus; extracts from the treatise, known through Eusebius' *Evangelical Preparation,* contain most unusual information concerning rules given by the oracles for worship and for the fabrication of statues. The treatise *On Images,* also abstracted by Eusebius, is more Stoic than Platonist; it gives numerous details about the symbolic significance of statues as well as the way in which they are made, their attitudes, their colors, and the attributes ascribed to them. Explication of a passage from Homer provides him in *The Nymphs' Cave* with an opportunity to outline his views on the destiny of the soul. Finally, against Atticus, a late second-century Neo-Platonist who holds that matter is a reality independent of the ultimate principle, he defends the Plotinian thesis that the last hypostasis is also derived from the principle. Such is the portrait of the theologian who wrote a violent attack *Against Christians* in which he states explicitly (according to extracts preserved by

Eusebius) that the worship of Jesus is incompatible with the worship of Aesculapius.

We should add that Porphyry was also a historian and commentator. The author of a *Life of Pythagoras* also wrote a *History of Philosophers* down to Plato, which has been partially preserved; an *Introduction* (isagoge) to Aristotle's *Categories*, which was of great historical importance during the Middle Ages; a commentary on the *Categories*, which has been preserved in part and of which Boethius' commentary is but the translation;[32] and an *Introduction to Ptolemy's Tetrabiblos*, which shows that he had an interest in astrology.[33]

IV *Iamblichus*

Under Diocletian (284–305) and Constantine (306–337) the teaching of Iamblichus of Chalcis dominated the last stage of Neo-Platonism. Then Platonism was highly esteemed by public authorities. The Platonist Sopatros presided at the rites celebrating the founding of Constantinople, and there was speculation as to whether the new city would realize the Plotinian dream of a Platonopolis.[34] Iamblichus was less a mystagogue than a philosopher, and the manner in which he suggested that Plato be studied (following an order that had perhaps become traditional) is characteristic: ten dialogues should be studied systematically, beginning with the *First Alcibiades*, which deals with knowledge of the self, and continuing through the *Gorgias*, which deals with political virtues, to the *Parmenides*, which relates to the supreme principle. Thus the dialogues, when correctly read, are but one vast guide to the spiritual life.[35]

We know nothing concerning Iamblichus' speculations on the soul other than through fragments of a historical treatise preserved in

[32] Cf. Bidez, *Comptes rendus de l'Académie des inscriptions* (Oct. 1, 1922).
[33] Boll, *Sphaera*, p. 7, note.
[34] Piganiol, *L'Empereur Constantin* (1932), p. 159.
[35] According to Proclus *Commentary on the First Alcibiades*, ed. V. Cousin (1864), p. 297, 11–20.

Stobaeus' *Eclogues* (i. 40.8; 41.32–33). What interests us is that he seeks to cut through the veil of accretions and to identify Platonism. According to one school of thought that does not go beyond Numenius, the soul is an essence identical to the essence of the higher reality from which it derives, but according to the true doctrine of Plato (and also of Aristotle and Pythagoras), the soul is a substance distinct from the higher reality and endowed with characteristics of its own. Here we see distinctly the opposition between a Platonism that is inspired by Stoicism — that of Numenius, who holds that souls are simple particles of the divine intelligence — and a Platonism that multiplies the members of the hierarchy of realities by taking pains to preserve for each its distinctive and original character.

The tendency to multiplication that appears here is the distinctive trait of the last stage of Neo-Platonism, the stage inaugurated by Iamblichus. He provides the method and the example that will inspire Proclus and yield, instead of the simple Plotinian triad, a supersensible reality composed of a great number of ternaries arranged in ascending order. Is this the continuation, as it has often been said to be, of the trend initiated by Plotinus? Plotinus is supposed to have inserted the hypostases of mind and soul between the ultimate Principle and the world in order to re-establish the continuity negated by the transcendence of the Principle; and his successors, following the same course, are supposed to have inserted still other members, just as we might add a series of points to approximate a continuous line.

The fact is, however, that there was a veritable reaction against the Plotinian spirit under the leadership of Iamblichus. Completely in keeping with the spirit of Iamblichus, Proclus shows in his *Commentary on the Timaeus* (241 ff.) that Eternity was a hypostasis to be inserted between the Good and the Animal in itself (just as Time must be inserted between the intelligible world and the sensible world). He makes the following observation about the authors whom he does not name and who must be Plotinus and the members of his school: "The others misinterpret everything, and since they suppose that only Mind separates Soul and the Good, they are forced to acknowledge the identity of Mind and Eternity." His simplistic criticism shows, not that he can clarify something misinterpreted and falsely identified by Plotinus, as one might assume after reading only Proclus, but that he misunderstands the spirit of Plotinus who, without in any way confusing eternity and the intelligible world, saw eternity in the motion of mind returning to the One.[36] Thus Plotinus inquired into the genesis and method of operation of eternity and did not, like his successors, treat it as a fixed term. Proclus follows the same pattern in criticizing Plotinus' theory of daimons. Plotinus destroyed the very notion of daimons by following the Stoic practice of making them a part of us.[37] Here, too, Proclus neglects the subtle Plotinian theory of the soul according to which the higher part of our self or the contemplative part (the daimon) is within us but is not our self; it is our self when we attain to it, but it ceases to be our self when we descend to a lower level.

The great problem of Iamblichus (and of Proclus) is to find a method that combines the Aristotelian method of classifying concepts on the basis of characteristics ranging from the most general to the most specific and the Platonic dialectic. The method must also allow him to trace and situate in the intelligible world the myriad forms identified by paganism: gods, daimons, heroes, etc. His vast classification is devoid of the spiritual life that animated the *Enneads* but now degenerates on the one hand to applied theology and on the other to practical theurgy.

In fact, the Plotinian triad (Good, Mind, and Soul, which collectively constitute the intelligible world) contrasts strikingly with Iamblichus' famous ternary even though the second issued from the first. We recall how Plotinus had pictured the production of the lower hypostasis from the higher one: procession starts from the higher hypostasis and continues until the derived being turns back-

---

[36] *Enneads* ii. 7.
[37] *Commentary on the First Alcibiades*, pp. 382–5, with reference to Plotinus *Enneads* iii. 4. 5.

ward in a double rhythm of outgoing and return and contemplates its source. Plotinus had added, particularly with reference to the way in which soul is derived from mind, that the prior principle of the soul does not proceed but remains in its own place. Iamblichus' ternary isolates the three factors in any production.[38] Each production has as its principle a ternary that includes that which remains (τὸ μένον), that which is produced (τὸ προίον), and that which makes the derived being turn backward (τὸ ἐπίστρεφον). But Iamblichus sees the factors of production as fixed forms: each ternary is like a world or rather a system (*diacosmos*) that includes that which makes the system one, that which makes it diverse (procession), and that which makes it remain unified in spite of its diversity (retroversion). Furthermore, the three factors which in the case of Plotinus merely outlined the general form of any production are for Iamblichus the totality of reality. There are for him only ternary systems or diacosmoi arranged one above the other and in such a way that each lower system is a specialized form of a higher system. Thus the first ternary comprises a principle of identity (the unit), a principle of procession or distinction (the dyad), and finally a principle of retroversion (the triad). Beneath the first ternary is a second ternary which when considered from three different viewpoints is seen as three tetrads: the first tetrad, the square of two (2^2), is a subsistent unit; the second, the product of two in the dyad (2×2), proceeds; the third, which implicitly contains the perfect decad ($1 + 2 + 3 + 4 = 10$), turns backward. Beneath the second ternary is a third ternary whose first member is the principle of resemblance and relates to identity, whose second member permeates all things in the manner of a soul, and whose third member makes things return to their sources.

These principles radically transform Neo-Platonism. Iamblichus' ternary is not simply added to Plotinus' triad; it replaces the triad. The rhythm of the ternary is no longer that of the triad — One, Mind, Soul — in which there is continuous progress toward further

[38] According to Proclus *Commentary on the Timaeus* 206a.

division and expansion. Instead, we see in Iamblichus' ternary a unity that expands and contracts, and the substitution of the triad of Being, Life, and Mind for the triad of One, Mind, and Soul.[39] Mind is subsequent to life and consequently to soul, as we readily observe in the evolution of the visible world, where birth is followed by the development of life and the latter by the development of mind, and where there is obvious progression in complexity from being to living being and from living being to intelligent being. Mind corresponds to the moment of retroversion: it produces nothing, but it orders and organizes what has been produced.

v *Proclus*

The foregoing traits are elaborated in the writings of Proclus of Byzantium (412–484), one of the last scholarchs of the Academy. He succeeded Plutarch at Athens and won acclaim as a teacher at the Academy, where he tried in vain to concentrate instruction. Born to a wealthy family of judicial officials and schooled in law, he became a philosopher by choice. Punctilious in his devotion, each month he performed ceremonies honoring the Great Mother, observed the days of mourning of the Egyptians, fasted regularly on the last day of the month, and prayed daily at sunrise, midday, and sunset; he searched for exotic divinities to whom he addressed hymns and practiced a theurgical art taught to him by Asclepigenia, who had learned them from her father, Plutarch.[40] Such is the portrait of the devout man who was the great systematizer of the Neo-Platonist school and the author of summaries, abstracts, and diverse commentaries whose coherence, clarity, and simplicity are remarkable in view of the abstruse nature of his material. His main works include vast but incomplete or uncompleted commentaries on the *Timaeus,* the *First Alcibiades,* the myth in the tenth book of the *Republic,* the *Parmenides,* and on the *Euclid;* theological treatises —

[39] *Ibid.* 252e.
[40] According to Marinus *Life of Proclus.*

a long treatise *On Plato's Theology* and a brief account of the *Elements of Theology;* and a dissertation *On Evil,* preserved in a Latin translation dating from the Middle Ages.

The *Elements of Theology,* which gives a complete idea of the supersensible reality, is remarkable for its method. It consists of theorems proven according to the Euclidian method, and Proclus exhibits a predilection for proving one proposition by showing the logical impossibility of others. Take the fundamental theorem in his treatise, the one that might be called the theorem of transcendence: "A term equally present to all terms in a series can explain them all only if it is not in one of them or in all of them but prior to all of them." He demonstrates this by showing that the term is either in all the other terms and shared by them, with the result that it requires another term to unite its parts, or it is in only one of the other terms and not present to all of them, and so forth. This important theorem is the demonstration of Platonic realism; it means that there are no good things unless there is first goodness, no eternal things unless there is first eternity, etc. In accordance with his theorem Proclus identifies three terms with respect to each series of things endowed with a common characteristic. For example, in the series of good things he identifies: an *unshared* or transcendent term, goodness; a *shared* term or the characteristic common to all things, good; and finally *sharing* things, that is, good things. We might express this in logic by saying that the unshared term is the apprehension of the concept, the sharing term its extension, and the shared term that which unites apprehension and extension.

Thus Proclus evolves a method of classifying terms according to decreasing generality, and by resorting to the brilliant stratagem of considering each general term as the cause of the things comprised in its extension, he makes the resulting classification a system of metaphysics. For instance, one or unity is the cause of everything that can be reduced to one, and it follows that the more general and simple a term is, the higher it ranks; in contrast to this, the simpler a sharing thing is — that is, the greater the degree to which it shares exclusively general characteristics — the lower it ranks.

Thus being, an abstract characteristic, is superior to life (that is, has a more extensive range than that of life), and life to mind; conversely, intelligent being is superior to mere living being and living being to mere being, more especially as the presence of a less universal attribute in a subject implies the presence of more universal attributes. For example, if a thing is a man, it is *a fortiori* an animal and, if it is an animal, it is a being.

Here then are his *series* (a series or σείρα being the reunion of an unshared, a shared, and a sharing element, such as life and beings that possess life) classed hierarchically according to the degree of generality or simplicity of the unshared element that dominates them: at the summit, the One; beneath the One, the series of unities (ἐνάδες); beneath this, the series of Being (beneath because any being is one whereas any one, for instance a privation, is not a being); beneath this, the series of life, and finally soul. Proclus states positively (Proposition 3) that series is genus, only for him genus is cause — that is, in its unity the genus indiscriminately contains every species. This means that each series is like a world (diacosmos) and in its own way contains every possible reality; whatever is contained in a series of henads in the form of the henad is contained in a series of being in the form of being and so forth. Each part of the content of the henad is therefore matched by a part of the content of being, life, mind, and soul. Faithful to his terminology, Proclus calls the totality of the corresponding parts, taken at different stages, an order (τάξις).

Something like a law of development or distribution of reality is common to every series: beings are distributed as unities, living beings as beings, minds as living beings, souls as minds.

Let us try to understand this law of distribution. The primary One or source of all things, as we recall, has diverse functions with respect to dependent beings: it makes them complete beings (τελεσιουργεῖ), holds together the parts of their essence (συνέχει), and protects their boundaries against invasion by other essences (φρουρεῖ). It is by virtue of the One that there is a system of defined and systematized beings. Now these diverse functions, completely undivided in the One, must be separated, and from their separation arises the series of henads or gods, each of whose terms defines a god or a class of gods. There are gods who complete, gods who contain, gods who retain, and still other gods if other properties of the One are identified. The composition of the series of henads or gods reappears in each lower series, which means that each series has the function of completing, containing, and retaining with respect to its subordinate: being determines the system or *series* of minds, mind determines the series of souls and, finally, souls exercise the same functions in the sensible world.

But there is more: each series contains the characteristics of every other series. Take the characteristics of the five subordinate series: from unities are derived essences or fixed, intelligible beings; from beings, Lives that are but these beings when seen as constituting a system analogous to a living being (the animal in itself in Plato's *Timaeus*); from Lives, Minds or intellectual subjects that apprehend and contemplate; and from Minds, souls that animate the sensible world. Now each series (this is the necessary consequence of the fact that the genus contains the species) contains terms that correspond to the whole chain of series. One, being, life, mind, soul: such is the structure not only of the chain of series but also of each series. In the series of unities there are, besides unity in itself, intelligible unities or gods corresponding to being, intelligent gods corresponding to mind, and intercosmic gods corresponding to souls. The same holds for each of the series: each has at its summit a unity corresponding to the divine series — Mind one, soul one, etc. — and contains in its own right — *qua* mind, soul, life, or being — everything contained by superior or subordinate series.

In each series, therefore, we find two themes of classification juxtaposed but not united, one based on the division of the One into its functions and the other on the principle that everything is contained in everything. This is completely different from Plotinus' philosophy. In Proclus' system everything conspires to keep each reality in its place in a fixed hierarchy that constitutes a more or less self-sufficient series. For instance, minds in the fourth series do not contemplate minds in the second, but within the fourth series there is a term — intelligible minds — that corresponds to the second series and is the object of intelligent minds. In Plotinism every avenue was open to the soul, the "traveler in a metaphysical land," [41] but there is nothing in Proclus that corresponds to the mobile, spiritual self that traverses every level between matter and the One. The notion of the spiritual life has almost disappeared. Proclus ceases to identify evil with matter. "Evil is neither in the form that seeks to dominate matter nor in matter that desires order; it is in the lack of symmetry (ἀσυμμετρία) between matter and form." [42] It does not exist as a hypostasis, but as a "parahypostasis" or a derived being. There could be no worse betrayal of Plotinus. Just any event presupposes creation and denies the eternity of the universe. "Why, after an infinite period of idleness, would God start to create?" Proclus asks the Christians. "Because he thinks it is better to create? But previously he either knew or did not know this fact; to say that he did not know it is absurd, and if he knew it, why did he not start earlier?" [43]

VI *Damascius*

With Damascius, whose *Life of Isidorus* reveals him as a man no less devout than Proclus, we come to the last intellectual circles of the pagans, those who gathered in Alexandria to talk of old times and about whom we now have many suggestive details, thanks to a recently discovered papyrus. [44] The long treatise entitled *On the First Principles,* which has been preserved, is a commentary on the last part of The *Parmenides;* it generally takes the opposite course to that of Proclus. The whole rigid hierarchy of realities as conceived by the almost juridical mind of Proclus crumbles and is replaced by an intense spiritual and mystical life that everywhere re-

---

[41] W. B. Inge, *The Philosophy of Plotinus* (3d ed.; 2 vols.; New York, 1928).

[42] *Commentary on the Timaeus* 115e.

[43] *Ibid.* 88c.

[44] J. Maspero, "Les Papyrus Beaugé: Horapolion et la fin du paganisme égyptien," *Bulletin de l'Institut français d'archéologie orientale,* vols. X and XI.

establishes the relations or avenues that lead to the higher realities. The chief preoccupation of Damascius is to destroy the categories established by Proclus and to show that they find no support in the *Parmenides.* To begin with, the first principle is not the transcendent One responsible for the unification of reality. Beyond the One in the Ineffable, "inaccessible to all, lacking any co-ordination, separated to such a degree that he no longer possesses the quality of separation; for that which is separated is separated from something and retains a relation with that from which it is separated." [45] We must therefore place the Principle outside and above any hierarchy and must refrain from investing it, even as a model, with any semblance of order or hierarchical arrangement. "Does something nevertheless come from it to the things in this world? Why not, if everything in some way comes from it (17. 13)?" This something is the ineffable or impenetrable quality contained in any reality, and the higher we ascend, the more ineffable it becomes. "The One is more ineffable than Being, Being than Life, Life than Mind." We are nevertheless on difficult ground when we try in this way to construct a hierarchy of ineffable qualities, for we run the risk of re-establishing a new hierarchy on the basis of an ineffable One responsible for an ineffable reality, and of having finally to refuse to say that it communicates anything of itself to the realities that issue from it. The Ineffable is posited by the first hypothesis in the *Parmenides,* which states that it is not even one: the soul first posits one, then eliminates the One because of its superiority, which makes it inaccessible.

Damascius reveals a predilection for intuition, which he tries to bring to a successful issue by making one affirmation limit another in an animated dialectic more characteristic of Plotinus than of Proclus. The Ineffable is an absolute initiative, similar to the One in Plotinus' treatise *On the Will of the One.* In contrast the One, being the cause, is defined as a function and a relation.

In a general way Damascius distrusts the mechanical method of determining principles that triumphed with Iamblichus and Proclus.

[45] *On the First Principles* (2 vols., ed. Ruelle, Paris, 1889–1891) i. 15, 13.

In his view, it is a serious mistake to apply to principles notions that logically apply only to processions. For instance, wishing to show how the collective one or the totality of intelligible realities proceeds from the primary One, proponents of the mechanical method make the former the synthesis of two opposing principles which they call the One and the Dyad, the Limited and the Unlimited, or the Father and the Power. The fact is that reality is not reached directly in such a manner but rather through images; accustomed to using such syntheses to explain without difficulty the mixtures contemplated by our minds and our souls (for example, a chord as a fixed relation determining the indefinite dyad of a high tone and a low tone), we simply transfer the opposing principles to the supreme reality (Section 45). Proof that the resulting analogy is at best uncertain is provided by the diversity of names used to designate each of the two opposing principles: Monad, Limit, Father, or Existence for the first and Dyad, Power, or Chaos for the second (Section 56). Separation and opposition, procession and return appear only in realities derived from the reality supposedly explained by the union of two distinct principles. This reality is the Union or the United, that is, the reality in which all things are still in the undivided state. How then could it issue from the fusion of two distinct realities? Principles that exist before the United, and therefore before anything has attained to the state of distinctiveness, could not be distinct.

The result is a new conception of the primitive ternary in which the three moments — persistence, procession, and return — are replaced by three terms whose triplicity does not alter their unity: the first of the three terms is One-All, one independently and all as the source of the second term; the second is All-One, all independently and one as the product of the first; the third receives from the first "one-ness" and from the second "all-ness." Each of Damascius' terms is an aspect or a facet of the same reality.

By criticizing as he does the method of Proclus, Damascius comes close to abandoning Neo-Platonism. An analysis of the details of his immense work reveals that for almost every explanation of the

Parmenides offered by Proclus, Damascius interposes his own contradictory explanation, motivated by a different spirit. For example, he rejects explanations that would base conclusions concerning the properties of the model on the properties of the created world,[46] and he stresses the fact that the sensible world is not an image of the totality of the supersensible reality but only of a tiny portion of it, the world of Ideas.[47] Furthermore, he recognizes and states forcefully that procession and retroversion apply only to intellectual natures (had Plotinus said anything else?) and cannot be used as a general explanation of the totality of reality.

Damascius' teaching, which in some instances shows remarkable depth and originality in spite of occasional lapses and inconsistencies, was unfruitful because of unpropitious historical factors. When Justinian ordered the closing of the Athenian schools of philosophy in 529, the University of Athens, which had flourished in the time of the Sophist Libanius, the friend of Julian and Himerius, had died away for want of pupils and perhaps of professors. Damascius in his *Life of Isidorus* calls attention to the inferiority of philosophical instruction in Athens during the time of Hegias (*ca.* 525), who put more stress on pious practices than on the study of philosophy. That Alexandria was not a mecca for philosophers is proven by the persecution to which they were subjected by the patriarch Athanasius and by the murder of the Neo-Platonist Hypatia, who was killed in 415 by a fanatical mob. In addition, the city had lost much of its splendor, and the new capital of the empire was not conducive to philosophical studies. Neo-Platonism died with the death of Greek philosophy and culture in general, and the sixth and seventh centuries were marked by a profound silence.

[46] *Ibid*. 52. 16–53, 17.
[47] *Ibid*. 156. 31–160, 22.

Bibliography

Texts and Translations

Plotinus. *Enneads* (with Porphyry's *Life of Plotinus*). Edited and translated by E. Bréhier. Budé Collection. Paris, 1924–38. Vols. I and II, 1924. Vol. III, 1925. Vol. IV, 1927. Vol. V, 1931. Vol. VI¹, 1936. Vol. VI², 1938. — *Opera.* Edited by P. Henry and H. R. Schwyzer. Paris and Brussels, 1951. Vol. I (*Enneads* i–iii), 1951. Vol. II (*Enneads* iv–v), 1959. Translations of the *Enneads* include the complete English version by S. MacKenna and B. S. Page (2d revised edition, London, 1957), and selections translated with introduction and notes by A. H. Armstrong (London, 1953)

Porphyry. Among the separate editions of Porphyry's works are the following: *Sententiae.* Edited by B. Mommert. Leipzig, 1907. English translation by T. Davidson in *Journal of Speculative Philosophy,* III (1869). — *De abstinentia.* Edited by A. Nauck. Leipzig, 1885. English translation by S. Hibberd, 1857. — *Ad Marcellam.* Edited by A. Nauck. Leipzig, 1885. English translation by A. Zimmern, 1896.

Iamblichus. *De mysteriis.* Edited by W. Pharthey, 1857. — *Theologumena Arithmeticae.* Edited by De Falco. Teubner edition. Leipzig, 1922. Cf. *Rivista indo-greo-italica,* VI (1922), 49.

Proclus. Teubner edition of Commentaries *On the Republic* (2 vols., ed. Kroll, 1899–1901); *On the Timaeus* (3 vols., ed. Diels, 1900–1906); *On the Parmenides* (ed. Pascuali, 1907); *Outline of Astronomical Theses* (ed. Manitius, 1907); *The Elements of Physics* (ed. Ritzenfeld, 1912); and *On the Euclid* (ed. Friedlein, 1873). See also *The Elements of Theology.* Edited and translated by E. R. Dodds. Oxford, 1933.

Damascius. *On the First Principles.* Edited by Ruelle. 2 vols. Paris, 1889–1891. French translation by Chaignet, 1898.

General Studies

E. Vacherot. *Histoire critique de l'école d'Alexandrie.* 3 vols. Paris, 1846–1851.

J. Simon. *Histoire de l'école d'Alexandrie.* 2 vols. Paris, 1845.

T. Whittaker. *The Neoplatonists.* 1901. 2d edition, 1918. 4th ed. Hildesheim, 1961.

W. R. Inge. *The Philosophy of Plotinus.* London, 1918. Reprinted 1948.

F. Heinemann. *Plotin.* Leipzig, 1921.

P. Merlan. *From Platonism to Neo-Platonism.* The Hague, 1953.

J. Pépin. "L'intelligence et l'intelligible chez Platon et dans le néoplatonisme," *Revue philosophique* (1950), pp. 38–64. — *Mythe et allégorie.* Paris, 1958.

R. Arnou. *Le désir de Dieu dans la philosophie de Plotin.* Paris, 1921.

E. Bréhier. "La philosophie de Plotin," *Revue des cours et conférences,* 1922. Also published separately, Paris, 1922. 2d. edition. See also *Etudes de philosophie antique.* Paris, 1955. Section D.

H. F. Müller. "Ist die Metaphysik des Plotinos ein Emanationssystem?" *Hermes,* XLVIII (1913), p. 409.

Paul Henry. *Etudes plotiniennes.* Vol. I: *Les Etats du texte de Plotin,* Museum Lessianum, 1938–1941; Vol. II: *Les manuscrits des Ennéades,* 1941, 2d edition, 1948.

M. de Gandillac. *La sagesse de Plotin.* Paris, 1952.

Jean Trouillard. *La purification plotinienne.* Paris, 1955. — *La procession plotinienne, ibid.* — "La genèse du plotinisme," *Revue philosophique de Louvain* (1955), p. 469. — "La méditation du Verbe selon Plotin," *Revue philosophique* (1956), pp. 65 ff. — *Entretiens de la Fondation Hardt.* (*Les sources de Plotin,* Vol. V). *Geneva,* 1957. Reprinted 1960.

F. Cumont. *The Oriental Religions in Roman Paganism.* Translated by G. Showerman. New York, 1956.

Cochez. *Les Religions de l'Empire dans la philosophie de Plotin,* 1913.

Special Studies

III, IV

J. Bidez. *Vie de Porphyre.* Ghent, 1913. — "Jamblique et son école," *Revue des Etudes grecques* (1919), pp. 29–40. Cf. *Bulletin de l'Académie royale de Belgique* (1904), p. 499.

Klibansky and Labovsky. *Parmenides . . . nec non Procli commentarium in Parmenidem.* London, 1953.

V

J. Trouillard. "La monadologie de Proclus," *Revue philosophique de Louvain,* LVII (April, 1959), p. 309–20. — "Convergence des définitions de l'âme chez Proclus," *Revue des Sciences philosophiques et théologiques* (Paris, January, 1961), pp. 1–20.

E. Bréhier. "L'idée du néant et le problème de l'origine radicale dans le néoplatonisme grec," *Revue de Métaphysique et de Morale* (1919), p. 443. — *Etudes de philosophie antique.* Paris, 1955. P. 248 and *passim.*

Cousin (ed.). William of Moerbeke's Latin translation of separate works by Proclus: *On Providence, Freedom and Evil,* and *Commentary on the First Alcibiades.* Paris, 1864.

VI

C. E. Ruelle. *Le Philosophe Damascius*. Paris, 1861.

Studies in English

A. H. Armstrong. *Introduction to Ancient Philosophy*. 3d edition, London, 1957. — *The Architecture of the Intelligible Universe in the Philosophy of Plotinus*. Cambridge, 1940.

E. Bréhier. *The Philosophy of Plotinus*. Trans. by J. Owens. Chicago, 1958.

E. R. Dodds. *The Greeks and the Irrational*. Berkeley, Calif., and Cambridge, 1951.

J. Katz. *Plotinus' Search for the Good*. New York, 1950.

P. Merlan. *From Platonism to Neoplatonism*. The Hague, 1953. — *Monopsychism, Mysticism, Metaconsciousness; Problems of the Soul in the Neoaristotelian and Neoplatonic Tradition*. The Hague, 1963.

P. V. Pistorius. *Plotinus and Neoplatonism; An Introductory Study*. Cambridge, 1952.

L. J. Rosán. *The Philosophy of Proclus*. New York, 1949.

R. E. Witt. *Albinus*. Cambridge and New York, 1937.

HELLENISM AND CHRISTIANITY

CHRISTIANITY does not stand in opposition to Greek philosophy as one doctrine against another doctrine. The natural, spontaneous form of Christianity is not written, didactic instruction. The Christian communities, which were made up of artisans and people of small means, attached prime importance to brotherhood and mutual assistance in the expectation of the imminent consummation of the world. From the apostolic age we have only incidental writings — epistles, relations of events from the life of Jesus, the acts of the apostles — intended to strengthen and propagate faith in the kingdom of heaven; we have no reasoned, coherent doctrinal statement.

By the beginning of the Christian era there had evolved in Greek philosophy the image of a universe imbued with reason and shorn of mystery. Its design is revealed repeatedly in philosophical writings as well as in more popular forms (the treatise *On the World*, Seneca's *Natural Questions,* etc.). In the Greek universe the problem of the future life had vanished, supplanted either by the Epicurean idea of "immortal death" that in no way concerns the living or by Stoic acceptance of death as one of a number of events woven by universal fate; the myths of the gods had also vanished, reduced either to the proportion of a historical narrative by Euhemerus who would make such myths the history of deceased kings, or to a physical symbolism by the Stoics. The philosopher's practical attitude was inspired in its entirety by rationalism, and his words of

218

consolation or advice echo the same refrain as his ethical code: why complain? why entertain dread? why be disturbed in a world in which every event has its place and its hour?

While in Rome the philosopher was preaching rationalism, in Galilee Jesus was instructing uneducated people who knew nothing at all about the Greek sciences or the Greek conception of the world, and who could grasp parables and images more readily than the intricacies of dialectical argumentation. In such instruction the world, nature, and society intervene, not as realities imbued with reason and subject to apprehension by the philosopher, but as inexhaustible reservoirs of images replete with spiritual significance: the lily of the valley, the prodigal son, the lost sheep, and many others whose freshness and popular appeal contrast sharply with the conventional flowers and studied elegance of the diatribes. He, too, teaches people how to attain to happiness, but not through a heroic will that treats all external events with indifference. Poverty, sorrow, wrongs, injustices, persecutions — these are true evils but evils which, thanks to God's fondness for the humble and the downtrodden, open the gates to the kingdom of heaven. Suffering and expectation, joy in the midst of suffering as a result of the expectation of happiness — how different is this state in the disciple of Christ from the serenity of the sage who at each moment sees in its entirety the fulfillment of his destiny!

The teaching of Christ, which stands in stark contrast to Hellenism by virtue of its total lack of reasoned, theoretical views concerning the universe and God, forces the historian of philosophy to examine a problem that is actually but one aspect of a more general problem relating to the history of civilization: precisely what is the importance in the history of philosophical speculations of the fact that Western civilization, from the time of Constantine, became a Christian civilization? The question has elicited the whole gamut of replies. There are two reasons for denying that the fact has any importance: to preserve the purity of evangelical Christianity, which contains nothing other than the obligation of love and charity and salvation through Christ; and to guarantee the autonomy and independence of rational thought. The purists show (this was the viewpoint of the first Protestant historians of philosophy) that the Christian dogmatism superimposed on the Gospel and on the writings of St. Paul during the first five centuries, especially speculations concerning the nature of the Word and the Trinity, was a dangerous departure, under the influence of Greek speculation, from the primitive tradition.[1] The rationalists show that successive advances of the human mind to the rational viewpoint are directly related to the Greek intellectual heritage, and that Christianity played no part in the march of events leading from Greek mathematics to the infinitesimal calculus or from Ptolemy to Copernicus. According to late eighteenth-century theoreticians of progress, Christianity has at times been able to impede but has never aided the independent evolution of rational thought.

According to other historians of philosophy, however, Christianity marks an important revolution in our conception of the universe. The originality of Christianity is presented from two distinct but perhaps complimentary viewpoints. In the first place philosophers who tend to search for an internal dialectic in history call attention to the fact that Greek philosophy gives what is essentially an objective representation of things, an image of the universe as an object for the contemplating mind. The subject is to some degree absorbed in its known object when, as Aristotle says, it becomes identical to it through perfect knowledge, and in Stoicism the subject has no autonomy other than complete adhesion to its object. Against this, Christianity knows truly autonomous subjects which are independent of the universe of objects, which contemplate the universe without exhausting themselves completely, and which have a life of their own — a life of feeling and love that cannot be translated into terms of objective representation. In short, by ignoring all the speculations of the Greeks concerning the cosmos, Christianity has simply reasserted more forcefully the originality of its contribution to human thought, which is the discovery of that which is essen-

[1] See E. Bréhier, *The Hellenic Age,* trans. Joseph Thomas (Chicago, 1964), pp. 16 ff.

tially subject, heart, feeling, conscience. Only in a Christian civilization could there have been developed an idealism that makes of the innermost nature of the subject the principle of development of any reality.[2]

Furthermore, and this is a second side of the intellectual revolution brought about by Christianity, the cosmos of the Greeks is, in a manner of speaking, a world with no history. Its eternal order is not affected by time since it is either forever identical or forever returning to the same point following a chain of events relating to cyclic changes that are repeated indefinitely. Is not the history of humanity itself, for an Aristotle, a perpetual return of the same civilizations? The opposite idea that there are in the world of reality radical changes, absolute initiatives, veritable inventions — in a word history and progress in the general sense of the term — such an idea was impossible before Christianity overturned the cosmos of the Hellenes. A world created out of nothing, a destiny which is not thrust upon man from without but which he forges for himself through his obedience or disobedience to divine law, a new and unforeseeable divine initiative to save men from sin, a ransom obtained through the suffering of a God-Man — that is the dramatic new image of the universe. Here everything depends on crises or dramatic shifts and we would search in vain for fate, the reason that underlies all causes; here nature disappears and everything depends on the intimate, spiritual history of man and his relations with God. Man sees before him a possible future that he will create and for the first time is delivered from Lucretius' melancholic *sunt eadem omnia semper,* from the Stoic fate and from the eternal geometric scheme in which Plato and Aristotle enclosed reality.[3] It is this important trait that impressed the first pagans who concerned themselves seriously with the Christians. What complaint does Celsus lodge against the Christians in *The True Doctrine,* written near the end of the second century? That they believe in a God

[2] For example Hegel, *Philosophy of History,* trans. J. Sibree (London, 1857; new issue, 1947), Sec. III, chap. ii.

[3] Cf. L. Laberthonnière, *Le Réalisme chrétien et l'idéalisme grec* (1904), ii, iii.

who is not unchangeable since he takes the initiative and makes new decisions in accordance with circumstances, that he is not impassive since he is affected by pity, that they believe in mythology or in myths about Christ "which are not susceptible of allegorical interpretation," that is, which are offered as true history and cannot be reduced to a symbol of a law of physics. For a Platonist like Celsus, Christianity has serious intellectual defects.

Thus we have on the one hand pure Christianity fundamentally independent of Greek philosophical speculation and an autonomous intellectual heritage wholly Greek in origin and unrelated to the spiritual life of the Christian, and on the other Christianity that ushers in an entirely new vision of the universe, a dramatic universe in which man is something other than immaculate knowledge of the order of the world.

If we consider the question from a purely historical viewpoint, steering clear of broad generalizations concerning contrasts between paganism and Christianity and making use of detailed studies on the origin of Christianity carried out over a period of almost a century, we shall probably find that none of the proposed solutions is satisfactory. Let us examine each of them briefly. The pure Christianity of the Protestant historians is only an abstraction, perfectly legitimate from a practical viewpoint but wholly illegitimate in the eyes of the historian; in fact, during the first five centuries one and the same development carried pagan thought from the practical problem of inner conversion in men like Seneca or Epictetus to the refined theology of Plotinus and Proclus, and the Christian doctrine of spiritual and inner Christianity of St. Paul to the dogmatic theology of Origen and the Cappadocians, with the result that it would be difficult not to see the same forces at work in each instance. Besides, we are constantly reminded of a historical truth that is becoming increasingly apparent: what separates pagans and Christians is not a question of intellectual method and of speculation but only submission to prescribed forms of worship, particularly to the worship of the emperor.

As for the autonomous development of scientific thought, the facts seem to be confirmed, but it must be noted that with respect to Greek scientific education Christianity does not occupy a situation different from that of Greek philosophy itself. Origen, for example, carefully delineates a triple wisdom: "the wisdom of this world," which Seneca called the liberal arts and Philo the cycle of education — that is, grammar, rhetoric, geometry, and music, to which can be added poetry and medicine or "all that which contains no vision of the divinity, or of the mode of being of the world, or of a sublime reality, or of the institution of a good and happy life." Then comes "the wisdom of the princes of this world," that is, the occult philosophy of the Egyptians, Chaldean astrology, and especially "the diverse and multiple opinions of the Greeks concerning the divinity." Finally, there is the wisdom of Christ that is derived through revelation.[4]

It must be added that in "the wisdom of this world" there is room for a considerable amount of philosophy, namely logic and dialectic, for certain generalities concerning physics and astronomy, and finally for all the rigid training appropriate for the virtuous man — for instance, a comprehensive moral catechism like that of a Musonius. It is interesting in this context to consider the opinion of Hermias, a Platonist and a contemporary of Proclus. Hermias separates "human philosophy" from the special initiation that the Platonist reserved for his adepts. We are misusing the word, he says, when we refer to mathematics, physics, and ethics as philosophy, and he contrasts with human philosophy the enthusiasm of the initiated who has within him "theology, philosophy in its entirety, and amorous folly."[5]

Even though they were divided over its spiritual worth, the Christians did not reject traditional education in principle. Their ranks included cultivated men like St. Augustine and St. Gregory of Nazianzen, who became its ardent defenders, and others like the Latins Tertullian and St. Hilarius, who advocated the short course and had no sympathy for rigorous training or even criticized it

[4] *On Principles,* following the Latin translation of Rufinus, III, ii.
[5] Hermias *Commentary on the Phaedrus* 92. 6 (ed. Couvreur).

explicitly. But the divergence of views on the subject was no greater among the Christians than it had been among the pagans after Aristotle. With the appearance of Cynicism and Stoicism the philosophical sciences, which were for Plato the only means of access to knowledge of true realities, became either mere auxiliaries or servants of wisdom, incapable of achieving independently an understanding of their own principles, or even (among the Cynics and Cyrenaics) useless frills nourished by human pride.

The first centuries of the Christian era are obviously characterized by an intellectual order common to all. It is predicated on the feeling that there is a gap between ordinary education, which is universally accessible, and the religious life that is attained only through methods vastly different from the normal exercise of reason: through the moral training of the Stoic, through Plotinian intuition, or through Christian faith in revelation.

But Christianity is not responsible for the intellectual order. As we shall see in due course, Christianity accepted the existing state of affairs without ever reacting against it, and the intellectual revolution that brought it to an end at the time of the Renaissance in the West was inspired by something quite different from the Christian influence. In any event, during the first five centuries there is no distinctive Christian philosophy that implies a table of intellectual values fundamentally original and different from that of the pagan thinkers.

Still to be determined is the extent to which Christianity can be said to have renewed our vision of the universe. It would be dangerous to confuse Christianity as it existed initially with Christianity as it was interpreted after a lapse of several centuries. In the beginning there was nothing speculative about Christianity; its main concern was mutual assistance, both spiritual and material, in different communities. To begin with, however, the spiritual life practiced in these communities is not peculiar to Christianity: the need for the inner life or self-consciousness was felt throughout the Greek world long before the triumph of Christianity, awareness of sin and error is expressed in popular formulas by historians and poets,[6] and self-examination or spiritual consolations that are veritable confessions are frequent at the beginning of the Christian era. Furthermore, the spiritual life and practices of the Christians had not the slightest influence on the image of the universe that resulted from Greek science and philosophy. A unique and limited world, geocentrism, the contrast between heaven and earth: this image was to persist until the age of the Renaissance. The spiritual life of the Christians evolved alongside the Greek cosmos without giving birth to a new concept of reality. The spiritual life doubtless implies (and again we shall see under what restrictions) the notion of an unforeseeable crisis or absolute initiative that Greek cosmology had tried to obliterate, but this sense of history and evolution was to be realized as a comprehensive conception of reality only through the infinitely accumulated experience of man in time and in space and the methodical recasting of Greek curiosity, already censured by the Stoics.

We hope then to show that the development of philosophical thought was not strongly influenced by the advent of Christianity and, to sum up our thinking in one statement, that there is no Christian philosophy.

We do not intend, however, to offer even a summary history of the Christian dogmatism during the first centuries. Important names will be missing from our account since we are studying Christianity, not in isolation, but in relation to Greek philosophy.

1 St. Paul and Hellenism

Christianity passed through the same stages as paganism at the end of antiquity. To the moral teaching of the Roman Empire corresponds (as has often been observed with respect to Seneca) St. Paul's preaching and his epistles. To the formation and birth of Neo-Platonism toward the end of the first century corresponds the

[6] Polybius *Histories* xviii. 43. 13.

fourth gospel, the apologists, and the development of the Gnostic systems. To the ripening of Platonism with Plotinus correspond the vast theological syntheses made by the Alexandrian scholars Clement and Origen. Proclus and Damascius have as their counterparts during the same period St. Augustine, the Cappadocian fathers, then all those who could be called Neo-Platonist Christians, like Nemesius and Dionysius the Areopagite.

Christianity and paganism both exhibit the same pattern of spiritual evolution, the same tendency to pass from a moral, religious and essentially inner life based on confidence in God to a doctrinal and dogmatic theology that speaks of God in the absolute rather than of the relations between man and God.

St. Paul was an educated Hellene and his writings manifest, either directly or indirectly through doctrines that had become common property, a number of ideas, attitudes and expressions characteristic of Seneca and especially of Epictetus. Christianity like Stoicism is cosmopolitan, and it recognizes but one virtue common to all rational beings. "There is neither Jew nor Greek, there is neither bond nor free, there is neither male nor female: for ye are all one in Christ Jesus." Like the Stoics in their diatribes, St. Paul maintains that man's social condition has absolutely no bearing on his salvation.[7]

The apostle of the Gentiles and even the evangelists have the same feeling as Epictetus concerning their role and the duties incumbent upon them.[8] We know how highly Epictetus esteemed his moral mission, "giving himself over to it with all his soul" and considering himself as a soldier, and how St. Paul looked upon himself as "a good soldier of Christ." The source of their strength is their faith in God; both St. Paul and Epictetus know that they can do anything by the grace of God who gives them his strength. Their confidence in reason that judges and understands all things derives from the fact that it has been given to us by God; as St. Paul puts it, "he that is spiritual judgeth all things, yet he himself is judged

[7] Gal. 3:23; I Cor. 7:17–40.
[8] Compare Epictetus *Discourses* ii. 2. 12; iii. 24. 31, and St. Paul, I Cor. 9:7.

by no man." Like the Cynic whose ideal portrait was sketched by Epictetus, the apostle is God's envoy on earth.[9]

From their faith in God comes serenity under all circumstances, for all events result from God's goodness.

Like the Stoic preacher, the messenger of good tidings was often jeered by worldlings. We recall the old man with the golden rings who, in the presence of Epictetus, counsels the young man in this way: "One must philosophize, but one must also have brains; and these things are foolishness." [10] Similarly, St. Paul knows that Christianity is "foolishness" in the eyes of the "natural" man who cannot know "what he that is spiritual judgeth." It is precisely this ignorance of their own faults, this lack of awareness of their sin, that makes the preacher's task indispensable. Kindness toward the ignorant, fraternal forgiveness of wrongs, lack of concern over the judgment of others — such is the attitude that the philosopher and the apostle have in common toward the world.

All their common traits derive from similar conditions under which their preaching is conducted. They are answering a common need, poignantly felt, for an inner conversion. What matters is not the persuasive use of words in the manner of the Sophists or the spreading of a dogma. St. Paul's theology is as vague as Epictetus' Stoicism. What matters to St. Paul is not the discovery of the nature of God but the salvation of man, and that is why the Christ who explains all the relations between God and man is at the heart of his doctrine. Similarly, Epictetus shows little concern for the question of the substance of God; first place goes to man's divine filiation, expressed with a degree of tenderness unknown to old Stoicism. The result is the brotherhood of all men; like Epictetus, Marcus Aurelius uses the term *fellow man*. Man's divine filiation is symbolized by Hercules, the son of Zeus and savior who abandons his own and wanders through the land spreading justice and virtue.[11]

There remains of course the fundamental trait of Christianity,

[9] Compare Epictetus i. 6. 37 and i. 1. 4 and 7 with St. Paul, Phil. 4:13 and I Cor. 1:2, 15.

[10] Epictetus i. 22. 18. St. Paul, I Cor. 1:27, 3:18.

[11] *Discourses* i. 22. 14, ii. 12–7; *Manual* 33.

which is not found in Epictetus and which, as Pascal says, makes man his own savior: man's wretchedness. According to St. Paul, the sinner who knows good cannot practice it because of the power of sin, which is counterbalanced only by the grace of Christ. Instead of semi-abstract forces that succor man, or the divine word, or inner daimons such as those found in Stoicism or even in Philonism, St. Paul offers a historical personage whose death has saved mankind; his action, through its utterly mysterious efficacy, sets him completely apart from the pagan sage who merely teaches or offers himself as a model.

11　Second-Century Apologists

The apologists of the time of the Antonines, except for Tatian, are obviously concerned with spreading the new religion: Justin, the author of two extant *Apologies,* one addressed to Antoninus Pius (138–161) and the other to Marcus Aurelius (161–180); Tatian, whose *Discourse to the Gentiles* was written shortly after Justin; and Athenagoras, whose apology is addressed to both Marcus Aurelius and his son Commodus. They are concerned with pointing out what the new religion has in common with Greek thought, what can bring out its universal, human character, or in a word, what can make it acceptable to the pagans. This explains the sympathetic but cautious attitude of Justin toward Greek philosophy, particularly toward Plato whom he declares superior to the Stoics in knowledge of God even though inferior to them in ethics.

By identifying Jesus with the Logos or Word "that was in the beginning with God" by whom "all things were made," the author of the celebrated fourth Gospel had introduced theology into Christianity: theology, that is, preoccupation with divine or supersensible reality in itself and not in its relation to the religious life of man. Justin seeks to attain directly, by the grace of Christ, to the Word of God and to the intelligible world of which the philosophers had but vague presentiments.[12] But for their presentiments to have been

[12] A. Harnack, *Lehrbuch der Dogmengeschichte* (3d ed.; Freiburg and Leipzig, 1894–1897), I, 467 and 470.

possible, he has to admit that the God who revealed himself to Moses and in the Gospels also revealed himself partially to the philosophers and especially to Socrates and Plato. There is a unique Word or divine Logos whose revelation in varying degrees of completeness produces among all men innate notions of good and evil as well as the universal notion of God; most men possess these notions even though they are unable to put them to use. Universal reason, the revelation of the prophets, and the incarnate word are but different degrees of one and the same revelation. Reason is but a partial and diffuse revelation. "Each philosopher, seeing through a portion of the divine Word that which is related to him, gives expression to thoughts of extraordinary beauty." [13] It is hard to reconcile the thesis of partial revelation with another thesis that Justin may have found among the Jews associated with Philo: the thesis that Plato and the Stoics were the pupils of Moses. The common link between the two theses is the desire to discover some sort of unity of the human spirit, reflecting the unity of the Word. Furthermore, it should be noted that Justin proceeded with the Jews just as with the Greeks, trying to identify Christ with the Logos in the books of the Jews, with the Son, with Wisdom, with the Glory of the Lord.[14] Such a method was possible only on the basis of a very superficial knowledge of Plato. Like the Stoic moralists in the days of the Empire, he is acquainted with the *Apology, Crito, Phaedrus,* and *Phaedo,* but he knows nothing of the dialectical dialogues and focuses his attention on the *Timaeus,* mixing in many elements (as Philo of Alexandria had done before him) from the account of creation given in the Book of Genesis. He learns from the *Timaeus* that "God, through his goodness, started from formless matter and created everything for men," thereby confusing the philanthropy of the God of the Jews and the goodness of the Platonic demiurge.[15]

Thus the theme of a Christian Plato makes its appearance in his-

[13] *Apology* ii chap. xiii.
[14] *Dialogue Against Tryphon* 61.
[15] E. de Faye, *De l'Influence du Timée de Platon sur les idées de Justin martyr.*

tory. It is treated in detail in *Exhortation to the Greeks,* a work which was first attributed to Justin but which was actually written almost a century later. The author, much better informed than Justin, does not hide the contradictions between Plato and Aristotle or between Plato and himself concerning crucial issues: the eternity of the world, the immortality of the soul, monotheism, etc. Plato nevertheless had, according to him, a precise notion of the true God: *being* for him is the *I am that I am* of Moses if only one knows how to read him; he qualifies his stand on monotheism and posits unbegotten matter and begotten gods because he feared that if he gave a frank statement of his beliefs, like Socrates he would be brought to trial. This would explain Plato's rather involved account of the gods.[16]

The Christian Plato revealed through a reading of the *Timaeus* against the background of the Book of Genesis reappears in Tatian, the pupil of Justin. In contrast to his master, however, Tatian grants no knowledge of God through reason and explains the resemblance of Plato and the Stoics to Moses through an unacknowledged act of plagiarism on the part of the Greeks. Generally, Justin's rationalism seems to suffer a setback with Tatian; for instance, the Spirit or pneuma that receives the revelation exists only in those who are pure and is not a part of the soul — which is simple but subtile and penetrating matter that differs from the soul of beasts only by virtue of articulated speech — but is superimposed on the soul.[17]

With Athenagoras, however, Justin's rationalism receives a fresh impetus. The monotheism that he finds in poets, in the Pythagoreans and in Plato is supposed to indicate a divine inspiration common to Moses and the philosophers, and Plato is supposed to have gone so far as to conceive of the Trinity. Still, the fact remains that Plato, whom he knows much better than Justin, is a Christian Plato, that the Good or the unchanging being that he depicts as God has only the name in common with the first Plotinian hypostasis and is much closer to the God of the Stoics. If we recall how vigorously pagan

---

[16] *Exhortation to the Greeks* chaps. xx–xxii.
[17] A. Puech, *Les Apologistes grecs du II* siècle de notre ère* (Paris, 1912).

Neo-Platonism rejected Stoic religiosity, we can appreciate more fully the significance of Christian Platonism that retains all the theology of the Stoics and their arguments (in syllogistical form) based on providence and the beauty of the world.

III *Gnosticism and Manicheism*

Even as the apologists held sway the so-called Gnostic systems were being evolved. They are known to us mainly through the refutations of the Church Fathers of the following century, particularly the unknown author of the *Philosophumena,* Irenaeus in his *Against Heretics,* Tertullian in *Against Marcion* and, not least in importance, *Pistis Sophia,* a Gnostic work which is written in third-century Coptic but which is actually a translation of older Greek writings.

According to one thesis found in the *Philosophumena* and generally accepted down to the present time, the Gnostic systems are supposed to have resulted from an intrusion of Greek philosophy into Christian doctrine, and the Greek sects are supposed to be ultimately responsible for the Christian heresies, which as the product of Greek thought would be of direct interest in the history of philosophy. But contemporary studies that have succeeded in sifting the elements of true Gnosticism from the rather whimsical expositions in which the Church Fathers have hidden it, give the impression that Greek philosophy had little influence on the Gnostics. Their systems are nevertheless of capital interest since, as we shall see, they provide the counterproof for a truth that emerges, we believe, from our general exposition of Greek philosophy: Hellenism is characterized by the eternity of the order that it assigns to things; from the principle of the eternal the same consequences eternally flow. Now the common theme of the Gnostic systems is redemption or deliverance from evil, which at the same time implies destruction, and definitive destruction of the order in which we live. For the Hellene contemplation of the universe of which he is a part entails the disappearance of evil; for the Gnostic the suppression of the universe, or the elevation of the soul above and beyond the universe, brings about the disappearance of evil.

Basilides, Valentinus, and Marcion are the three best known Gnostics from the middle of the second century. But only Valentinus, it seems, offers a comprehensive conception of the Gnostic universe. Basilides is primarily a moralist, "obsessed by the problem of evil and of the justification of providence." [18] "Anything at all," he said, "to avoid attributing evil to Providence." And to explain the suffering of martyrs he is ready to concede that they have sinned in a previous life. Moreover, he attributes sin to passion and passion to an evil spirit that invades and defiles the soul. His views lead to a sort of ethical dualism that has its analogue in Plato.

But Valentinus, a man with a more metaphysical turn of mind than Basilides, necessarily arrived at conclusions antithetical to Platonism. For Valentinus seeks in the origin of man the explanation of his dualism. The dualism between spirit and flesh corresponds to a deeper dualism between the creator of the world — the demiurge, escorted by his angels, as we read in the Book of Genesis — and the supreme god or the good god. Following the account given in Genesis and, at least in part, the interpretation given by Philo of Alexandria, he shows how man was made by evil beings, the demiurge and his angels, who introduce the passions and are evil spirits. To this creature the supreme God or the good God has added a seed of the substance from on high, spirit.

The entire history of the world is the history of the struggle against the angels who seek to eliminate this seed, and the struggle ends with its deliverance. Redemption does not consist here, as in the case of St. Paul, in the efficacy of the death of Christ but derives, as we see especially in Heracleon, a disciple of Valentinus, from the gnosis or revelation brought by Christ.

After Valentinus the best known Gnostic is Marcion, who seems to have been the main exegete of the group, for through the study of texts he seeks to show that the God of the Old Testament — the cruel, vindictive, and warring god revealed by Moses — is not the

[18] E. de Faye, *Gnostiques et gnosticisme* (1913), pp. 24–6.

same as the God revealed by Christ as the God of goodness and the creator of the invisible world, in contrast to the visible world created by the god of Moses. They stand in opposition to each other in the same way as justice and goodness. He does not attempt to draw support for his thesis other than from the double revelation of the two testaments; his main concern is to show that Christ the redeemer who will deliver us from the power of the demiurge has nothing in common with the Jewish Messiah foretold by the prophets; and it is not hard for him to interpret the texts literally and to show that no trait of the Messiah is to be found in Jesus. On the other hand he cannot concede that Christ, the messenger of the supreme god, can actually have a corporeal nature, that is, that Christ can participate in any way in the world of the demiurge; he thinks, therefore, that Christ suddenly revealed himself as a man among men and that his body is only apparent. Marcion deduced from his views a most rigorous asceticism that proscribed marriage and made continence the prerequisite for baptism; in this way he provided for escape from the world of the demiurge.

Gnostic thought splintered after Valentinus and Marcion and is reflected in a number of systems known through the *Philosophumena,* each of which always deals with the same theme but offers variations that are at times most peculiar: deliverance through Christ of the soul that is of divine origin and is imprisoned in the sensible world created by a wicked demiurge.

Gnostic thought in general is characterized by the same comprehensive view of the spiritual life as Neo-Platonism: in each instance a soul of divine origin descends into an earthly body where it is defiled, and it must leave the body and return to its source. But here the superficial resemblance ends, and we need only read the treatise that Plotinus addressed to the Gnostics whom he knew in Rome around A.D. 260 to understand the aversion that a Hellene must have felt toward people who inclined to Gnosticism but drew support from the *Phaedo* and *Phaedrus.* The point on which they differ is apparently this: whenever the Gnostic is not satisfied with religious practices or asceticism and wants to understand the experience of his redemption or the origin of salutary or inimical spiritual forces, he arbitrarily superimposes a metaphysical drama on religion. Take as one of many examples the way in which the third-century Gnostic Justin relates the drama that culminates in redemption: at the summit are the three principles, the good God, then Elohim or the father, who is masculine, and Eden, who is feminine; Elohim through his union with Eden produces two series of twelve angels who collectively make up Paradise; Man is created there and receives from Elohim a pneuma or spiritual breath, and from Eden a soul; Elohim who previously knew nothing of the God of goodness, rises (like the soul in the *Phaedrus*) to the heights of creation and abandons Eden in order to contemplate him; Eden, to avenge herself, introduces sin into man; Elohim, wishing to save man, sends Baruch, one of his angels, first to Moses, then to Hercules, and finally to Jesus, the ultimate redeemer who, crucified by one of the angels in Eden, leaves his body on the cross.[19]

We need only read his lucubration, which makes man's fate hinge upon a metaphysical domestic wrangle, to understand the degree to which the generation of the Aeons or eternal realities issuing from divine mates as described by the Gnostics differs from the Plotinian generation of hypostases, and also the degree to which redemption predicated on a struggle between forces for possession of the soul (a popular representation that persists for a long time and reappears in many legends) differs from Plotinian salvation (if the term salvation is applicable to something that is but reflective knowledge of a rational order). Thus Gnosticism that culminates on one hand in fairy tales into which are introduced all the religious forms that appeal to the mind of an Oriental, and on the other in superstitious practices which have left monuments throughout the Roman Empire, is related only indirectly to the history of philosophy.

Consciousness of the reality of evil, born of a voluntary and radically evil power, is at the heart of Gnosticism. It is also at the heart of the trend that originated in the third century with the Persian

[19] *Ibid.*, pp. 187 ff.

Mani (205-274) and, under the name of Manicheism, spread throughout the Empire and reappeared in different guises in several heresies during the Middle Ages. Mani introduces the Persian dualism of the power of good and the power of evil, Ormazd and Ahriman; his dualism is quite different from the dualism of the Gnostics, who are essentially monotheists and subordinate the inferior creative power to the supreme reality. Mani posits two creative powers engaged in a struggle: Good counters each creation of evil with a new creation until destruction is complete. This accounts for the drama of the world:[20] the God of goodness who first created five powers or agents — Nous, Ennoia, Phronesis, Enthymesis, and Logismos (the five agents are obviously aspects of divine thought) — establishes no link between them and the world because they are "made for tranquility and peace"; as the need arises he creates other powers to struggle against evil — the Mother of the Living who in turn evokes the First Man, the Friend of Lights and the living Spirit, the Messenger who evokes twelve virtues, and finally Jesus — all destined to enter into relations with the power of darkness. The duality between the two types of powers, one corresponding to the Word or Mind of the Greek philosophers and the other to a religious drama in which everything appeals to the imagination, is most revealing. The Logos or Mind that supports the eternal order of things is not sufficient to explain a temporary order assumed to result from an abnormal crisis. In Manicheism the creation of the sensible world is not, as in Gnosticism, wholly the creation of a bad demiurge: primal man is assumed to have created in turn five elements that he wears like a suit of armor — clear water, cooling wind, the mild zephyr, bright light, and quickening fire — and each of these is matched by a token from the world of darkness — vapor, heat, mist, the sirocco, and darkness.

[20] According to the commentary on Manichean cosmogony written by Theodore Bar Khoûi, a late sixth-century bishop, whose work is analyzed by F. Cumont in *Recherches sur le Manichéisme: I. La cosmogonie manichéene d'après Théodore Bar Khoûi* (Brussels, 1908). (Cf. Académie des Inscriptions, session of December 2, 1932.)

IV *Clement of Alexandria and Origen*

The school that was founded in Alexandria by Pantaenus, a Stoic who was converted to Christianity, and later directed by Clement of Alexandria (160–215) and Origen (185–254), represents the first exhaustive attempt to provide Christian instruction equal in scope to the instruction given in pagan schools. The setting is quite different from that of the Gnostics; here for the first time we find men who are thoroughly grounded in Greek philosophy and who take a definite stand with respect to it.

Their stand is nevertheless complex. In his *Protrepticus* ("Exhortation to the Greeks"), for example, Clement takes it upon himself to compare Hellenism with Christianity; in Hellenism he finds gross errors or partial truths which are but timidly expressed and which can be fully understood only by Christianity. He shows that Greek theology, as expressed in forms of worship and in the mysteries, is erroneous or scandalous (Chapters V, VI). He divides philosophers into two groups: those who looked upon the elements as gods and those one degree higher who attributed divinity to the stars, the world or its soul; both were completely in error, for they confused God with his works. In contrast, however, he finds an element of truth in Plato's reference in the *Timaeus* to "the father and creator of all things"; in the same way Antisthenes and Xenophon attained to monotheism, and Cleanthes the Stoic, as well as the Pythagoreans, knew the true attributes of God. Christianity would then consummate Hellenism in much the same way that the New Testament reveals the errors of the Old Testament even as it consummates its teachings.

The same is true of ethics. Greek wisdom finds practical application in particular cases relating to marriage and public life, and Greek piety is "a universal commitment for a lifetime that tends always and everywhere toward the essential end." Christianity represents the complete realization of that which Stoicism and the other schools were seeking. By pretending to limit philosophy to the art

of practical counseling in matters of detail, Clement intends to replace it as a science of principles (Chapter XI).

The truth is that Clement casts Christianity in its entirety in the
mold of Greek philosophical instruction, particularly as practiced
by the Stoics who, until the second century, had the only fully
organized system of instruction. "Since the Word has come from
heaven into our midst," he says, "it is no longer necessary to have
recourse to human instruction." [21] But divine instruction retains the
same form as the human instruction that it replaced. When Clement
tells us that faith ($\pi\acute{\iota}\sigma\tau\iota\varsigma$), disparaged by the Greeks, is the path to
wisdom,[22] he is not deviating from Greek thought to the extent
that we might think; like the Stoics he defines faith as voluntary
assent, as assent to a fixed, secure term, as assent that is the prelude
to the Christian life just as it was a prelude to wisdom among the
Stoics. The true object of faith, he adds, "is not the philosophy of
the sects but gnosis or the scientific demonstration of things transmitted in true philosophy, which is Christianity." [23] And when we
examine the details of his teaching, we see that from start to finish
his *Paedagogus* ("Tutor") is constructed like a Stoic treatise on
ethics. The first book contains the criterion of right action, namely
right reason, identical to the Word; and it is worth noting that in
the third chapter Clement, evidently thinking of the Gnostics, shows
through a Stoic line of reasoning that justice is identical to goodness as he moves from an argument based on God's love for men
to his justice. The second and third books constitute a diatribe in
the style of Musonius and prescribe a simple, modest life for Christians. He incorporates into the teaching of Christianity the whole
doctrine of Stoicism blended, as we have seen, with Cynicism. In
the paradox, "only the sage is truly rich," he simply substitutes one
word: "only the Christian is truly rich."

Even with respect to method in the knowledge of God, Clement
does not hesitate to borrow everything he has to say from the teach-

---

[21] *Protrepticus* chap. ix.
[22] *Stromata* ii. 2.
[23] *Ibid.* chap. xi.

ing of the Pythagoreans or the Platonists. He identifies the series of abstractions through which we arrive at knowledge of pure unity and uses with reference to God the formulas found in Albinus' manual of Platonism: "God is neither genus, nor difference, nor species, nor individual, nor number, nor accident, nor subject; he is not a whole." Finally, his notion of the Son or Logos is not far from the Stoic concept of the intelligible world; the Father, who is undemonstrable, stands in contrast to the Son who is revealed as wisdom, science, and truth. For "he is all things; he is the circle of all the powers that turn around a unique center." [24]

Origen's attitude toward Hellenism is indicated clearly in his long reply to Celsus' pamphlet against the Christians. As a Hellene who believes in an eternal order of things, Celsus objects strongly to the event of the Incarnation: "If the slightest change is made in the things of this world, everything will be upset and will disappear." Or again: "So after an eternity God thought of judging men whom he had been neglecting all the while." [25] Now it is precisely this mythological or, we might say, historical character of Christianity that Origen takes pains to attenuate in his reply: "The only change produced by the presence of God," he writes in reply to the first objection, "is a change in the soul of the believer." [26] In this way he seeks to reduce the Incarnation to an inner event; in addition, he later presents the descent of God as "a figure of speech" (a tropology). To the second objection he answers that God "has never ceased being concerned with the ransom of men; with each generation the wisdom of God descends into blessed souls and prophets." And in a similar way he answers the objection against the creation of the world erected by the Hellenes on the basis of the impossibility of acknowledging an inactive god: rejecting the eternal recurrence of the Stoics, he reasons that God created other worlds before creating this one and in this way admits the cyclic concept of time

[24] *Ibid.* v. chap. xi and xii; iv. chap. xxv.

[25] Quoted by Origen *Against Celsus* iv. chap. iii; in *Griechische Christlicher Schriftsteller,* ed. P. Koetschau (1899), p. 278, l. 8, and p. 279, l. 9.

[26] *Against Celsus* iv. 182. 8.

that is the prime characteristic of Hellenism.[27] He manifests the same adherence to Hellenism when he considers the modifications of the Word in the creation or the incarnation, not as changes in the Word itself but as appearances due to the different capacities of beings for receiving the Word.[28]

Still, the same Origen distrusts Hellenism and especially Platonism. "All those who acknowledge a providence," he says, "believe in an increate God who created everything. We are not the only ones to proclaim that the increate God has a son; even though Greek or barbarian philosophers seem unable to accept the idea, some of them admit it when they say that everything was created by the Word and by the Reason of God. But it is by virtue of our faith in a divinely inspired doctrine that we believe in it . . . As for the Holy Spirit, the only ones who have had the slightest suspicion of it are those who know the Law and the prophets, or those who believe in Christ." [29] Here we see the exact limits of Hellenism and the way in which the Christian faith was superimposed on it without destroying it. But alongside its partial truths Hellenism also has errors, and these may relate to either the nature of the world or the nature of the soul. Origen's sensible world is in no way an order reflecting an intelligible model. In the first place, the world of ideas exists only in the imagination and could not produce the Savior or provide an abode for the saints.[30] Second, in the beginning God created only equal rational beings, but they are all endowed with a free will and can fall; this explains the diversity of souls and a corresponding diversity of bodies that do not have an absolute existence but are born at intervals by virtue of the varied motions of rational creatures that need them and are invested by them.[31] Finally, Origen does not believe that created souls can exist apart from bodies. Only God is incorporeal. One must

[27] *On Principles* ii. 3. 4.
[28] *Against Celsus* iv. chap. xviii.
[29] *On Principles* i. 3. 1.
[30] *Ibid.* ii. 3. 5.
[31] *Ibid.* ii. 9. 5; iv. 4. 8.

say only that the body varies in dignity and in perfection according to the dignity and perfection of the soul with which it is in constant communication.

v Christianity in the West in the Fourth Century

Christians not so closely attached to Hellenic civilization as Clement and Origen still stressed the impossibility of reconciling Christ and Greek philosophy. They are irreconcilable primarily because they do not carry divinity to the same point in the hierarchy of beings: Plato and the Stoics attribute divine reality to souls, the stars, and the world, all of which are divine beings; the Christians, however, restrict divinity to the Trinity alone. Arguing against the divine nature of souls, Arnobius (converted in 297) attacks Plato and his hypothesis of reminiscence, which implies that souls are fallen divine beings and are subordinate to gods and daimons. How is it possible, he asks, since whole races are ignorant, since men hold multiple and conflicting opinions in the sciences and, finally, since the famous cross-examination in the *Meno* would be truly probing only if addressed to a human being raised in the depths of a sealed cave, sheltered from any experience, and (unlike Meno's slave) not acquainted with the use of names? Besides, if the soul forgets when it enters the body, then it is capable of receiving action and consequently is corruptible and perishable.[32] Here is a line of reasoning whose full significance may have been beyond the grasp of Arnobius' mediocre mind but which accords with orthodoxy only through its empiricism. The argument advanced by Lactantius (d. 325) against the divinity of the stars is still more revealing: "The Stoic argument in support of the divinity of the celestial beings proves the opposite, for the assumption that they are gods because they follow a regular, rational course is completely unfounded; and precisely because they cannot leave their prescribed orbits, it would appear that they are not gods; if they were gods, we could see them move about like animate beings on earth that

[32] *Against the Pagans* ii. chap. xix.

go wherever they wish because their wills are free." [33] This is certainly a novel view; regularity alone is no longer sufficient to establish divinity and, conversely, as we see in Lactantius' fourth book, God manifests himself through unexpected decisions, inspiring prophets and sending his son to the world.

The foregoing observations, made by men who are not so much friends of the philosophers as Christians whose heritage is Greek, contradict the notion of a hierarchy of divine beings issuing from each other and constituting all that there is of true reality. The Nicene Council (325) affirmed the absolute equality of the persons of the Trinity in the famous statement, "The Son is consubstantial with the Father," put an end to any attempt to identify a similar hierarchy within divine reality, and excluded from divine reality all spiritual creations.[34] Soon we shall examine the conditions under which a Christian Neo-Platonism was nevertheless able to evolve.

St. Augustine (354–430) is one of those who contributed most to making the name of Plato respected among the Christians. His conversion to Christianity (387) almost coincided with the reading of Plotinus' works in the Latin translation of Marius Victor, and he was always impressed by the kinship between Christian spirituality and the spirituality of the Platonists. He holds that the Platonists alone are theologians. The other philosophers exhausted their faculties in their investigation into the causes of things, but the Platonists became acquainted with God and found in him the cause of the universe, the light of truth, and the source of happiness.[35] What they lack therefore is not the idea of the end that is to be attained but the idea of the path that leads to it, Christ. In his *Confessions* he has this to say about his reading of the Neo-Platonists: "I have read, though not in these exact words of course, that in the beginning was the Word, and that the Word was with God and that the Word was God, that the Word did not issue from the flesh or from the blood or from the will of man, or from the

[33] *Divine Institution* ii. chap. v.
[34] Harnack, *Dogmengeschichte*, II, 230.
[35] *The City of God* viii. 10.

will of the flesh, but from God; but I have not read that the Word was made flesh and dwelt among us . . . , that he humbled himself by taking the shape of a servant and by being obedient until death, and death on the cross." [36]

The opposition between the Platonist mediator and Christ recurs frequently in the thought of St. Augustine. Christ is the mediator not because he is the Word, for the immortal and supremely happy Word is remote from unhappy mortals, but because he is a man. Christ is not, as in the case of the philosophers, a principle that explains the physical universe; he is the one who delivers men by becoming a man. His incarnation is a transitory event that contrasts sharply with the eternal order that makes him eternally the intermediary between God and men. It follows that the divine mediator cannot be a daimon or an angel, as Apuleius would have it, since it is their nature to be happy and immortal and especially since in his thinking the intermediary serves to separate God from the world rather than to join him to it, to isolate God from the taint of mortal things rather than to save man. [37]

The foregoing citations will perhaps suffice to indicate the gap that separates St. Augustine, in spite of his sympathy for them, from the Platonists. The gap becomes still more obvious when he comes to the fundamental theses of Hellenism: the eternity of souls and the eternity of the world. With respect to the first he says: "Why not believe rather in the divinity in matters that cannot be investigated by the human mind?" Against the eternity of the periodic revolutions of the universe, he adduces only religious arguments: "How can the beatitude whose eternity is in question be a true beatitude if there is always a recurrence of the same misfortunes? Besides, Christ died but once." [38] We sense in his pronouncements a sort of affective ardor that is surely the mark of a saint. Just as he subordinated what he assumed to be the rational order

[36] Confessions vii. 9.
[37] The City of God ix. 15.
[38] Ibid. x. 31 and xiii. 13.

of things to the needs of the religious life, so he took issue with the Stoics and justified every passion of the human soul: desire, fear, and sadness may spring from the love of the good and from charity, and are not in themselves vices. The downfall of moral rationalism occurred at the same time as the downfall of philosophical rationalism.

Thus it is only with many precautions and reservations that we can speak of the Platonism of St. Augustine. After lavishing praise on the Platonists in his early writings — even going so far as to say that they are the only true philosophers and that philosophy and religion have one and the same object, the intelligible world that can be discovered in two ways, either by reason or by faith[39] — he takes a more sober view in his *Retractions:* "The praise that I bestowed on Plato and the Platonists displeases me, and not without justification, especially since the Christian doctrine must be defended against gross errors on their part." [40]

The spirituality of Augustine is far removed from that of Plotinus. We need only compare the famous passages in the treatise *On the Trinity* cited by Descartes' opponents, in which Augustine speaks of inner wisdom through which we know that we exist and that we live, with Plotinus' statements on hypostases that possess self-knowledge to see how different is the meaning attached to self-knowledge by the two writers.[41] For St. Augustine it is knowledge that thwarts every reason for doubting advanced by the Academicians; it is knowledge of a fact or an existence, not knowledge of an essence. For Plotinus it is something entirely different; it is knowledge of the intelligible essence of things, which is identical to the essence of mind or intelligence; to know oneself is to know the universe, and the important thing is not to feel that one is living or existing but to know realities. As in the case of self-knowledge, Augustine's interpretation of intellectual knowledge sets him apart

---

[39] *Against the Academicians* iii. 20. 43; written in 287.
[40] *Retractions* i. 14; written in 426.
[41] *On the Trinity* x. 13 and xv. 21; *Enneads* v. 3 (beginning).

from Plotinus. The trait that impresses St. Augustine is not an intrinsic property of intelligible things but the independence of the truths conceived by individual minds: "everyone who reasons, using his own reason and mind, sees the same thing in the same way — for instance, the reason and truth of numbers." [42] Such is the purely external characteristic that proves to him the existence of an intelligible reality. Here again, what matters is the disposition of the subject with respect to things, not things themselves.

It was also a form of Hellenic rationalism that St. Augustine attacked in the case of the heretic Pelagius, who held with the Stoics that we are wholly responsible for both our demerits and our merits. "If Adam's sin taints even those who do not sin," he said, "then Christ's justice must extend to those who do not believe." He added: "It would be unthinkable that God, who forgives us our own sins, should impute to us the sins of another." [43] Here the important thing for Augustine is that Pelagius' thesis rules out prayer and, along with prayer, any religious life; it separates us from God by making us search our will to determine which good is ours and which good does not come from God. By making God the author of our will and adding that it is through our own efforts that our will becomes good, the Pelagians were certain to reach this conclusion: that which comes from us (our good will) is better than that which comes from God (mere will).

These few examples suffice to show the mixed reception accorded to Greek philosophy in Latin circles. St. Ambrose (d. 397), who stressed discipline more than doctrine, chose as his model Cicero's treatise *On Duties,* which he imitated in his treatise that bears the same title and sets forth the obligations of the clergy. Before him Tertullian (160–245), acting as the faithful guardian of orthodoxy, praised Stoic ethics and acknowledged that "Seneca is often one of us"; but he had no intention of accepting the complicated metaphysical machinery of Neo-Platonism or even the liberal Greek education.

[42] *On Free Will* ii. chap. vii.
[43] According to St. Augustine, *To Marcellinus* iii. 2.

vi *Christianity in the East in the Fourth and Fifth Centuries*

The situation was entirely different in the East, where theology was "reserved for the clergy, for officials, and for the upper class, while the people practiced an inferior type of Christianity."[44] Here theology reflected the aristocratic tradition of the Greeks. For example, Eusebius of Caesarea (265–340) in his *Evangelical Preparation,* which was intended to show how Christianity is susceptible of clear proof and is not a blind faith, cites copious extracts from the Greek philosophers, many of whom are known to us only through him. Later we see Gregory of Nazianzen (330–390) defending the liberal education of the Greeks, that is, the sciences, against Christians who judge them useless.[45] The allusions to philosophical schools in his *Eulogies* of Caesarius and Basil are proof of his intimate acquaintance with Greek philosophy.[46] Still, the Cappadocians, Basil, Gregory of Nyssa (d. 395), Gregory of Nazianzen, and also St. John Chrysostom look upon the Greek philosophers as "alien sages" to be consulted on occasion when commenting on Scripture.[47]

St. John Chrysostom does not conceal the fact that "we should have no need of Scriptural help but should make our lives so pure that the grace of the spirit would replace books in our souls and would be inscribed in our hearts as ink on books." He adds that "because we have rejected grace, we must employ writing, which is a tergiversation."[48] Furthermore, in quarrels concerning the nature of the Trinity — which set Arius and his supporters, who believed that the Son was a creation of the Father, against orthodox Christians, such as St. Athanasius and the Cappadocians, who accepted the consubstantiality of the persons — it seems that the question

[44] Harnack, *Dogmengeschichte,* II, 273.
[45] *Eulogy of Basil* chaps. xi–xii.
[46] *Eulogy of Caesarius* xx. 4 and 5; *Eulogy of Basil* xx. 2; lx. 4.
[47] Gregory of Nyssa, in *Patrologia Graeca* xliv. 1336a (ed. Migne).
[48] *Commentary on St. Matthew* (beginning).

posed is completely alien to philosophy. Generation and procession, words used by the Christians to designate relations between the Son or Spirit and the Father, by no means retain the precise meaning that they have for Plato and the Platonists. This meaning, if preserved, would imply a doctrine such as Arianism since one of the absolute principles of Neo-Platonism is that the reality that proceeds is inferior to the reality from which it proceeds. But belief in the divinity of Jesus Christ contradicts this principle and prescribes a dogma that no longer has the slightest affiliation with philosophical speculation.

In other circles, however, Platonism met with much greater success. For example, the treatise *On Human Nature* by Nemesius (about A.D. 400), bishop of Emesa, is infused with Platonism. Not a trace of Christian inspiration is to be found in this work in which the bishop treats with the freedom of a philosopher the question of the union of the soul and the body and wonders how the two distinct realities can constitute a single being. His full sympathy goes to a doctrine which he attributes to Ammonius Saccas, the teacher of Plotinus, and which in any case bears a close resemblance to the doctrine of Plotinus himself. His doctrine compares the soul to an intelligible light which suffuses the body, and obviously assumes the divine origin of the soul, one of the theses that did most to widen the gap between Christianity and Hellenism.[49]

To understand the relations between educated Christians and philosophers in Egypt and Asia Minor during the fifth century, one must read the extraordinary dialogue, *Theophrastus,* by Aeneas of Gaza (about 500). A pagan philosopher, Theophrastus, has just come from Athens to Alexandria, where he is discussing the Christian thesis of the resurrection of the dead with a certain Euxitheos of Syria, a Christian who has studied under the Neo-Platonist Hierocles and who is going to Athens to study "with the philosophers" the question of the survival of the soul. The odd part is that the Christian Euxitheos uses the philosophical dialogue to defend the thesis of a created and perishable world and of the resurrection

---

[49] *Patrologia Graeca* xl. 592.

of the flesh. To the customary objections of the Greek, which we have already encountered several times, he replies that before the beginning of the world God was active in the eternal procession of persons, that "the Chaldeans, Porphyry, and Plotinus" teach the creation of matter, that according to Plato every sensible being is created. Furthermore, the world must perish, for according to the *Timaeus* it can perish inasmuch as any potency must pass to the act. Besides, God causes the world to perish for the sake of order: the order requires the production of contraries and, consequently, the production of the sensible that perishes in contrast to the intelligible that is eternal.

As for the resurrection of the flesh, Euxitheos tries to incorporate the thesis into a Hellenic dogma, not only by citing the resurrectional facts mentioned by the Greeks but also by stressing the efficacy of seminal reason, which is strong enough to reunite the disunited elements of the body. Besides, cannot the soul communicate its immortality to the body just as the sun communicates its warmth to water?

Finally we come to Pseudo-Dionysius, the mysterious personage who throughout the Middle Ages was assumed to have been St. Paul's companion, Dionysius the Areopagite. The confusion results in part from the extreme authority attached to his writings, and it is impossible to say how many Neo-Platonist ideas entered Christian mysticism under cover of his name. Quoted for the first time at the Council of Constantinople (533), Pseudo-Dionysius must have written after Proclus (d. 485), who influenced his development. His writings fall into two classes. The first includes *Celestial Hierarchy* and *Ecclesiastical Hierarchy,* which study the complete series of creatures capable of receiving divine revelation, from the highest (the first order of angels who are in direct contact with God) to the lowest (the faithful who have been baptized); each being receives revelation from a higher being and transmits it to a lower one. The second includes *Divine Names* and *Mystical Theology.* These works, together with two others that have been lost (*Theological Sketches* and *Symbolic Theology*) constituted a complete course in theology. The outline for the course is given in the third chapter of his *Mystical Theology*. The first three works — *Sketches, Names,* and *Symbolic Theology* — embraced positive theology: first, in *Sketches,* the Trinity that is above the intelligible world; next, in *Names,* the denominations of God borrowed from the order of the intelligibles — good, being, life, mind, etc.; finally, in *Symbolic Theology,* the attributes of God borrowed from the sensible world — anger, jealousy, promise, etc. The last work, *Mystical Theology,* contains his negative theology and shows, by reversing the order of positive theology, that no demonstration borrowed from the sensible world or the intelligible world is applicable to God.

Pseudo-Dionysius never clarifies his position with respect to pagan Neo-Platonism. In his letters he refuses to engage in any controversial discussion with the pagans, but he does acquaint us with the opinion of a "pagan Sophist," Apollophanes, in connection with his writings: "This Sophist curses me and charges me with parricide because I impiously pit one Greek against another," he says.[50] Here we see that he was accused by the pagans of using Neo-Platonism to advance Christianity, and indeed, even though he boasts of drawing all his "philosophy" or "theosophy" from Scripture,[51] his thought is nevertheless impregnated with the ideas of Proclus.

The foregoing conclusion is supported by three considerations. In the first place, God, since he is the cause of all, contains all just as a cause contains its effect. Putting it another way, we can attribute to God the names of all his creations — Life, Wisdom, etc. — if we interpret these names in the sense of Cause of life, Cause of wisdom, etc. So much for positive theology. But since God is the cause of all without being any part of that which he causes, we must deprive him of all these attributes, and this is the principle of negative theology, which is superior to positive theology. Second, in examining the denominations of God in *Divine Names,* Pseudo-Dionysius adopts the order of hypostases accepted by the Neo-Platonists beginning with Iamblichus: the Good is followed by the

---

[50] *Letters* 6 and 7 in *Patrologia Graeca* 1080a and 1080b.
[51] *Ibid.* 588a.

triad of Being, Life, and Mind. Thus he goes from the abstract to the concrete, and in exactly the same way as Proclus he explains how, although Being is superior to Mind, intelligent beings are superior to mere beings.[52] Third, it is for reasons similar to those adduced by Proclus — reasons that go back ultimately to the *Parmenides* — that he accepts the following principle, which is essential to his theology: although the effect is similar to the cause, the cause is not necessarily similar to the effect.

Still, there are traits that set his doctrine apart from the doctrine of Proclus. In the first place, the order of divine names or hypostases in no way represents an order of divine generation: of divine Life proceeding from divine Being and divine Mind from divine Life. All is identical in God, and he therefore makes no attempt to justify this order. Furthermore, and consequently, God as the Trinity of Father, Son, and Holy Spirit, as discussed in *Sketches,* transcends divine names. Finally, he renounces any true deductions with respect to things: the three triads of angels in his *Hierarchy* are not linked to each other by rational considerations, nor is there a link between each term in a triad and the other two terms; they are the numerical frames of Neo-Platonism without the content.

Appearance to the contrary, one must refrain from attributing these important modifications to the influence of Christian orthodoxy, which rejects outright the necessary procession of the forms of reality. The truth is that the evolution of Neo-Platonism is the same in both Pseudo-Dionysius and his contemporary Damascius. As we have seen, Damascius states explicitly that the procession of hypostases and the hierarchy that extends from the highest to the lowest are but inept metaphors insofar as the identification of first principles is concerned. He, too, renounces rational deduction, and he has recourse to the tradition of the *Chaldean Oracles* to determine the succession of the forms of reality. Finally, the negative theology of Pseudo-Dionysius links him more closely to Damascius than to Proclus. Instead of accumulating negations on the first term in the series, the Good or the One, both of them define a

[52] *Ibid.* 818a.

still higher term; Damascius calls it the Ineffable, and Pseudo-Dionysius, citing the *Parmenides,* says that it is beyond language, nameless, and unknowable.[53]

Such, then, was the diversity of the intellectual currents within Christianity during its first centuries. The gap between the teaching of St. Paul and the work of the man long presumed to be Dionysius the Areopagite is as wide as the gap that separates the preaching of Musonius and Epictetus from the complicated metaphysics of Damascius. During the whole period there was no semblance of a true Christian philosophy.

[53] *Ibid.* 1043a.

BIBLIOGRAPHY

General Studies

A. Harnack. *Lehrbuch der Dogmengeschichte.* 3d edition. 3 vols. Freiburg and Leipzig, 1894–1897. (English translation, *History of Dogma.* 7 vols. 1894–1899.)
J. Tixeront. *Histoire des dogmes dans l'antiquité chrétienne.* 4th edition. Paris, 1915. 6th edition, 1919. 8th edition, 1921.
Corbière. *Le Christianisme et la fin de la philosophie antique.* Paris, 1921.
A.-J. Festugière. *L'Idéal religieux des Grecs et l'Evangile.* Paris, 1932.
E. Bréhier. *Etudes de philosophie antique.* Paris, 1955.
O. Cullmann. *Immortalité de l'âme ou résurrection des morts?* Neuchâtel and Paris, 1956.

Special Studies

I

E. Renan. *Saint Paul.* (*Histoire des origines du christianisme,* Vol. III). Paris, 1869. Volume IV in *Oeuvres complètes,* 1949.
C. Toussaint. *L'Hellénisme et l'apôtre Paul.* Paris, 1921.
A. Bonhoeffer. *Epictet und das neue Testament.* Giessen, 1911.
J. Babuzi. *Création religieuse et pensée contemplative.* Paris, 1951.

II

A. Puech. *Les Apologistes grecs du IIe siècle de notre ère.* Paris, 1912.
Justin. *Apologies.* Greek text and French translation by L. Pautigny. 1904. — *Dialogue with Tryphon.* Greek text and translation by G. Archambault. Paris, 1909. (In Hemmer and Lejay's collection of texts and documents; Paris: A. Picard.) (For English translations consult the "Oxford Library of the Fathers" and the "Ante-Nicene Library.")
M. Spanneut. *Le stoïcisme des Pères de l'Eglise de Clément de Rome à Clément d'Alexandrie.* Paris, 1957.

III

E. de Faye. *Introduction à l'histoire du gnosticisme.* Paris, 1903. — *Gnostiques et gnosticisme, étude critique des documents du gnosticisme chrétien aux IIe et IIIe siècles.* Paris, 1913.

W. Bousset. *Die Hauptprobleme der Gnosis*. Göttingen, 1907.

F. Cumont. *Recherches sur le manichéisme*. I: *La Cosmogonie manichéenne d'après Théodore Bar Khôni*. Brussels, 1908.

S. Pétrement. *Le dualisme chez Platon, les Gnostiques et les Manichéens*. Paris, 1947.

F.-M. Sagnard. *La gnose valentinienne et le témoignage de saint Irénée*. Paris, 1948.

Corpus hermeticum. Edited by Festugière and Nock. Vols. I–IV. Paris, 1954.

A.-J. Festugière. *La révélation d'Hermès-Trismégiste*. Vols. I–IV. Paris, 1944–1954.

H.-C. Puech. *Le manichéisme, son fondateur, sa doctrine*. Paris, 1949. — "Les nouveaux écrits gnostiques," in *Coptic Studies in Honor of E. Crum*. Boston, 1950.

IV

E. de Faye. *Clément d'Alexandrie*. Paris, 1898. 2d edition, 1903. — *Origène*. Vol. I: *Sa biographie et ses écrits,* 1923; Vols. II and III, 1928.

J.-F. Denis. *De la Philosophie d'Origène*. Paris, 1884.

C. Bigg. *The Christian Platonists of Alexandria*. Oxford, 1913.

R. Cadiou. *Introduction au système d'Origène*. Paris, 1932. — *La jeunesse d'Origène*. Paris, 1936.

H. de Lubac. *Histoire et Esprit, L'intelligence de l'Ecriture d'après Origène*. Paris, 1950.

Mme Harl. *La fonction révélatrice du verbe incarné dans l'oeuvre d'Origène*. Paris, 1957.

V

P. de Labriolle. *Histoire de la littérature latine chrétienne*. Paris, 1920. 2d edition, 1923. — *La réaction païenne*. Paris, 1934.

C. Guignebert. *Tertullien*. Paris, 1901.

L. Grandgeorge. *Saint Augustin et le néoplatonisme*. Paris, 1896.

J. Martin. *Saint Augustin*. Paris, 1901.

P. Alfaric. *L'Evolution intellectuelle de saint Augustin*. Paris, 1918.

C. Boyer. *L'Idée de vérité dans la philosophie de saint Augustin*. Paris, 1920.

G. Bardy. *Saint Augustin*. Paris, 1940.

St. Augustine. *Works*. Vols. IV and V: *Philosophical Dialogues*. Edited and translated into French by Desclée. Paris, 1939.

Paul Henry. *Plotin et l'Occident*. Louvain, 1934.

R. Thamin. *Saint Ambroise et la morale chrétienne au IVe siècle*. Paris, 1895.

J. Guitton. *Le temps et l'éternité chez Plotin et chez saint Augustin*. Paris, 1933.

H.-J. Marrou. *Saint Augustin et la fin de la culture antique*. Paris, 1933. — *L'ambivalence du temps de l'Histoire chez saint Augustin*. Paris, 1950.

P. Courcelle. *Les lettres grecques en Occident de Macrobe à Cassiodore*. Paris, 1943. — *Recherches sur les Confessions de saint Augustin*. Paris, 1950.

VI

C. Gronau. *De Basilio, Gregorio Nazianzeno Nyssenoque Platonis imitatoribus*. Göttingen, 1908.
J. Durantel. *Saint Thomas et le pseudo-Denis*. (Introduction: "La question du pseudo-Denis.") Paris, 1919.
J. Daniélou. *Platonisme et théologie mystique, essai sur la doctrine spirituelle de saint Grégoire de Nysse*. Paris, 1944.
Dionysius Areopagita. *Œuvres complètes. Edited by M. de Gandillac*. Paris, 1943.

Works in English

B. Altaner. *Patrology*. English translation by H. C. Graef. Freiburg, 1960.
R. W. Battenhouse (ed.). *A Companion to the Study of St. Augustine*. New York and Oxford, 1955.
C. Biggs. *The Christian Platonists of Alexandria*. 1886. 2d edition, 1913.
V. J. Bourke. *Augustine's Quest for Wisdom*. Milwaukee, Wis., 1945.
Phillip Carrington. *The Early Christian Church*. Cambridge, 1957.
H. Chadwick. *Origen: Contra Celsum*. Trans. with intro. and notes. Cambridge, 1953.
J. Danielou. *Origen*. Trans. W. Mitchell. New York, 1955.
M. Dibelius. *Paul*. Philadelphia, 1953.
Dionysius. *Celestial Hierarchy*. Edited by G. Heil. English translation by J. Parker. 2 vols. 1897–1899.
F. Homes Dudden. *The Life and Times of St. Ambrose*. 2 vols. Oxford, 1935.
E. H. Gilson. *The Christian Philosophy of St. Augustine*. Trans. L. E. M. Lynch. New York, 1960.
E. R. Goodenough. *The Theology of Justin Martyr*. Jena, 1923.
R. M. Grant. *Gnosticism and Early Christianity*. New York, 1959.
A. M. Hunter. *Paul and His Predecessors*. Revised edition. London, 1961.
H. Jonas. *The Gnostic Religion*. Boston, 1958.
J. N. D. Kelly. *Early Christian Doctrines*. London, 1958.
E. F. Osborn. *The Philosophy of Clement of Alexandria*. Cambridge, 1957.
J. E. L. Oulton and H. Chadwick. *Alexandrian Christianity*. Selected translations of Clement and Origen with introductions and notes. London, 1954.
H. Pope. *Saint Augustine of Hippo*. London, 1937.
J. Quasten. *The Beginnings of Patristic Literature* (Vol. I in *Patrology*. 4 vols.). Utrecht, 1950.
S. Sandmel. *The Genius of Paul*. New York, 1958.
W. D. van Unnik. *Newly Discovered Gnostic Writing*. Naperville, Ind., 1960.
R. M. Wilson. *The Gnostic Problem*. London, 1958.

INDEX

3849